Beyond *the* Bookstore

Beyond *the* Bookstore

How to Sell
More Books Profitably
to Non-Bookstore Markets

Brian Jud

Reed
Business Press

BEYOND THE BOOKSTORE:
How to Sell More Books Profitably to Non-Bookstore Markets

Copyright © 2004 by Brian Jud

A *Publishers Weekly®* Book
Published by Reed Business Press™
360 Park Avenue South
New York, NY 10010

www.reedpress.com

Library of Congress Cataloging-in-Publication Data

Jud, Brian.
    Beyond the bookstore : how to sell more books profitably to non-bookstore markets / Brian Jud.
        p. cm.
"A Publishers Weekly book."
    ISBN 1-59429-002-4 (hardcover with CD-ROM : alk. paper)
    1. Books—United States—Marketing. 2. Booksellers and bookselling—United States. 3. Selling—Books—United States. I. Title.
Z471.J83 2003
381'.45002—dc22

2003018541

Book design and composition by John Reinhardt Book Design

Published in the United States of America

10 9 8 7 6 5 4 3 2 1

This book is dedicated to my wife and best friend, Nicki,
for giving me all the hours it took to write this
that really belonged to her.

And also to my business partners, Art Salzfass and Jerry Labriola,
for helping me through the difficult times.

Acknowledgments

The following people contributed to the content of *Beyond the Bookstore*

Peter Abresch, Alice Acheson, Nick Allen, Vivian Antonangeli, Judith Applebaum, John Arnold, Lorilyn Bailey, Robin Bartlett, Bruce Batchelor, Hajni Blasko, Michele Bledsoe, Wendy Brickman, Beth Bruno, Dick Bruso, Roberta Buland, Austin Camacho, Larry Carpenter, Helma Clark, Charlene Costanzo, Tami DePalma, Dean Eaker, Pat East, Paulette Ensign, Tracy Erickson, Tonya Evans, Frank Forchetta, Rick Frishman, Louise Gaylord, Eric Gelb, Greg Godek, Robert Goodman, Jim Gurfein, Mark Victor Hansen, John Harnish, Richard Harris, Stephen Harrison, Brian Harvey, Mike Heim, Tom Hill, Shel Horowitz, Jim Houtz, Rita Ippolitti, Tordis Ilg Isselhardt, Nicki Jud, Eric Kampmann, George Klein, Patty Kondub, John Kremer, Paul Krupin, Antoinette Kuritz, Jerry Labriola, Jane Leventhal, Ellen Levine, Len Liebenhaut, Jen Linck, Steve Linville, Jane Martin, Tim McCormick, Nanette Miner, Shelly Motz, Jan Nathan, Sally Neher, Patrick O'Connell, Deb Percival, Raleigh Pinskey, Dan Poynter, Ron Pramschufer, Lori Prokop, Ellen Reid, Fern Reiss, Mark Resnick, Melanie Rigney, Carla Ruff, Art Salzfass, Jane Salzfass, Penny Sansevieri, Jack Short, John Simone, Marcella Smith, Michael Smith, Joan Stewart, Cathy Stucker, John Styron, Millie Szerman, Sherri Valenzuela, Robin Veronesi, Martin Warzala, Carol Waugh, Deb Werksman, Mary Westheimer, Kathleen Willoughby, Tom Woll, Randy Yarbrough, Mary Jean Young.

Contents

9 Capitalize Your Special-Sales Efforts Sufficiently and Price Your Books Profitably   125

10 Energize Your Implementation   137

11 Special Distribution Markets   143

12 The Commercial Sales Segment   177

13   Selling to the Niche-Market Sector   219

14   How to Contact Prospective Buyers   245

15   Scrutinize Your Relative Success and Make Necessary Corrections   269

16   Realize Your Goals   279

Appendices   283

Index   297

To write books is easy. It requires only pen and ink and the ever-patient paper.

To print books is a little more difficult, because genius so often rejoices in illegible handwriting.

To read books is more difficult still, because of the tendency to go to sleep.

But the most difficult task of all that a mortal man can embark on is to sell a book. SIR STANLEY UNWAIN

Introduction

THE SAGA LEADING TO THE WRITING of *Beyond the Bookstore* began when I wrote and published the title *Job Search 101* in 1991. I quickly found that marketing books through bookstores was not as lucrative as I thought it would be. Distribution discounts, returns and extended payment terms wreaked havoc on my net income.

In search of profits, I performed grassroots research in different markets, broadened my product line with new titles, published a series of booklets and produced audio and video packages. With this expanded line, I sought sales in new markets such as colleges, corporations and state governments. These strategies led to the sale of over 500,000 units in non-bookstore markets.

That, in a nutshell, is special-sales marketing. It is the process of finding out what information consumers need and in what form they want it, and then delivering it to them where they are located. It sounds simple, and it is. But it is not easy. There are four hints that will make it somewhat less difficult and more lucrative for you.

1. *Stop thinking in terms of books and start thinking in terms of the delivery of information.* Some publishers believe the key to increased income and profits is to publish more titles. However, the quest for a revolving frontlist can actually limit your profitability as it depletes your limited resources of time, energy, creativity, attitude and money.

Instead, find out if the people in your target audience want the information you have, whether fiction or nonfiction, delivered as a booklet, in a three-ring binder or as a DVD. A book may be the best way to communicate your content, but at least be open to considering new product ideas. An open book and an open mind have a lot in common. They can both stimulate your thinking in unknown areas.

2. *Stop thinking in terms of frontlist and backlist.* Most non-bookstore buyers are less concerned with the publication date than they are with how the content of your book can help their constituents. Assuming your information is relevant, corporations may use it as a premium, magazines as a way to increase subscriptions or cereal makers as an in-pack sales promotion. In each case, the format of your information may have to be changed to accommodate the buyers' needs.

   Given the fact that you probably already have a frontlist and backlist, evaluate your complete inventory of titles, and then devote your attention to marketing those with the greatest potential. One way to accomplish this is to reduce your reliance on bookstore sales and seek nontraditional opportunities such as selling to schools, colleges, hospitals, corporations and/or associations. These groups might purchase them for resale, as premiums or as gifts for customers.

3. *Start thinking in terms of long-range results.* The sales process for a large order to a corporation may take several years. Book fairs may test your title over a long period and then wait a year before placing an order. Rarely are people in as much of a hurry to buy your book as you are to sell it; so be patient.

4. *It is not necessary to choose between marketing to either traditional-bookstore or to special-sales markets.* It may make good sense to do both. Just keep an open mind and look for new places in which to sell your books.

   Beginning on the path to special-sales marketing is like starting the day looking at a misty landscape. At first you can see little, but you can sense something great about to happen. You will experience exhilaration and anticipation as you embark into the unknown territory that awaits you *beyond the bookstore.*

1

The Buck Starts Here

What Is Special-Sales Marketing and How Can You Use It to Increase Your Profits?

THERE ARE TWO PLACES IN WHICH you can sell books—in bookstores or outside of bookstores. That is an obvious statement, but sometimes publishers overlook apparent opportunities because they are blinded by tradition when it comes to selling their books. "I've always done it this way" has become their mantra, its soothing familiarity lulling them into a feeling of security befitting the passengers of the *Titanic* as they began their journey.

The bookstore market—embracing the top chain stores and superstores, independent bookstores and major online stores—is a familiar system that rarely challenges a publisher's marketing prowess. One contracts with a distributor to sell its frontlist titles, and perhaps a wholesaler to sell them to libraries, then settles in for a period of promotion to stimulate demand.

But there are less familiar places in which publishers can sell their books, daring them to exceed their strategic comfort zones. *Special sales, nontraditional sales, non-bookstore sales* are all terms defining the enormous opportunity that exists to sell your products outside of the traditional channels, like gold buried in mines awaiting the persistent prospector.

What and where are these mines of cash? They are all around you, but you probably do not recognize them because they do not have canyons of bookshelves. To publishers, they do not look like traditional sales outlets. They are disguised to look like discount stores, airport stores, home shopping networks, warehouse clubs, premium and incentive companies, catalogs, associations, gift shops, online communities and forums, retail stores, corporations, foundations, organizations, government agencies, schools, military bases, supermarkets and drug stores.

Once you get past the differences between these marketing alternatives, you will see their similarities. In both traditional and nontraditional distribution you can sell fiction and nonfiction titles through distributors to resellers dealing with the consumer. These sales entail discounts, and there are circumstances in which you could receive returned books. While there is greater emphasis on personal selling in nontraditional markets, you still need to promote your works with press releases, reviews, media appearances, direct marketing and sales promotional tactics.

Today, the worldwide book market approximates $90 billion. Almost one third of those sales occur in the United States.[1] Over the past ten years, the amount of sales through traditional outlets has decreased by 11 per cent (down 19 per cent without factoring Internet sales), and sales through non-bookstore outlets have increased by 8 per cent.

Traditional Book Marketing

Bookstores have historically been the traditional source of book sales. Even though bookstores are losing ground as *the* source for books, they are still the most likely place people go to buy books. But, as Dan Poynter says, they are "a lousy place to sell books."

Bookstores rely on the publishers to promote their books, moving them off the shelves. But what happens when a prospective buyer goes to a store looking for your title? Since similar titles are placed in the same area, he or she is presented with alternative selections right next to yours, awaiting immediate comparison, like commodity products lined up on a grocery-store shelf. Your promotion may help you, or it may help your competitors.

---

1. Data provided by Chuck Williams of AMS.

Change Since 1991	
Traditional	
Chain Bookstores	23% (Down 1%)
Independent Bookstores	15% (Down 17%)
Internet	8% (Since 1998)
Used Bookstores	3% (Down 1%)
Total	49%
Special Sales	
Book Clubs	20% (Up 3%)
Mass Merchandisers	9% (Up 2%)
Warehouse Clubs	7% (Up 4%)
Mail Order	3% (Down 1%)
Food/Drug	3% (Down 2%)
All other	10% (Up 2%)
Total	52% (Totals exceed 100% due to rounding)

This immediate comparison limits your pricing flexibility, too. The fixed price range may squeeze your profits, since your costs are high due to the distribution fees that are typically set within a narrow range of negotiation. The constraints imposed by fixed distribution fees, an artificial price ceiling and relatively high unit costs resulting from small print runs all conspire to limit the revenue and profits you can derive from each sale.

Additionally, bookstores return books they do not sell in what they consider to be a reasonable amount of time. If the books are sold, you receive payment in 90 to 120 days. Given this system, there are circumstances in which you can actually owe money to your distributor. A basic precept in the publishing industry is that a singular focus on traditional book marketing will doom most independently published books. Still, many publishers choose that route as their sole source of revenue.

Nontraditional Marketing

Nontraditional marketing strategy, as described in *Beyond the Bookstore*, is the process of selling your books to individuals or buyers in businesses *other than bookstores*. In special-sales marketing, a successful title is written in response to an identified need, is published in the form desired by the reader, then is properly priced, distributed and promoted directly to a defined group of prospective customers.

There are three major advantages of special sales over traditional bookstore marketing. These are *control*, *customization* and *segmentation*.

1. CONTROL. You have more control over your destiny. The responsibility for success falls squarely upon your shoulders as you direct and control the journey of your titles to the appropriate buyers.

PRICING CONTROL. Competitive titles are not on a shelf next to yours, so immediate price comparisons are unlikely. The price ceiling is raised, if not eliminated. At the same time, distribution discounts may be eliminated and your print run could be higher. A strategy of pricing your titles based upon the value they offer the customer is more the rule. The result is more pricing flexibility and more leeway to offer price incentives, discounts, two-for-ones or coupons (as you will see in Chapter Twelve). There are instances in which you could actually lower your list price and still be more profitable.

PRODUCT CONTROL. Restrictions placed on books to conform to bookstore standards no longer hinder your creativity. Now you can publish your content in the format most suitable to your target readers. This could be a book, or it could be a three-ring binder, DVD or other packaging.

PROMOTION CONTROL. You no longer have to cringe when a careless newspaper editor misinterprets your press release, or when a reviewer pans your book. Instead, you can create your own publicity, advertising, sales literature and sales promotional tools to tell your story in your way. You may also decide to contact people directly by telephone or personal visit to present your story and negotiate the terms of sale.

DISTRIBUTION CONTROL. In non-bookstore marketing you can devise your own sales channels. You might sell your business books through airline magazines or career coaches; your book about dogs, in kennels; or your book about car safety in schools or automobile dealerships. You might choose to sell your romance novel to discount stores, or negotiate with Godiva Chocolate Company to use it as a premium, or have limousine services purchase it as a gift for their passengers.

This is not to suggest that you ignore traditional distribution. On the contrary, market your products along parallel channels in a way that will optimize your revenue. *The Marketing Planning* CD-ROM accompanying *Beyond the Bookstore* shows you how to place proper emphasis on each channel in each market.

2. CUSTOMIZATION. Bookstore marketing requires that you sell *books*, probably 6" x 9" softcover books with a wide spine for easy visibility on the shelf. In special-sales marketing you are not necessarily selling books, you are selling the intangible *content* of your books. People are interested in what the information in your books will do for them—educate, inform or entertain. The beauty of nontraditional marketing is that the categories of frontlist and backlist are irrelevant. Buyers are concerned with the relevancy of your content to the solution of their problems, and the format in which it is delivered, while relevant, is not mandated as a book.

Buyers want to buy helpful information, not necessarily *books*. This gives you the flexibility to customize the form in which the information is delivered. It may be a comb-bound or spiral-bound manual that lies flat when used as a workbook during your seminars. Or, it may be a three-ring binder allowing people to add or change pages easily. You may choose to serve the needs of your potential customers with a video program, DVD, CD or saddle-stitched booklet.

3. SEGMENTATION. Some people looked at Goliath and thought he was too big to hit. David looked at him and thought he was too big to miss. You might look at special-sales marketing and think, "Is the nontraditional market big enough to approach, or is it too big?" The answer is *yes*. A U.S. market of $13 billion is too big to pass up, but it is too big a market in which to compete profitably—if you look at it as one goliath market.

Selling books is similar to selling automobiles in the sense that neither is one homogeneous market. In the latter, there are many groups of people, each with a preference for economy cars, luxury cars, sports cars, SUVs, used cars or antique cars. Within each segment, some people may also demonstrate a unique preference for style and color. There are demographic breakdowns in age groups that buy certain brands or styles, as well as psychographic differences among people who buy particular cars to express themselves.

The essence of special-sales marketing is this same concept of *segmentation*, the act of breaking the mass market down into smaller pieces, each more relevant to your particular title. The total non-bookstore market is actually made up of hundreds of "mini-markets," each with varying degrees of suitability for your title. These could be separated geographically, demographically and psychographically.

As an example of nontraditional market segmentation, consider the market for selling job-search books to unemployed people. Not everyone in that total market has the same career needs, skills or aspirations. There are college students seeking their first position. There are fifty-plus people with families and greater financial obligations. Women, minorities, blue-collar workers and Hispanic people all have different needs, require different information and may look for job-search assistance in diverse places. A title describing the basic functions of how to get a job could—and should—be marketed differently to each segment.

The title *Skiing in Colorado* demonstrates geographic segmentation. Your marketing instincts might immediately suggest selling this book in ski resorts in Colorado. But think not only of the book's geographic setting, think of where people who might want to buy your book would congregate. Skiers may come to Colorado from every state and you might reach them in ski shops or travel agents around the country.

This concept applies to fiction, as well. Fred Fenn's *Journey to Common Ground* is a historical fiction novel set in New England during the Civil War. This book could be sold in Civil War museums, or in airport stores, gift shops and bed-and-breakfast inns in New England.

Segmentation also applies to publicity. You might seek a review for your science fiction book in the *Fantastic Daily Book Reviews* e-zine, your romance novel in *Romantic Notions* or your mystery in *The Drood Review* instead of submitting them to the *New York Times Book Review*.

Award competitions are also segmented. The Publishing Marketing Association's (PMA's) Benjamin Franklin Awards competition has many different categories for fiction and non-fiction titles. You may also enter your science fiction book for the World Fantasy Award, or your mystery for the Dagger Award presented by the Crime Writers' Association. If you have a book on women's basketball, you might propose it for the award presented by the Women's Basketball Coaches Association.

Segmentation helps you market your book where interested, prospective buyers congregate. This may save you from wasting time, effort and money—all valuable commodities to the independent publisher.

Below are additional benefits that accrue when selling books in special-sales markets. The bottom line is an improved bottom line, since these benefits translate into greater profitability for your business.

1. *Increase your sales in a marketplace equal in size to the bookstore market.* If you do not seek book sales outside of bookstores than you may be missing half of your potential. Or, to look at it from a different perspective, you could double your sales with additional marketing effort directed to non-bookstore markets.
2. *Experience growth that is virtually limitless.* You can create an

entirely new segment for your books simply by conducting some basic research (see Chapter Two). Mandeville Press was able to breathe new life into its line of spirituality titles by finding new sales in yoga-center bookstores and meditation centers, in bookstores at retreat centers and through marriage counselors.

3. *Take your titles to the potential buyers rather than waiting for them to go to a bookstore, browsing among all the competitive titles.* When you call on large corporations or small gift shops you have the buyers' undivided attention. Most likely, no other author or publisher has tried to contact them. And when you call on people who more regularly deal with publishers—such as book clubs and catalogs—the buyers are usually receptive to your presentation.

4. *Reduce the competition because most publishers ignore the segments in which you are selling.* The majority of publishers ignore special-sales markets, with the possible exception of libraries, and relies upon bookstores as their sole source of revenue.

5. *Minimize discounting since buyers do not have immediate access to competitive pricing.* Bookstore buyers know how your book compares to competitive titles. That is their job. But if you go to product managers in a corporation who are looking for a premium to boost the sales of their products, they do not know if yours is priced above or below competitors' titles. They are only concerned with its cost—how the information in your book can help them sell more of their products profitably.

6. *Sell books on a nonreturnable basis.* Although some buy on a returnable basis (discount stores, warehouse clubs, supermarkets) most special-sales buyers do not expect to return books.

7. *Stimulate increased exposure.* Confer multiple *hits* upon your target buyers through a variety of promotional tools such as articles in niche magazines, trade shows, direct mail and media performances. If you are selling a title about improving someone's tennis serve, a review or article in *Tennis* magazine would more efficiently reach prospective buyers than it would in *People*.

8. *Increase your flexibility in negotiations since there are few fixed distribution fees.* Discounts are more flexible, and are typically based on the number of books purchased. Even if you negotiate a 50 per cent discount with a buyer, you are 5–20 per cent better off than selling that same book through bookstores. There are also nonprice variables open to negotiation, such as format, terms and payment periods.

9. *Improved cash flow, since some businesses purchase your products at list price.* Government agencies are obligated to pay you interest if uncontested invoices are not paid within thirty days. In special sales markets, many orders are for multiple copies, minimizing your costs to fulfill orders. Shipping charges are typically prepaid and added to the invoice. Returns are less prevalent and payments may be made in 30 days from your invoice date.

10. *Make your marketing expenditures more efficient.* Segmentation of your prospects and pinpointing promotion reduce waste and increase the efficiency of your expenditures. Below is a table comparing the marketing techniques necessary for selling books in traditional and nontraditional markets.

A QUICK-COMPARISON CHART

Characteristic	Traditional Book Marketing	Special Sales Marketing
Demand	Reduced during slow economic periods; discretionary purchases reduced	Stable or increased during slow economic periods; companies use promotional items to increase share
Concentration of Buyers	Generally dispersed, with some geographical/ regional differences	Industry differences; target segments are more concentrated
Buying motives	Buying becomes more subjective as the degree of similarity among titles increases	Experienced and trained buyers seeking good ROI; buying motives are more rational and objective as the degree of similarity of quantifiable factors among titles increases
Contact with decision-makers	Rely on distributors' sales representatives to sell your titles	Direct contact with the decision maker(s)

Purchasing influencers	Distributors' sales reps create personal relationships with store buyers and employees	Publisher creates and maintains relationships with people who influence the sale
Buyers' source of information	Distributors' sales reps, publicity, media appearances	Personal selling; advertising; direct mail, publicity, media appearances
Decision-making process	Short, usually during two or three selling periods per year; emphasis on front list	Deliberate; large companies may take a year or more to make a decision; emphasis on content rather than frontlist or backlist
Impact of price	Compare to competitive titles	Value-based decisions; focus on cost vs. price; business buyers seek positive ROI
Returns	"... the return rate for hardcover bestsellers has risen to 37%... compared to 29% in the year-earlier period..." (*Publishers Weekly*, May 12, 2003)	Some special sales are made on a returnable basis, but most are nonreturnable sales
Distribution	Distributors, wholesalers and sales rep groups	Distributors, wholesalers and sales rep groups to Special-Distribution markets; direct to most
Distribution Discounts	Standard distribution discounts range from 55% to 70%	Book clubs, catalogs, warehouse clubs, discount stores require substantial discounts; many opportunities for negotiated discounts and sales at list price

Strategy	Rely on distributors to move product to bookstores; utilize publicity and media appearances to sell through	Emphasize direct sale and distribution to the customer; push marketing (sell-to)
Product line	Standardized; commodity; sell one title to many different customers	Customized to needs of buyers; sell many units to few customers
Promotion	Promotion is primarily the task of the author; push marketing to channel members; pull marketing to consumers (sell-through)	Primarily two-pronged, push communication strategy to buyers in Commercial Sales and Niche Markets; sell through Special Distribution
Promotional material	Fact sheets to provide data to distributors, reviews; press releases for media	Creative material that connects the benefits of the titles to the buyers' needs

▰▰▰ Will Your Title Have Life after Birth?

The term *special sales* has come to be defined simply as selling books in non-bookstore markets. According to this definition, you are pursuing special sales if you sell your title to libraries, discount stores and book clubs. While this is true, it is only part of the opportunity available. In reality, special-sales marketing is a strategy for growing your business profitably.

Figure One depicts this concept. It shows the revenue from its bookstore sales (line ABC) going through the traditional life cycle stages of Introduction, Growth, Maturity and Decline.

Since the period of greatest profitability lies in the Growth Stage (between Points A and B), it behooves the marketer to extend this period as long as possible. Selling more books to new markets is certainly one way to do this, and *Beyond the Bookstore* describes how to do that. In this case, the Growth stage is extended to Point D, maximizing the profits generated from this particular title.

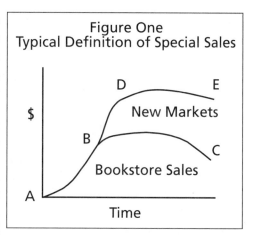

Figure One
Typical Definition of Special Sales

But what if you expand the definition of special sales to include more opportunities? Then *special sales* takes on a new connotation, i.e., it becomes a business-growth strategy. For instance, what if you were able to produce your title in different formats, to new users, for new uses and with more creative promotion? Then you have demonstrated a new concept of marketing that can extend the title's growth stage almost indefinitely. In essence, this is what Mark Victor Hansen and Jack Canfield did with the *Chicken Soup for the Soul* line.

The illustration in Figure Two demonstrates this idea. When you approach the growth of a title from a total-marketing perspective, you can extend its growth stage using a variety of marketing techniques. Below is a discussion of the ways in which you can market to these prospective buyers.

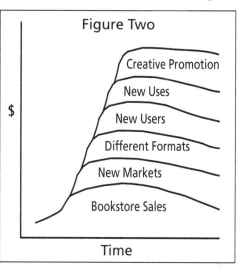

Figure Two

Strategy # 1: Find New Markets for Existing Titles

The signature application of special sales is finding new markets in which to sell your books. Fortunately, this is not too difficult because the special-sales marketplace for most titles is made up of three mutually exclusive component parts. The first is Special Distribution, the sector that utilizes distributors and wholesalers to reach retail outlets, similar to traditional bookstore marketing. The second entails marketing directly to Niche Markets made up of people who have an identifiable need for the information in your book. The third is marketing directly to the Commercial Sales sector encompassing sales to entities that use books as sales-promotional devices.

SPECIAL DISTRIBUTION

The segment most similar to traditional bookstore marketing is Special Distribution. This applies the distribution channels that most independent publishers currently use to market books, i.e., distribution partners ⇨ retailers ⇨ consumers. Examples of this network are having Advanced Marketing Services sell your book to warehouse-buying clubs, or Anderson Merchandisers reselling to Wal-Mart or Levy Home Entertainment to supermarkets.

The similarities to the traditional bookstore distribution channels do not end here. Retailers prefer to buy directly from publishers, and their choice of titles is a marketing decision, not a literary one. Distributors know what their customers are likely to sell—either fiction or nonfiction—and will reject others. In addition, returns are endemic, the discount schedule can reach 70 per cent and payment terms may exceed ninety days. Conversely, the rewards of immediate national distribution can be significant.

However, there are other channels of distribution using middlemen that act as distributors, but sell directly to ultimate consumers. Book fairs, book clubs, mail-order catalogs, home-shopping networks all exact a high percentage for their services to sell your books. Some, not all, return

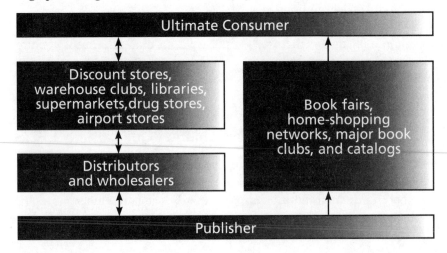

unsold books. See Chapter Eleven for detailed information on reaching prospects in the Special Distribution sector.

NICHE MARKETS

Niche marketing entails selling to definitive groups of people that share a common need for the information in your book. For example, you could sell your book about healthy eating to doctors' offices, fitness centers and stores that sell clothing, cookware, gourmet foods, groceries and health foods. A children's book could be sold to day-care centers, toy stores, pediatricians' offices, children's hospitals and children's museums.

Greg Drambour demonstrated an example of niche marketing by contacting spiritual centers and approaching targeted magazines, awards competitions, online communities, newsletters and niche reviewers while marketing his New Age title *The Woodstock Bridge*.

This strategy results in relatively small orders from many customers. A key to profitability under these conditions is to find clusters of prospective customers and then sell to the group's buyer. As an example, instead of selling books to individual day-care centers, sell to a chain of centers such as KinderCare.

There are niche book clubs, such as those for children, religions, foreign languages and teachers. John Palmatary marketed his Christian title *It's About Time* to the book club at *www.christianbookclub.co.uk*. Victoria Kinnear marketed her line of children's learning titles to the book club at *www.kidsonlinebookclub.com*. Additionally, mail-order catalogs can be segmented into demographic (for seniors, pet owners and individual sports), psychographic (health, new age and alternative catalogs) and geographic concentrations.

The thought of speaking before a group makes some people feel pressure that catches them in the chest like a giant fist. But if you are proficient at public speaking you could sell your books at the back of the room at full list price. Effective platform skills will also enable you to conduct library tours during which you can sell your books with little or no discounts. Jerry Labriola sold thousands of copies of his book *Famous Crimes Revisited* during personal presentations at libraries just in Connecticut (see pp 170–172).

Publishers that market through Amazon.com, Books-A-Million.com or bn.com consider online bookstores a traditional sales outlet. In reality, there are many other niche stores online, some of which may serve your needs. These include *www.coffeetablebooks.com*, *www.DealPilot.com*, *www.BookNook.com*, *www.1Bookstreet.com*, *www.AdventurousTraveler.com*

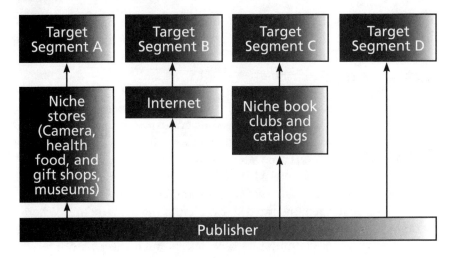

and *www.SmartBooks.com*. Chapter Thirteen provides extensive information on reaching niche segments.

COMMERCIAL SALES

In the Special Distribution and Niche Marketing segments the most typical product is a book. But in the Commercial Sales sector content is king, customization the prince and their servants run the gamut of all product formats. This gives you flexibility to change the form of the product to deliver your content as a book, CD or booklet, or for use as a fundraising item, premium, incentive or gift.

Of course, some customers may purchase your books as they are. Rita Ippoliti approached parachute equipment manufacturers to use her book *Falling into Place* as a premium. Michael Heim is creating a series of state-specific travel guides. The first is for the state of Wisconsin and is an excellent item to market to the Wisconsin Bed and Breakfast Association, the Wisconsin Association of Convention and Visitors Bureaus as well as local chambers of commerce to use as premiums or gifts.

Another factor differentiating this segment from Special Distribution is that in Commercial Sales you contact, negotiate with, ship directly to and bill the people representing these firms. There are no distributors to deal with, you can bargain for the terms, returns are rare and payment is generally made in 30 days.

Buyers for these organizations may not be aware of the value of books as sales-promotional tools. In this case, the sales process may be a two-step venture where you first convince them of the value of books as a marketing tool. This requires an understanding of successful selling techniques, numerous cold calls and the ability to accept rejection. The selling period is long—sometimes a year or more—but the payback can be enormous when one customer buys tens of thousands of nonreturnable books.

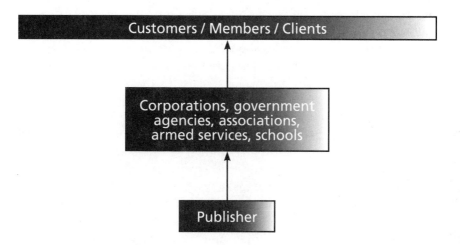

The Internet serves as a unique conduit for reaching all three sectors, vastly reducing your time and expense per sales call. For instance, if you are selling a children's book, you could contact online gift-registry agencies for babies and have them use your book as a gift item or premium and submit to *www.iBaby.com* and online niche bookstores such as *www.JustForKids.com*. You could also offer your book as a sales-promotional item for companies that provide baby-shower services such as that found at *www.baby-showers.com*.

CASE HISTORY

Perhaps an example will help clarify this process. Michael Andrew Smith's *Business-to-Business Golf: How to Swing Your Way to Business Success* is a book that can help salespeople develop successful business relationships while playing golf with their clients. Here are examples of nontraditional sales opportunities for *Business-to-Business Golf*, in each of the three sectors.

1. **SPECIAL DISTRIBUTION.** Distribution partners can be utilized for selling to libraries and to sporting-goods stores such as Sports Authority and

Herman's. Every sporting-goods store in the U.S. could be a prospective customer, as could general discount stores such as Target and Wal-Mart.

2. **NICHE MARKETS.** There are online stores such as *www.GolfWarehouse.com* that could sell Mr. Smith's book. *Business-to-Business Golf* is also a great title for sales through gift stores and golf pro shops. The author could pursue media events on web forums and write articles and stories for golf magazines (*Golf* and *Golf Digest*). The readers of airline magazines might be interested in articles about business-to-business golf, as would magazines whose readers include sales people and business executives. And there are niche mail-order catalogs catering to golf books, including *www.GolfSmart.com*.

3. **COMMERCIAL SALES.** *Business-to-Business Golf* could be purchased by managers in companies to give to their salespeople or by firms that manufacture golf equipment and accessories for use as a premium or self-liquidator. Companies that make golf software could also use it as a sales-promotion item. The national PGA and the state PGAs might use it as a sales promotional tool to promote golf as a business sport. Similarly, The Club Managers Association of America could use it as a fundraiser or to resell on their website to its members.

FICTION TITLES AND NON-BOOKSTORE MARKETING

These principles of segmentation apply to fiction, too. Louise Gaylord wrote *Anacacho*, a murder mystery that took place in Texas. It was published by Little Moose Press and marketed with the assistance of Book Shepherd Ellen Reid (*www.smarketing.com*) in each of the three sectors.

1. **SPECIAL DISTRIBUTION.** Special distribution can be utilized by submitting the book to distributors reaching libraries, discount stores, supermarkets, and independent bookstores that carry mystery titles.

2. **NICHE MARKETS.** Niche markets are widespread for *Anacacho*. There are mystery communities and forums online on which to visit, communicate with and sell to fellow mystery enthusiasts. There are mystery awards programs as well as reviewers that specialize in reviewing mystery titles. There are a variety of mystery newsletters, magazines and e-zines seeking articles by the author and willing to write stories about appropriate titles. There are also myriad mystery book clubs, catalogs and online bookstores that carry mystery titles.

3. **COMMERCIAL SALES.** The commercial sales category is probably the least likely of the three to be kind to fiction titles. However, there are premium and incentive companies that represent fiction, and some companies purchase fiction titles to give to customers and employees as gifts. In addition, there are associations such as Crime Writers of Canada, Sisters in Crime and Mystery Writers of America, Inc., that hold annual conferences at which this author could speak and sell books as back-of-the-room sales. Opportunities abound for the innovative marketer of fiction titles.

There are companies that perform selling activities for most titles,[2] but there is no reason why publishers and authors cannot pursue these lucrative avenues themselves. It takes some investigation, persistence and creativity and in many cases this can be accomplished online. Do not be intimidated by the term *special sales*. Divide it into its component parts and conquer them as you see fit for each title.

Strategy # 2: Provide Your Information in a Different Format

The form of the product that delivers your information is flexible, simply a means to an end. Form is simply the shape of the product, which becomes an armature upon which your content carries the message. A book is malleable, and may be modified or even abandoned to serve the greater purpose of communication.

As you focus on selling the contents of your book instead of selling the book itself, you can deliver the generic information in different ways. *Job Search 101*, a book describing creative techniques for finding employment, was sold to bookstores via traditional distribution channels. As the economy worsened, bookstore shelves became saturated with competitive job-search books. Incremental growth through conventional outlets became less profitable so a strategic marketing decision was made to seek growth elsewhere.

Research among college students determined that they wanted job-search information in a more easy-to-use format. In response, a series of eight, thirty-two-page booklets was created, each devoted to one traditional job-search tactic such as writing a resume or interviewing. With a little rewriting, the booklets were easily adapted to meet the needs of other markets. With minor changes, they were marketed to unemployment offices in all fifty states. With further changes in content and strat-

---

2. See *www.bookmarketingworks.com* for more information.

egy, they were sold to corporations to help employees who had been, or were about to be, laid off.

Another example of offering information in a different format was the video, *The Art of Interviewing.* In this case, the job-search interviewing techniques of correct posture, eye communication, gesturing and voice control were more easily communicated in a video format than in writing.

Strategy # 3: Locate New Users for Your Existing Information

Continuing with the *Job Search 101* example, additional research discovered an absence of career information available for the Hispanic market. Hence, *Job Search 101* was translated into Spanish and published as *Elementos basicos para buscar trabajo.* This required a new distribution network, one more knowledgeable in servicing a market unfamiliar to the publisher.

Further research uncovered another opportunity for entering the college market. *Job Search 101* was sold to college career departments where students receive job-search assistance. These sales were invoiced at list price with no distributor discounts and no returns. Additional sales of *Job Search 101* were made to instructors of job-search courses who used it as a textbook. This strategy also increased sales to college libraries.

Seek new opportunities with a clear eye and an alert imagination. Be open to at least evaluating a different concept, a different way of reaching the goals you have set for your business. Special-sales marketing is like electricity. It gives energy and power to the publisher, author and title. It brings good books to life.

Strategy # 4: Find New Uses for Your Basic Information

The titles *Job Search 101* and *Help Wanted: Inquire Within* describe many of the basic techniques for finding employment. Together, they explained where to find the names of prospective employers, how to contact them and how to interview effectively. Fortunately, these are the same steps required by authors to secure and conduct performances on television and radio shows. Even the interview techniques of correct posture, eye communication, gesturing and voice control are similar. But these were as difficult to portray to authors as they were to jobseekers.

This observation bore an entirely new product line, using as its foundation the basic fundamentals of job-search communication. This versatile content was repurposed and presented to a new market as the video program, *You're on the Air*.[3] This media-training product now helps authors get on and perform on television and radio. Its two companion guides, *Perpetual Promotion* and *It's Show Time* extended this initial product offering.

Strategy # 5: Implement Creative Promotional Campaigns

The marketing technique of *bundling* occurs when two or more associated products are packaged together and sold as one item. This tactic proved successful in a direct-mail campaign directed at parents of graduating college students. A package comprised of *The Art of Interviewing, Help Wanted: Inquire Within* and *Job Search 101* was offered at a discounted price to this target segment.

Examples of special-sales promotional techniques abound. Seek new ways to take your titles to new markets, in different formats to meet needs of new prospects. The combined impact of all these strategies will act as the waves pounding on the shore; they eventually wear down anything that gets in their way.

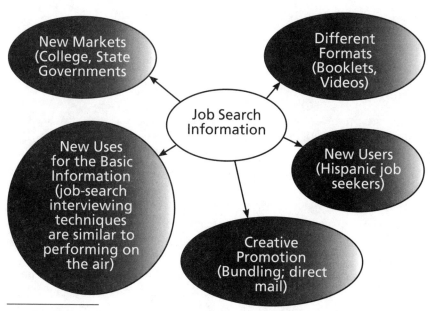

3. Produced by Publishing Directions, LLC; *www.bookmarketingworks.com, imarketbooks@aol.com.*

Continue to pursue sales in non-bookstore market segments and you should experience extensive growth in unit sales and profitability. These actions will prolong the profitable life of the original title while creating additional revenue and profits through the line extensions. These utilize all the marketing strategies that, when taken together, create the marketing process called *special sales*.

Strategy # 6: Organize Your Approach to Special-Sales Marketing

Special sales is a relatively uncharted area, a hidden market that awaits your discovery. Yet, too many publishers use the Christopher Columbus method of planning to reach this market. They do not know where they are going. When they arrive they do not know where they are. And when they return, they do not know where they have been. This is not a good way to run a business.

Avoid this situation by developing a coordinated, systematic, strategic approach to your nontraditional marketing efforts. Create a plan that identifies the most promising business opportunities and describes the actions you will take to exploit them efficiently and profitably. It should integrate all the elements of a complete promotional mix into a strategic program that unfolds as a coordinated attack. Remove the blinders and look through these "ize" for a view of a new planning formula:

RECOGNIZE. Finding new markets, new uses and different users is like writing nonfiction. You take raw information and mold it into meaning. Sometimes it is obvious, sometimes not. But the focus is always on people—the recipients of your final work.

A basic premise for successful marketing is to sell people what they want to buy rather than trying to sell what you have. In other words, find a need and fill it. This is especially important in special-sales marketing since you are directing your sales to the specific needs of individuals in well-defined groups.

How do you discover these needs? By researching in three major areas. First, discover what product opportunities exist. Second, learn the demographics (quantitative measurements such as age, income and education), geographics (the physical location of your targets) and psychographics (qualitative measurements of values, attitudes and beliefs) of your prospective customers. Finally, determine your potential market's size, growth and competitive status. Chapter Two describes simple ways to conduct effective market research.

CRYSTALLIZE. According to a proverb, a journey of one thousand miles begins with a single step. But what if that step is in the wrong direction? Start your voyage by deciding where you want to go. Write a specific objective and the date by which you will accomplish it.

STRATEGIZE. With your destination etched indelibly in your mind, plan how you will reach it. Start by creating strategies in each of the Four Ps of marketing: Product, Place (distribution), Price and Promotion. Based on your research, should your **product** be a book, a CD or a video program? Will you market it through existing distributor/wholesaler channels or directly to selected niches? Answers to these questions will dictate your **distribution** network and discounts, which in turn impact your **pricing** strategy and net revenue. Finally, describe how you will coordinate the elements of your **promotion** mix by manipulating your advertising, publicity, sales promotion and personal selling strategies.

ORGANIZE. Once you determine your general strategies you must plan the specific actions you will take in each of the Four Ps. If your product is to be a book, what size, color and shape will make it most saleable? At what price? Which distributors will you contact? To which reviewers will you send galleys or review copies? What will be in your press kit, and to what television and radio stations will you send it? Which trade shows will you attend? When and to whom will you conduct a direct-mail campaign? Part Two of *The Marketing Planning CD-ROM* takes you step-by-step through the process of creating a customized marketing plan.

PRIORITIZE. There are literally thousands of nontraditional places in which to sell most titles outside of bookstores. Unfortunately, not all are equally interested in buying your books. Any time you waste trying to persuade an uninterested buyer detracts from the time you could spend toe-to-toe with an interested prospect. You can maximize your selling time by listing your potential customers according to their interest, need and ability to buy.

CAPITALIZE. There are hundreds of different actions you can take to market your products. However, most publishers do not have unlimited funds to perform them all. Therefore, create financial statements allocating your projected revenue and expenses.

This is a good point at which to review your entire marketing program. If expected revenue will not cover your planned expenditures and no outside funds are available, what tactics can you eliminate? And what impact will their removal have on your income? For example, if you try to save money by eliminating a planned direct-mail campaign, you will also have to reduce your forecasted revenue by the amount you projected that program would generate.

ENERGIZE. Without action, planning only gives the illusion of progress. A vision must be accompanied by the ability and willingness to execute, or it is merely a hallucination. Now it is time to put your plan into action. Marketing a book successfully requires perpetual promotion and it is up to you to do it. Passionately perform each step according to the way you planned it.

> The author puts the energy behind the book to make it stand out. That's what makes the difference between a book that sells, has a life of its own, and a book that gets returned. MARCELLA SMITH, *Small Press Business Manager, Barnes & Noble*

People, products and markets evolve. They develop and grow, defying yet demanding definition. And you will change with them as your skills and intuition mature. The results of your actions are increased or diminished as you and your targets transform.

SCRUTINIZE. Action is not synonymous with accomplishment. You may be busy promoting your titles but not getting closer to your goal. Periodically assess your progress and make any changes that are necessary to get back on track. Few things move as quietly as the future. Avoid getting left behind by knowing where you are at all times.

REALIZE. The "ize" planning formula organizes and directs your thinking and actions to best exploit available opportunities. It coordinates and unifies your efforts to make your budget more efficient. And it helps you regain your bearings and look back to see how far you have come. You are more likely to reach your goals and maybe you will have some fun in the process.

◼ Strategy #7: Chart Your Path to Special-Sales Success

Marketing is both sequential and reiterative. Take the steps prescribed in the method below, backtracking where necessary to reevaluate your

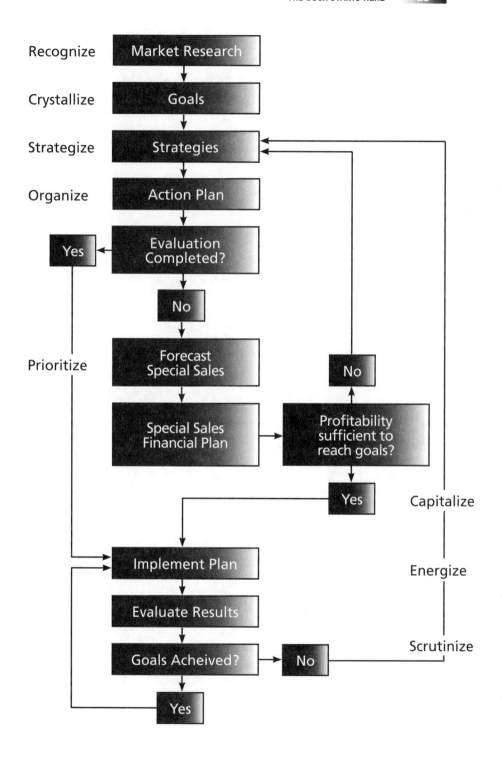

goals, strategies, actions and results. But when future analysis shows something is amiss, you may need to backtrack and change your plans. Below is a flow chart depicting this winning formula and defining the sequence in which the information will be presented in the remainder of *Beyond the Bookstore*.

2

Recognize Where to Find Special-Sales Markets for Your Title

F A COMPANY WERE TO SELL ballpoint pen sharpeners, how many would you buy? Probably none. What if the company cut the cost and made it easy to order them online? Now how many would you buy? Still probably none, because you do not need a ballpoint pen sharpener. Yet metaphorically, this is exactly what publishers do when they publish a book before they find out if there is a market for it, and if there is a market, how large and where it is.

Strategy # 8: Define the Opportunities for Your Titles

There is a significant amount of revenue that can be yours in special-sales marketing, but you may not quite know where or how to start mining it. Determining market opportunity is actually a three-part process.

1. DEFINE YOUR TARGET MARKETS IN TERMS OF POTEN-TIAL BUYERS. The operative words here are *markets* and *potential*. If you have a title on estate planning, you might sell it in bookstores. But how much more money could you make if you sold it in other segments including retirement planners, divorce counselors, divorce lawyers, estate planners, banks, retirement communities, senior centers and associations such as the American Academy of Estate Planning Attorneys? That is what Mark James did with his title *Estate Planning Success™ for Pennsylvania Residents*.

Potential buyers are not customers they are *suspects*. Before you make them customers you must locate them and find out what they want, the form in which they want it and how many they might purchase. Potential buyers can be found in bookstores, airport stores, supermarkets, drug stores and military bases.

2. CONDUCT SIMPLE MARKET RESEARCH to learn what people want, the form in which they want it, where they are, how many they might buy, the price they may be willing to pay and what competitive information exists (see Strategy #10 for information on how to do that).

3. CREATE A PROFILE OF THE TYPICAL BUYER, an image of the perfect prospect in each niche. Keep this image in mind as you develop your content, decide upon the form in which it will be disseminated, and promote your titles to them. See Strategy #11 for more guidance.

This process makes forecasting and marketing easier. If you know there is some demand for your title, and you know the approximate number of people who desire that information, you will have a better handle on your expected revenue, the number of books to print and where and how to spend your marketing budget.

A new title does not have to deliver earth-shattering content to be successful in non-bookstore markets. But it must meet an existing need and be sufficiently different from the other titles addressing the same topic in the same niche. Therefore, first find out what that existing need is and then publish books that satisfy it. This process is dynamic, and for many reasons actually makes the marketing process simpler, but not necessarily easier.

The people who get on in this world are the people who get up and look for the circumstances they want, and, if they can't find them, make them. GEORGE BERNARD SHAW

Strategy # 9: Segment Your Markets

When asked who the target reader is for their book, many authors reply, "This book is for everybody." Few statements will kill a book more quickly. The special-sales market is extremely diverse in its reading and buying requirements. You will be more effective and efficient finding groups of people who, as a whole, exhibit some similarity of need for your title.

A key is not to market a title that everybody likes a *little*, but to market one that fewer people need and are willing to purchase. These smaller groups of people are called market segments, or niches. They consist of an identifiable number of people within the total population that exhibit a common need for the books you publish. And each may buy your books for different reasons.

Think about the process of selling a mystery title. The author might think it is meant for anyone who likes mysteries. But people buy mystery novels for different reasons. Just look at examples in the three special-sales sectors, and the reasons people have for buying a mystery title in each:

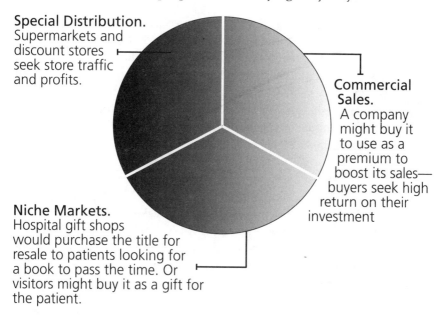

Special Distribution. Supermarkets and discount stores seek store traffic and profits.

Commercial Sales. A company might buy it to use as a premium to boost its sales—buyers seek high return on their investment

Niche Markets. Hospital gift shops would purchase the title for resale to patients looking for a book to pass the time. Or visitors might buy it as a gift for the patient.

Each of these would require a separate marketing strategy with different implementation. That is the essence of special-sales marketing. Organize people of similar needs into unique segments and market to them according to *their* reasons for buying your title.

There are three steps involved in the process of finding these groups and communicating a message that will motivate them to buy. The first step is market segmentation, where you make a list of everyone who could be a potential customer. The second is market targeting. Here you prioritize the segments according to their need for your titles. Third, creating a market position that communicates the reasons why people in each market would benefit by purchasing your titles. These steps are performed before, during and after the research is completed.

Market Segmentation	Market Targeting	Market Positioning
Identify distinct groups of people interested in buying (or who could be persuaded to buy) the titles you are selling.	Evaluate the opportunity each segment represents in its ability to purchase your books. Rank them in order of importance.	Identify what the people in each segment feel is important and communicate a positioning statement for each.

Publishing Directions, LLC, published a series of eight, thirty-two-page booklets describing the basic functions of finding and securing a job (writing a cover letter and resume as well as employing interviewing techniques). These could have been sold to all eight million unemployed people, but the buyers are so diverse that they would be difficult to reach. Instead, the processes of 1) Market Segmentation, 2) Market Targeting and 3) Market Positioning were implemented to make the marketing of these booklets more effective and efficient.

Market Segmentation

The saddle-stitched booklets are not suited for Special Distribution markets where a wide spine, a striking cover design and a formal distribution network are required. Instead, there are several major groups of potential customers who could use this content in booklet format. These are college students, government unemployment agencies, corporations, employment agencies, military exchanges and Internet outlets.

Market Targeting

College students comprise the largest single opportunity among these segments. They 1) are a captive audience that is easy to reach, 2) have an immediate need, 3) seek information in bite-size increments, 4) embody an educated audience and 5) represent a market that provides recurring income annually.

State unemployment agencies represent the second greatest opportunity because 1) there are only fifty decision makers to contact, 2) they have an immediate need, 3) their constituents seek basic information suited to people at various levels of education and 4) they represent a market that provides recurring income annually. Military exchanges exhibit similar characteristics.

Corporations might represent a viable market at first glance, but there are tens of thousands of large companies, each with a variety of decision makers who would be difficult to locate. In addition, the decision-making process is sufficiently long that the need may be nonexistent by the time a purchasing decision is made. There are similar reasons to eliminate employment agencies.

The Internet represents an outlet and the opportunity to use the booklets as a premium item (see Strategy #53). On your website, you might offer a condensed version of your title in booklet form, as a sample.

Market Positioning

Your positioning statement must communicate your title's distinct benefits as they relate to each segment, by demonstrating how your title meets its unique needs. Here are examples of positioning statements for different segments:

Segment Positioning Statement—communicated in each message

COLLEGE STUDENTS: Free (the colleges pay for them and give them to the students), easy-to-use job-search tips to help you get the job you want, at the salary you want, immediately upon graduation.

GOVERNMENT AGENCIES: Job-search information in an easy-to-use format for people at all career levels.

Positioning is a communication strategy that forms a certain image of your titles in the buyers' minds. It is a means to influence the way a prospect thinks about your title, and what it means to him or her.

Antoinette Kuritz relates this story about positioning her title *1001 Ways to Celebrate America*. "It was a book I thought of after September 11, but it was not a September 11 book," said Antoinette. She and her co-author, Greg Godek, contacted Triumph Books to publish it. Triumph agreed to do so if they could stimulate interest among bookstores beforehand. Triumph's initial attempts to sell it to bookstores were rebuffed because the stores had already bought all the September 11 books they could handle. "I told them that it was not a September 11 book, and I suggested a different approach," Antoinette advised. She concludes her tale by saying, "Triumph called back a few days later and said they had made their first $7,500 sale of the book, and they sent us a contract. They later sold one hundred thousand copies to Scholastic for distribution into schools."

Market segmentation, targeting and positioning offer publishers several benefits over mass marketing. You can fine-tune your content to meet the needs of an identifiable group of people. You have more pricing flexibility. Your marketing costs may be lower, presenting a greater opportunity for profits. Your choices of marketing strategy, distribution system and communication channels become clearer. You may face fewer competitors when focusing on a unique market segment. Finally, you will establish your position as the market leader on your topic in each niche.

It's the first company to build the mental position that has the upper hand, not the first company to make the product. IBM didn't invent the computer; Sperry Rand did. But IBM was the first to build the computer position in the prospect's mind. AL RIES

Strategy # 10: Conduct Market Research

Do you wear a watch? Glasses? Earrings? If so, were you thinking about them before you were reminded? The principle of *accommodation* asserts that we become so comfortable with certain things that we stop paying attention to them. Only when your watch is missing and you habitually look at your empty wrist, are you reminded about how frequently you consult it.

This principle can be applied to book marketing, too. We become so accustomed to one process of publishing a book and submitting it to a distributor that it becomes routine. This also applies to promotion, when a press release that seems to work for one occasion is duplicated for all. Sometimes the same message is projected verbally during media performances, personal presentations and store events. That is not necessarily wrong unless it becomes routine, delivered without passion or promise.

Special-sales opportunities are so ubiquitous that we fail to see them. We become so used to seeing a gift shop, toy store, beauty salon or museum for what they are that we do not think of them for what they could be: potential outlets for book sales. As you become aware of these new opportunities you can develop them into revenue. It simply entails conducting grassroots market research to discover the best prospects for your books, where they are located and why they would be interested in the information or entertainment you provide.

Special-sales marketing involves finding pockets of need and demonstrating to the people in those pockets that your titles have information important to them. How do you know where the need is? How many people are interested in your titles and what are the best ways in which to reach them? The answers are found through market research.

This is probably not the response you want to hear, since it conjures images of conducting focus groups, creating long questionnaires and then performing statistical analysis. Although this can be done, it is not necessarily the process suggested here.

Market research can be as simple as keeping an open and inquisitive mind as you go about your daily activities. For example, the number of women homeowners has grown by 53 per cent since 1989.[4] Publishers have been slow to recognize this trend, and home-repair manuals were traditionally aimed at males. A pair of enterprising authors recognized an opportunity in this situation and wrote a home-repair manual aimed at women: *Dare to Repair: A Do-It-Yourself Guide to Fixing (Almost) Anything*. It was picked up and published by HarperCollins in September 2002. According to *Publishers Weekly*, "The book worked because of the combination of a great cover, an intriguing angle, bookable, energetic authors and a void in the media for topics like this." Be ready to open your mind, evaluate its contents, and do not be afraid to change it.

START AT THE BEGINNING

The way to find a better mousetrap is to ask people how they would change their existing one. And if it were changed to their specifications, how many would they buy? Find out what people want by asking questions. Until you get all the answers, you will not have a complete sense of the market. This process may lead you to discover that you already have an existing title that solves their problems, but the marketplace does not know about it. Then your strategy becomes one of improved communications.

Do not fall prey to the conclusion that a good book will overcome the need for research. People do not care how much you know until they know how much you care ... about them.

Market research is more feasible when conducted among people in specific market segments, rather than the general populace. Reinforce-

---

4. *Publishers Weekly*, Jan 13, 2003

ment of this fact can be found in the job-search market beginning with the assumption that there are eight million unemployed people in the United States. If you could afford the time and money to survey all these people, you would probably find that each wants different information, customized to his or her specific needs. But you would not want to publish eight million unique books.

So, the first step is to look for points of similarity among your potential customers. Graduating college seniors have different requirements than do graduating high-school seniors. Fifty-five-year-old unemployed white corporate executives have different needs for information than do blue-collar workers looking for employment. Your opportunity lies in your ability to find out how many people need what information, and the number and content of competitive titles.

Suppose you decide to create a new title to help graduating college students find a job. The next step is to contact career-development offices, bookstore managers and librarians at colleges by mail, telephone calls or personal visits (see Chapter Fourteen). Ask them questions about how the needs for job-search information are currently being satisfied. Look for areas of unmet need.

What titles are currently available? What are their strong and weak points? What title is the segment leader, and why? Without that information you might blindly forge into this segment, erroneously thinking that the information you have is unique and necessary.

Much of that information may be gleaned from a quick search on Amazon.com. Margot Silk Forrest did this with her title, *A Short Course in Kindness*. She searched in the *kindness* category and found 336 competitive titles. She then sought the bestselling titles by sorting them in order of their sales. A quick review showed what people were looking for in this category, since they usually voice their opinions with their wallets. This quick scan also provided competitive information on the segment leader and the price range people seemed to be willing to pay.

Marketing research may be expressed in the form of creativity. Why not sell *A Short Course in Kindness* to religious bookstores, to gift shops, to support groups, to retreats and perhaps even to anger management centers? Insurance companies might even use it as a tool to reduce road rage.

What opportunities and trends do you see that others do not? Where are the holes in competitors' product lines? A case in point is typical job-search titles focusing on the basics of writing resumes and cover letters, and conducting interviews. Rather than duplicating existing titles, an author might decide to publish a title about how to dress for interviews, on job-search skills for women or one relating tips for performing during the first few months on the job. These are all subsets of the umbrella category.

Remember that your competition may not be a book—it may be a state of mind. College students are typically frugal. They can get free information from the career-development offices or their colleges' libraries. Why should they pay money to buy your book? This information might lead you to sell your books to buyers in career-development offices and school libraries or to instructors to use as a textbook.

At the end of 2003, research by Unity Marketing found that *connecting* is the next major trend in the $14 billion stationery and greeting card market. Among other findings, it determined that "The connecting trend relates to consumers' need to reach out and communicate meaningfully with others."

"Consumer trends reflect the emotions of the times," said marketing expert Pam Danziger, author of the study and president of Unity Marketing. "The consumer psychology of the nineties gave rise to conspicuous consumption and a passion for collecting more and more stuff to fill up our 'nests.' In the new millennium, however, consumers are focusing on enhancing their relationships with others." How might you use that information to enhance your product line, or launch a new one?

Find out where potential buyers look for information about your topic. Readers of romance novels would not be surprised to find them in hospital gift shops, at Victoria's Secret stores, flower shops (brick-and-mortar or online) or on cruise ships. You might sell golf books at golf driving ranges, business books to local chambers of commerce or diet books in beauty salons. Sell your books where people interested in your topic congregate.

WHERE DO YOU FIND THIS INFORMATION?

There are many sources of information that require more time than money to survey. Use those below to uncover information that can serve as fodder for your creative thinking.

1. ONLINE STORES. Search online for competitive information such as pricing, cover design, book size, number of pages and binding.

2. BOOKSTORES. You can perform RBWA (Research By Walking Around) in bookstores. Talk to employees and ask them what books are selling well, particularly in your category. Why are they selling? Is it the size, price, cover design, number of pages or internal layout? Peruse the shelves for examples of cover designs that you like. This information will benefit your sales wherever your books are displayed face out, such as in airport stores, supermarkets, catalogs or drug stores.

3. WEB SITES. Go to *www.google.com* and conduct a search using your topic as a keyword. An excellent by-product of this exercise is that you will find many ideas for new places in which to sell your books.

4. DISTRIBUTORS. If you have a relationship with a distributor, talk to your contacts there. Otherwise, go to their exhibits at BookExpo America (BEA) and talk to their representatives. Ask them why one book sells over another? How can you work with their sales representatives to increase your sales to non-bookstore markets?

5. TRADE SHOWS. BookExpo America (BEA) is perhaps the single best source of firsthand information about the book-publishing industry in the United States. Here, most of the top companies in the publishing industry gather to introduce their new titles. Talk to the exhibitors. Attend the seminars and other events that usually occur there. PMA-University is an intensive book-marketing extravaganza that is held during the three days prior to each BEA.

Publishing Directions, LLC, had the title *Job Search 101* translated into Spanish. The publisher took the translation, new title (*En busca de trabajo 101*) and proposed cover design to a BEA show and asked Hispanic exhibitors for their comments. He found that not only was the translation too literal, but the title was inappropriate. In the United States, a basic course in a subject is usually numbered (or referred to as) 101. This has no meaning to Latinos outside the U.S. This informal research enabled the publisher to change the title and sell a large quantity of books.

If you cannot attend BEA there are regional booksellers events annually (see sidebar). Most industries have a trade show you could attend to learn more about it. A good list of trade shows in most major industries, cities and countries may be found at *www.expocentral.com*.

6. PUBLISHER ASSOCIATIONS. Publishers Marketing Association is the largest association for independent publishers. Go to *www.pma-online.org* for helpful, free information and a list of local affiliates. SPAN (Small Press Association of North America) has a similar list of their partners (*www.spannet.org*) and an annual seminar. Find and join one of these local groups of publishers. Attend their meetings and educational events to network and learn.

7. LISTSERVES. Join online groups and participate in the discussions. Ask questions and read the posts of others. Keep in mind that while the participants mean well, their postings contain their opinions that may or may not be in your best interests to adopt. Evaluate what you read and apply that which seems most relevant to you.

8. READ. Subscribe to and read all the major industry magazines such as *Publishers Weekly* and *Writer's Digest.* Purchase and read the books by top authors Dan Poynter, John Kremer, Fern Reiss, Shel Horowitz, Ron Pramschufer, Marilyn and Tom Ross, and Brian Jud.

9. YOUR BACKLIST. Workman combined two seemingly unrelated pieces of information to sell over one hundred-thousand copies of one title. First, it found that American's spending on pets—mostly dogs and cats—increased from $17 billion in 1997 to $31 billion in 2003. Second, it looked to its backlist and noted a 1997 title with 762,751 books in print: *97 Ways to Make a Baby Laugh.* Armed with this research data, Workman published *97 Ways to Make Your Dog Smile*, which sold 112,000 after one week. It was sold through a dual-distribution network including bookstores, specialty stores, gift shops and pet stores.

> **Regional Booksellers Associations**
>
> Great Lakes Booksellers Association
> www.books-glba.org
> Mid-south Independent Booksellers Association
> www.msiba.org
> Mountains & Plains Booksellers Association
> www.mountainplains.org
> New-Atlantic Independent Booksellers Association
> www.naiba.com/index.cfm
> New England Booksellers Association
> www.newenglandbooks.org
> No. California Independent Booksellers Association
> www.nciba.com
> Pacific Northwest Booksellers Association
> www.pnba.org
> Publishers Association of the South
> www.pubsouth.org
> Southeast Booksellers Association
> www.sebaweb.org
> Upper Midwest Booksellers Association
> www.abookaday.com

It doesn't take a lot of work to discover pockets of opportunities. Simply ask yourself questions. "What should I be doing, or what *could* I be doing similarly or differently than I have in the past?" If you have existing titles that might address new markets, ask, "How many other people could use the information in this title? In how many other places could we sell this book?"

Or, ask yourself, "In what other forms would the information in my books be useful?" Perhaps you could present the content of your books in the form of audiobook, a CD, videotape, or conduct personal presentations and sell your books at the back of the room (at list price).

In how many ways could your title attract interest among corporate buyers to use as a premium? Barbara Pate Glacel and Emile A. Robert, Jr., wrote a book with the title *Light Bulbs for Leaders*. The obvious connection possible with Sylvania and GE notwithstanding, thoughtful market research suggests sales through corporate libraries and executive coaches.

No problem can stand the assault of sustained thinking.
FRANCOIS MARIE AROUET (VOLTAIRE)

Strategy #11: Create a Buyer Profile

After you have compiled sufficient information about your target audience, create a profile of your typical prospect or customer. Organize your prospects into well-defined pockets of buyers, each with similar reasons for needing the information in your books. For instance, Jim Houtz wrote the book, *Seize the American Dream: Ten Entrepreneurial Success Strategies*. He found distinct segments among corporate libraries, book clubs for entrepreneurs, small business consultants and through catalogs aimed at entrepreneurs.

The more carefully you define the buyers in each niche, the more successful you will be in demonstrating that you understand their needs, and that your title has information they will find important. Define each subset demographically (sex, occupation, income, education), psychographically (attitudes, beliefs and habits) and geographically (i.e., regional pockets of opportunity).

1. DEMOGRAPHICS are objective, quantitative points of classification. People who are of similar ages, genders, educational levels and income brackets may exhibit similar buying habits. If you can define a typical buyer for your book, by these objective criteria in each category, you may find your sales efforts more successful. As an example, if you find that readers of your book are fifty-five-plus years of age, you might plan to lay the book out with a larger type size and greater leading. Or, if you have a book on improving one's golf game, people in a high-income bracket may purchase it in pro shops at country clubs.

Armed with demographic information, John Assaraf, author of The *Street Kid's Guide to Having It All*, sought sales for his title among associations for businesswomen/mothers who work from home, and through newspapers at business schools in the Northeast (*Babson University Free Press*).

Bookspan established the Black Expressions Book Club in 1999 serving the African-American market and offering fiction, history, biography, finance, self-help, children's books and more. Bookspan is also targeting Hispanics, now the largest minority in the United States, in a major push by its Spanish-language book club Mosaico.

Consider how Good Books publishing company segments their markets. They have a line of religious books for children in sequential age groups, including the titles *My Very First Bible* and *My Very First Prayers* for ages birth to four years. Children from five to seven years of age would go on to *My First Bible*. Those in the seven- to twelve-year-old age group graduate to *The Bible for Children*.

Peter Abresch is the author of a series of mystery novels involving Elderhostels. Elderhostels are learning adventures that senior citizens take to places around the country and around the world. By using them as the settings for his stories, Abresch has not only targeted mature readers as his specific market, but has actually made use of the Elderhostel Inc. (a not-for-profit organization) name as a promotional tool. As his exciting and fun books promote the Elderhostels, people who go on Elderhostels will naturally be tempted to promote his books. In this way, he has established a comfortable niche.

Another practical application is the fact that warehouse club members offer a unique set of demographic characteristics compared to customers at other retail formats.[5] Todd Hale, an analyst at ACNielsen said, "More than 50 per cent of the heavy shoppers at warehouse clubs are consumers we classify as affluent." These members typically have annual incomes between $50,000 and $70,000. However, George Whalin, president of Retail Management Consultants, said, "You also have a class of shoppers who literally live paycheck to paycheck and they've found that a membership at Costco, BJ's or Sam's Club is the best way to stretch the dollar." RoperASW (*www.roperasw.com*), a worldwide marketing intelligence firm, provides the following club member demographic information:

- 68% of club members own a personal computer.
- 66% are married.
- 66% are homeowners.
- 57% have Internet access.
- 27% are college graduates.
- 27% have children ages eight to seventeen.

---

5. *Warehouse Club Focus* newsletter, Volume 7, Issue 133

- 26% have children ages zero to seven.
- 20% are sixty years old or older.

That information can be very helpful in proving to a warehouse-club buyer that your titles are perfect for its members. It may also be vital to you when creating the appeal to use in your press releases and other promotional material.

2. PSYCHOGRAPHICS. Of course, not every fifty-five-year-old, female college graduate has the same values, beliefs and attitudes. Your promotional campaigns will be more effective if you also define your target audiences qualitatively, or subjectively. If your title is about staying healthy and fit while traveling, and your target audience is comprised of active retired couples, you may try to market it on cruise ships, in ski resorts, through travel agents or in airline magazines.

3. GEOGRAPHICS. Your target consumers may congregate in certain geographic areas, too. Knowing this information could be helpful to your marketing efforts in at least two ways. First, you could sell to people residing in the book's topical area. David Rosane's title, *The Biodiversity of New York City*, would probably be of interest to a certain segment of people living in New York City. They could purchase it in the Museum of Natural History or The Botanical Gardens.

Another valuable audience might be people living outside the New York metropolitan area, but who expect to travel there. David could reach them through hotel gift shops, in airport stores or by selling it to travel agents in Europe to use as a sales-promotional tool.

> No great marketing decisions have ever been made on quantitative data alone. JOHN SCULLEY, IN THE *INTUITIVE MANAGER*

Strategy # 12: Find New Special-Sales Opportunities Through Creative Thinking

How could a wine press change the future of the publishing industry? Gutenberg combined the wine press and the coin punch to create moveable type and the printing press. You can apply the same innovative thinking to overcome obstacles that are keeping you from improving your business. The power of an idea—properly developed and implemented—can liberate a title to greatness.

WHAT IS CREATIVITY?

Creativity is simply the ability to find something new by rearranging the old in a new way. It is not necessarily a "bolt out of the blue" although it can be. There are techniques you can use to stimulate your thinking to come up with new ways of solving marketing problems or seeking new directions. Creativity is …

… a tool, not an end unto itself. It is a technique you can use to stand out from the crowd in a positive way. It is a system that can make your promotional efforts more unique and perhaps more memorable and successful. You can use this tool to plan new titles, implement a new pricing program or sell your books to a different target market.

… a different way of doing something. It is an outlook, an attitude, the ability to search for more than one right answer and the capacity to look at what everybody else sees but think something different. You apply your creative talents when you think of a new cover design for a book, or when you decide to sell your books in airport stores or to the military in addition to bookstores.

… fun. Innovation can be as enjoyable as it is productive. What if you, as an author, set a goal of writing three pages every day. You can still write your three pages on those days when your writer's block is larger than a city block. Just set your computer to display your work in 72-point type.

SO WHAT?

An old adage says, "If you do what you always did, you'll get what you always got." If you are content with your present circumstances, continue selling only to bookstores as you have done in the past. But if you want to improve your situation, find different and new places and ways to market your books.

HOW CAN YOU BE MORE CREATIVE?

Most of us are born creative, but that flair is suppressed as we grow up with the admonition to "fit in" or to "not rock the boat." Here is an eight-step method to help you release the imaginative child within you. It begins with the decision to change something, and leads to taking action so you "do not get what you always got."

Genius is childhood recaptured at will. CHARLES PIERRE BAUDELAIRE

STEP 1. Decide to do something differently than you have in the past. This is usually sparked by the realization that something is amiss. It could be the revelation that returned books are greater than forecast or that your profits are less than what they were one year ago. Or, you may want to introduce more new titles, sell into different markets or improve a publicity campaign.

STEP 2. Next, define the challenge so you know exactly what you need to solve. Another proverb tells us, "A problem well stated is a problem half solved." Describe it in broad terms to give you maximum leeway when seeking an answer. For instance, if you want to reverse a decline in sales, do not seek to answer the question, "How can we sell more books?" Instead, think, "What is the non-market? Who else could buy our books that are not buying them now?" This may open the door to sell your travel books to bed-and-breakfast inns, erotic titles in Victoria's Secret stores or adoption books to the National Foster Parent Association.

STEP 3. Conduct a creative-thinking session to come up with new ways to tackle the challenge you have defined. Gather two to five people in a room and start thinking. Have some fun while you are at it. There are three general concepts that will help your creative sessions become more productive.

1. Stimulate as many responses as possible. Think quantity, not quality at this point. Do not judge any idea at the time it is offered, so people feel free to contribute. This also encourages far-fetched responses, many of which will not be practical. However, an implausible idea may lead to a more realistic one.

2. Record your ideas. Use a flip chart, chalkboard or some other means of recording all the responses that is visible to everyone.

3. Discard unusable ideas at the end of the session. Once the idea-generating portion of the meeting is finished, go back and decide which of the responses are not applicable.

Use these techniques to inspire and fuel your idea-generating session:

1. *Ask questions beginning with "What if...?"* What if you condensed the information in your book and made a series of booklets? What if you sold your book as a premium to corporations? What if you sold your job-search books to prison libraries or your children's books to nannies?

2. *Ask questions in a way that will stimulate multiple responses.* If you say, "Where else can we sell this book?" then the first plausible idea will answer the question. Instead, ask, "*In how many other markets*

can we sell this book?" This will generate other possible solutions such as discount stores, government agencies, book clubs or academic markets.

3. *Think about your ultimate consumers.* Where do they seek the information in your book? In libraries? Then sell your books to librarians. Are your titles of interest to business travelers? Then sell your books in hotel gift shops or airport stores. Do they buy through catalogs? Then there is where your books should be. In how many ways can you make your books more accessible to prospective buyers?

   Special-sales marketing gives you another advantage here. A title that is even marginally "me-too" can appear unique to the publisher if the competition is unknown. When you sell a children's book to home-schooling groups, or a book listing the top retirement locations to alumni associations, you reduce comparison of information or price.

4. *Take a broader view of your potential.* The video program *You're On The Air* trains authors to create and perform on television and radio shows. It also helped train members of the Association of Civil Engineers to perform on the air when they were called upon to do so as the local expert. How many other people can utilize the information in your books?

5. *Stop selling your books.* Start selling the benefits that people receive from buying your books. Discount-store managers want increased traffic and profits. Demonstrate how your promotional efforts will drive people into their store. Librarians are not profit driven, but they want to help their patrons. What do your customers need and how can you help them meet their needs?

6. *Emulate successful people.* When you hit a mental block, think about what others have done to sell millions of books. What would Patricia Cornwell, Spencer Johnson or Robert Kiyosaki do in your situation?

7. *Break the rules.* Mark Victor Hansen and Jack Canfield were told that a book of short, emotional, feel-good stories would never sell. Their *Chicken Soup for the Soul* series has sold over 70 million copies. What obstacles are in your path, and how can they be removed or sidestepped?

8. *Just do something.* When one author was asked how to be creative, he replied, "It's simple, you just take something and do something to it. Then you do something else to it. Pretty soon you've got something."

9. *Use manipulation verbs to force you to think from a different perspective.* Apply these concepts judiciously so you do not reduce the quality of your final product.

Combine several titles together as a bundle. Add a CD. Would the text be improved with a co-author?

Reduce the size of your book, or its price, or its cost. How could the presentation be minified? What could you subtract? Condense? Make shorter or lighter? Omit? Streamline? Split up? Understate? How would you change your book if it were to be inserted as a premium into boxes of cereal?

Enlarge your book or its price, or expand its market in special sales. Sell it internationally or sell its foreign rights.

Adapt your book to other uses such as a calendar, a board game or the script for a movie or a television series.

Turnaround your thinking. Ask not only why people buy your books, but also why they do not. What could be rearranged? Can you interchange components? Use a different layout or another sequence? Change the pace? Change the schedule? Transpose positive and negative? Turn it upside down?

Eliminate elements to reduce the cost (without reducing quality), such as embossing, color photographs, die cutting or odd shapes.

STEP 4. Now is the time to sort through your ideas and eliminate those that are unrealistic. Discuss how your ideas can be applied, giving them shape and substance. Organize them according to their fit with your company's mission, their relative feasibility and the resources you have to execute them. Rank them in the order in which you feel they may be implemented.

Evaluate your ideas. Are there any drawbacks? Is the timing appropriate? How much will it cost? Does the potential return on your investment make the idea worthwhile? Are your assumptions still valid? Has anyone else tried it? What happened? Why? Do you have a *Plan B*?

STEP 5. Go do something else. Put your ideas on a mental back burner. While you are immersed in other activities your ideas will simmer. Other nuances, different assumptions or a totally new idea may come to you while your attention is placed elsewhere. Poet Doug King said, "Learn to pause or nothing worthwhile will catch up to you."

STEP 6. At some point one great idea percolates to the top and things fall into place. This has been called the "A-ha!" point where a new direction becomes clear. Passion and a sense of immediacy erupt.

STEP 7. It is not enough to have an idea. You have to believe in it to bring it to life. Take action. Do not let your analysis lead to paralysis. Just try something, make mistakes and then improve it.

If you use this process it is highly likely that you will find new markets, new sources of revenue, and solutions to obstacles you previously felt were insurmountable. Turn your stone walls into stepping stones by applying innovative thinking and creative strategy. It involves risk and a strong belief in yourself, but in the end you will open new niches, find new opportunities, improve your business, grow personally and have a lot more fun.

Creativity is being able to see what everybody else has seen and think what nobody else has thought so you can do what nobody else has done. TOM MAXWELL

Case History: Phantoms of the Market

An engineer can look at the foundation of a building under construction and tell you its eventual height. The deeper the base, the higher the structure will be.

A solid foundation for supporting book sales in nontraditional markets is built upon information about your present customers, prospective customers, your suppliers and the segments in which you now (or could) operate. Conduct a situation analysis to learn, and to create a benchmark for these people and places. Market research is a useful tool only if the information is interpreted and applied correctly. Your analysis must go beyond the numbers to understand the people they represent. If this is not done, the planning process will be less effective.

DISCOVERING THE PHANTOMS

Several years ago Publishing Directions, LLC, performed research among the country's eight million unemployed people. A typical bell-shaped curve evolved pointing to an opportunity for six million unemployed people who needed help with interviewing and writing a cover letter and resume (Market A). The research also uncovered two fringe segments (Markets B and C), each comprised of about one million people who did not need that information.

Given the option of selling to a potential market of six million or one

Potential Market:
8,000,000 unemployed people

General Job-Search,
Resume, Cover-Letter
and Interviewing Skills

1,000,000	6,000,000	1,000,000
Market B	Market A	Market C

million people, the publisher chose Market A, published *Job Search 101* and attempted to sell it through bookstores exclusively. That decision, based upon good information but erroneous analysis, proved disastrous. The numbers that appeared so real on paper were actually hallucinations.

PHANTOM DEMAND. The masses of people may have the desire for certain information but not the resources with which to pay for it. Unemployed people, like most people, are unwilling to pay for any item they can otherwise get for free. Job-search information was available at no charge from libraries and state unemployment offices. Market potential cannot be determined simply by counting heads.

PHANTOM CONSUMPTION. Additional analysis proved that the total market was actually divided into many sub-markets, partitioned demographically, geographically and psychographically. People seeking white-collar jobs approached their search differently from those seeking blue-collar work. The same principle applied to college students and senior executives. And there was also a Hispanic segment presenting a completely different set of needs.

PHANTOM POTENTIAL. Competitors were looking at the same numbers thinking they could also sell six million books. The potential market was now divided among four hundred titles. This yielded an average opportunity of fifteen thousand units per publisher if each achieved 100 per cent of its fair share.

THE EXORCISM

The publisher's response to these phantom opportunities was to create an assorted marketing mix. It implemented a strategy of market segmentation to exploit Market A. As described earlier, it sold the full-length book, *Job Search 101*, to the general public through bookstores and libraries and to college instructors as a textbook. Next, it created a series of thirty-two-page booklets, each on a different job-search function. These were easily adaptable to different market segments and continue to sell well among colleges and state unemployment offices. Then, the publisher approached corporate executives with the video program, *The Art of Interviewing*. Finally, *Job Search 101* was translated into Spanish as the book *Elementos basicos para buscar trabajo*, to address the Hispanic market.

The important point is that during this time Markets B and C became much more attractive, creating a virtually noncompetitive market of two million people. Those in Market B knew the requisite job-search skills but did not know where to find prospective employers. Consequently, Publishing Directions published *Help Wanted: Inquire Within* to satisfy that demand. People in Market C had the skills and contacts, but had poor attitudes. Prolonged unemployment, family pressures and financial problems eroded their self-esteem. Therefore, Publishing Directions published *Coping With Unemployment* to help them triumph over the demoralizing grip of these negative forces. By concentrating its efforts on these smaller markets, the publisher was able to increase its sales dramatically.

Segmentation, market research and target profiling will keep you from being fooled by mirages and help you create successful marketing strategies. Look beyond the numbers to learn the needs of people in each segment. Do not market to the number of people but to the needs of the people. You will find this to be a more lucrative long-term strategy.

Because its purpose is to create a customer, the business has two–and only two–basic functions: marketing and innovation. Marketing and innovation produce results; all the rest are "costs". PETER DRUCKER

3

Crystalize Your
Special-Sales Mission

I F YOU HOLD A MAGNIFYING GLASS over a flammable substance on the brightest day of the year, you will never start a fire as long as you keep the glass moving. But when you concentrate the sun's energy on a specific point it will begin burning quickly. Similarly, you will ignite your publishing business with a visionary mission statement that is translated into everyday practice by focusing on clear and specific goals.

Focus is important, and so is vision and clarity. You might expect to hear these words from your ophthalmologist, but they are important to special-sales marketing professionals, too. Vision is a compelling image of an achievable future. If you know where you are going, and concentrate all your efforts on getting there, you can define your own path to special-sales success. The concept of creating your personal path is reasonable because the non-bookstore marketplace is not well defined. In fact, it is different for almost every publisher.

A publisher of self-help books creates a different path to success than does the publisher of a science fiction novel. The publisher of a mystery novel will sell to different markets than will the publisher of children's books. And the publisher of children's Title A may blaze a different trail to the hidden market than does the publisher of children's Title B. You have your way to success and others have their ways. *The way* to special-sales success does not exist.

Therein lie the beauty, opportunity and challenge in nontraditional marketing—it is what you make it. Become passionate about your future. Get involved with your journey and it will benefit you more than you expect.

Some people think that planning reduces passion because it eliminates spontaneity. But consider writers as they begin to create their works. Their outlines set the stage for their plots to unfold, and soon the characters' actions begin to take over and rewrite the story lines. They use words to move an idea from one point to another; from thought to paper. Each author's passion is not reduced, but engaged and released. Planning begins, organizes, concentrates and then liberates passion just as the magnifying glass does to the sun's rays.

An amazing thing happens when you look at special-sales planning not as a burden but as a guide, a Marketing Sherpa that helps you release invigorating, productive energy. It awakens the sleeping tiger within each title to give it a life of its own.

Publishers are not always analytical people and tend to be less systematic in nature. They often need some help writing their first plan. Appendix A has an outline for a simple marketing plan that you can use to organize your thoughts. And *The Marketing Planning* CD-ROM that accompanies *Beyond the Bookstore* has a template you can use to write your special-sales marketing plan.

There are two parts to every marketing plan. Part One sets direction, and is comprised of your mission statement, an analysis of the current market situation and a declaration of your objectives. Part Two defines the actions you will take to reach your objectives and fulfill your mission within the reality of the marketplace. Strategies # 13 and # 14 embrace Part One. They will help you set your direction by defining your mission statement and identifying your objectives—as they apply to non-bookstore marketing.

The first of Stephen Covey's 7 *Habits* is to *have a vision* of where you want to go. The second reminds us *to begin with the end in mind*. The next two Strategies recognize the validity of those principles. They are designed to enhance your vision, clarify your objectives and help you focus on your future. Always look ahead; there are never regrets in that direction.

Do not follow where the path may lead. Go, instead, where there is no path and leave a trail. RALPH WALDO EMERSON

Strategy # 13: Define What You Want Your Business to Be

Your overall mission statement in your complete business plan describes what you want your publishing company to be *when it grows up*. But since your special-sales plan is a subset of your business plan, it requires its own mission statement to keep you on the path upon which you are about to embark.

Your special-sales mission statement is a concise answer to the question, "Who are we trying to serve, and what do they want to be served?" In traditional marketing your vision may go no further than the bookstore. Special-sales marketing goes beyond the bookstore to describe the ways the information in your books can satisfy the needs of different people. The way in which you interpret your mission defines your special-sales programs.

Strategic planning is worthless–unless there is first a strategic vision.
JOHN NAISBITT, *business writer*

Your mission statement helps position your business in the minds of your target audiences, including the people who work for you. If you are publishing a line of titles about gardening, you and your employees may think you are in the business communicating information about flowers and plants. But you are really in the business of helping people enjoy and appreciate life without spending a lot of money. A sign in the employee's lounge might look like this:

Rule # 1: The customer is always right.
Rule # 2: If the customer is wrong, see rule # 1.
Rule # 3: Help people enjoy and appreciate their lives
without spending a lot of money.

Translate the definition of your company into terms that tell people what doing business with you (or working for you) means to them, and you will transform your business into a profitable venture for everyone. Here are some points that may help you create a mission statement.

- It should quickly convey who you are, what you do and what you are trying to accomplish.
- Do not confuse it with a slogan or advertising headline. It is not

for bragging about how great you are but about what you believe in; what makes you passionate about doing what you do every day.

- Think of it as the twenty-second elevator speech for your business, as a sound bite to answer the question, "What do you do for a living?"
- Do not write your mission statement and then file it away until the next planning period. Use it. Write it on every press release you send. Post it where all employees can see it. Get them to buy into it so it becomes your company's living philosophy.
- Keep it simple.

A special-sales mission statement should be broad enough to allow interpretation, but narrow enough to sustain focus. It might read: *Provide preschool children with information that will educate them while keeping them entertained.* You could do that by selling your books through bookstores. But you could also do it by selling your books to day-care centers, nannies, au pairs and parents involved with home schooling.

If your special-sales mission statement were to read: *Describe the top retirement locations in the country to help people fifty-plus years of age plan for their postcareer lives.* You could reach them by selling books through bookstores. But you could also do it by selling books to Century 21 for their brokers to give as gifts to people selling their homes, to alumni associations to use as fundraising items, through the bookstore of the National Council of Teacher Retirement or by listing it on Boomers International (*www.boomersint.org*), the worldwide community for baby boomers.

Your mission statement does not have to be elaborate. The mission of Publishers Marketing Association (PMA) is *to advance the professional interests of independent publishers.* The mission of the American Library Association is *to promote the highest quality library and information services and public access to information.*

Go now to *The Marketing Planning* CD-ROM and write your Special-Sales Mission Statement. Use it to 1) direct your thinking as you search for fresh groups of people in need of your content, 2) keep you focused on the needs of the ultimate readers of your books and 3) stimulate your passion for going to work every day. Do this and the paths to reach your new target segments will become obvious and abundant.

A strong passion for any object will ensure success, for the desire of the end will point out the means. WILLIAM HAZLITT, *English writer, essayist*

Strategy # 14: Begin with the End in Mind

Have you ever thought about how an airplane gets from New York to Los Angeles? The pilots' mission is to have a safe and timely flight even though for 99 per cent or more of the time they cannot see their final destination. But they know it is there. They follow their written flight plan, checking their instruments along the way to make sure they stay on the right flight path.

These same concepts apply to selling your books. Your goals keep your destination in your mind as each book takes flight. Your objectives supply a standard against which you can gauge your progress. They divide your vision statement into manageable steps and provide a flight path to its realization.

Purposeful objectives are written, functional, measurable, specific and time-oriented. However, objectives must be more than that or they simply remain good intentions. Objectives should be operational, motivating those responsible for their attainment. Dynamic aspirations become the inspiration, for work and achievement. Finally, clear intentions concentrate and allocate your resources of money, effort, attitude and time.

"How could that be?" you ask. Let's say that your objective is to sell fifty thousand books through Special Distribution, one hundred-thousand books into Commercial Sales markets and ten thousand books into Niche Markets by December 31, 200X. This forces you to allot time for marketing to each segment.

One order in the Commercial Sales sector could yield a sale of one hundred-thousand or more books, but it takes concentrated and sustained effort to close. Since the buying-decision process is typically longer than it is in the other segments, you could start here. Then as this long-term course is evolving you can work on shorter-term opportunities.

With your Commercial Sales efforts set in motion, focus on the Special Distribution sector where a sale of fifty thousand books could be comprised of several smaller orders. So your next task is to organize your distribution network. You also know that selling ten thousand books to niche buyers will probably entail many small orders, but the income from those sales will sustain you while you are working on the longer-term orders. The *Fastart*™ Checklist in Appendix B shows how you can allocate sufficient time to various special-sales marketing programs.

Goal setting is a strategic tool, and like any other device is useful only if used correctly. Goals are worthless unless they are...

... **CLEAR, SPECIFIC, MEASURABLE, TIME-SENSITIVE AND WRITTEN.** This admonition is almost a cliché, but it bears repeating. Objectives must be clear so there is no misinterpreting their intent; specific so there is no doubt about whether or not you reached them; measurable in their objectivity, eliminating indeterminate goals such as "be the best in the business;" attainable in a limited time period (which could be a month, a year, ten years or more); written to make them indelible and not subject to later interpretation.

... **REALISTIC.** You might intend to sell one million books through Wal-Mart stores in the next six months. This is certainly clear, specific, measurable, time-sensitive and written, but it is not likely to happen unless you have a desirable product, a formidable distribution network and an enormous promotional budget in place. Set goals within the realm of what is possible to accomplish. This does not mean you shouldn't stretch to meet a worthy objective, but only that your optimism should not exceed your ability to fulfill. Set goals just beyond your reach but not out of your sight.

> A good goal is like a strenuous exercise–it makes you stretch.
> MARY KAY ASH, *U.S. businesswoman*

... **ARRANGED HIERARCHICALLY.** The third of Stephen Covey's 7 *Habits* is to *do first things first.* Follow this advice and list your goals in order from the most to the least important so you focus on doing the essential tasks. This produces a sense of control over your actions and reduces the pressure to put out the fires that appear urgent, but may not be important.

... **PART OF A PLAN.** The word *planning* is a verb, suggesting a series of sequential actions. Preparing objectives is the start of the planning process, the foundation upon which your implementation and evaluation occur. Your strategies and tactics emit from your goals. Refer to Strategy # 26 for more discussion on this topic.

... **MOTIVATING.** Your goals should *energize* you into taking action. They should make you dance upon your feet like a boxer at the sound of the first bell.

... **DERIVED FROM FUTURE REVENUE, NOT FROM EXISTING RESOURCES.** You may think you do not have the money to exhibit at an upcoming conference. That thought results from focusing on *lack.* Instead, look at the expenditure as an investment. What if you sell one thousand books as a result of attending, networking, exhibiting and perhaps speaking at the event? How much would that trip be worth to you then? Use the Trade Show Break-Even Point calculator in *The Marketing Planning* CD-ROM to find the answer.

... **SET WHEN YOU ARE IN A POSITIVE FRAME OF MIND.** If your answer to the question in the paragraph above is, "But what if I do not sell any books?" then take time out to reevaluate your circumstances. Negativity can overpower your thoughts when revenue and profits are down. That is not the time to be setting growth goals. Instead, set a goal to turn your attitude around, wait until you have regained control of your thoughts and then get back to work.

... **EVALUATED TO ASSESS YOUR RELATIVE PROGRESS AND FORCE NECESSARY CORRECTIONS.** Are your actions taking you closer to, or further from your goals? How do you know? Scrutinize your relative progress to determine if it is forward and goal directed. If it is not, make the corrections necessary to get you back on course.

... **FOCUSED ON THE SOLUTION AND NOT ON THE PROBLEM.** Murphy's Law is alive and well in most parts of the special-sales marketing process. The number of orders you could receive, particularly in the Niche Market sector, may be many times what you have experienced in the past. The likelihood of errors becomes daunting. But if you dwell on the things that did, do or could go wrong, that is where your attention will be focused. Therefore, set goals to sell more books, not to avoid returns. Do not fight problems—right problems.

... **DERIVED FROM A SENSE OF PURPOSE.** Non-bookstore marketing is different from traditional marketing. You will apply your efforts in several directions at the same time, making it difficult to maintain a sense of direction. Purpose breeds passion, the lasting belief in yourself and your ability to make your goals become reality. Your objectives will rarely motivate you to sustained action if they are not derived from an unfailing sense of destiny.

... **FLEXIBLE.** Your mission statement should be etched in granite, but there must be some flexibility in the way you implement your plan to fulfill your vision. Mental blinders could obstruct your view and prevent you from seizing unexpected opportunities. Rigidly adhering to a goal of selling one hundred-thousand books to Corporation A may distract you from considering the more feasible goal of selling twenty-five thousand books to each of Corporations B, C, D and E. Use goal-setting as the tool it was meant to be, as part of the process that transforms your vision statement into reality.

... **FOLLOWED UP TO MAKE THEM WORK.** Once your preparation is complete, move to the implementation phase, taking action to reach your objectives. As the age-old maxim tells us, plan your work and work your plan.

The importance of special-sales planning should now be apparent. Your mission statement controls the formulation of your objectives. Your objectives begin to direct your thinking toward the actions you will take to fulfill them. Your forecast will subdivide your overall objective and point out the number of each title you will sell to each customer segment. This assigns a dollar figure to your objective that you can then use to create your financial statements.

First, have a definite, clear practical ideal; a goal, an objective. Second, have the necessary means to achieve your ends; wisdom, money, materials, and methods. Third, adjust all your means to that end.
ARISTOTLE, *Greek writer, philosopher*

4

Strategize Your Special-Sales Efforts

I F YOU WERE PREPARING TO DRIVE to an unfamiliar destination, one of the first things you might do is consult a map to plan your trip. You would compare different routes and chart the best course to minimize your time, maximize your enjoyment and avoid detours. Most likely, you would take this map with you and refer to it regularly, evaluate your progress according to predetermined checkpoints to make sure you were still on course.

This concept of creating a map applies to special-sales marketing. Your objective has set your destination, so now you have to create a map to reach it most effectively and efficiently. This chart is nothing more than a description of strategies that direct your actions to create your content and then distribute, price and promote it.

Special-sales marketing is new territory for many publishers. Even those with experience selling books into non-bookstore markets face different opportunities every year. New potential buyers enter the fray and you will discover fresh markets in which to sell your books. And innovative ways must be found to get existing customers to reorder, hopefully in larger quantities. A marketing plan will help you close the gap between what is and what could be.

When selling to bookstores, the need to strategize is diminished. You publish X number of new titles annually, usually 6" x 9" with a perfect bound, four-color soft cover. There are a few distributors and wholesalers from which to choose, and each has its standard terms with which you must abide. Bookstores return books at will, and you are paid for your sales in 90 to 120 days. You have limited flexibility in your pricing, and the actual selling price is often beyond your control. The bulk of promotion is usually conducted in the form of publicity, media appearances and book signings.

There are similarities, but many differences between this system and special-sales marketing. Here the overall markets for your titles are divided into smaller segments. Each of these submarkets may require a different strategy and different tactics, and delivers different results.

> All you need is the plan, the road map and the courage to press on to your destination. EARL NIGHTINGALE

Strategy # 15: Create Your Marketing Mix

The four controllable elements of any marketing mix are the product you sell, its price, the distribution system you choose and the ways in which you promote it. In non-bookstore marketing there are countless combinations in which you can organize and manipulate these weapons.

1. PRODUCT STRATEGIES (See Chapter Five). The word *product* is a *hard* noun. It conjures thoughts of a physical product with a front, back, top, bottom and sides. The word *content* is a *soft* noun, with no shape or boundaries. While used regularly throughout *Beyond the Bookstore*, there are subtle nuances between the two.

In special-sales marketing, the product form is a variable. It becomes a marketing decision, based upon what will satisfy the most needs and sell the most units. It may be a perfect-bound book, or it may be a spiral-bound manual. A critical difference is that in bookstore marketing you are selling books, but in special sales you are satisfying needs with your content.

Luckily, many of these needs are met with a book, so you do not have to go out and learn all new production techniques. Your strategy may only be to make minor changes to meet market segment needs. Librarians prefer a sturdy binding that will stand up to repeated use. Corporations may want to change the cover design to add their logo or a notice that it is offered as a "courtesy of Company A." If you intend to use your books during your seminars, a comb binding may make them lay flat and be more useful to the people in your audiences.

2. PLACE STRATEGIES Place refers to the process of physically moving your books from your storage area to the people interested in buying them. Non-bookstore marketing utilizes a variety of distribution strategies, with multiple paths to success. Selling books in the Special Distribution sector (discount stores, warehouse clubs, libraries) utilizes an indirect network: distributor ⇨ wholesaler ⇨ retailer. Direct distribution in the Commercial Sales sector and Niche Markets eliminates the middleman. Here, you sell directly to your prospective customers; you stock, sell, ship, bill and collect for your sales. In most cases, the optimum distribution strategy is a combination of traditional and nontraditional channels. (See the Distribution Profitability Calculator in *The Marketing Planning* CD-ROM).

3. PRICING STRATEGIES Price is the element of your marketing strategy with the greatest impact on revenue. Yet, some publishers establish the prices for their books by following the rule of thumb that says the price should be seven or eight times printing cost. Others price their titles the same as competitive ones. There are problems with both of these strategies.

First, printing cost is directly related to the quantity printed. Multiplying the cost by eight may have little bearing on the most profitable list price.

Similar problems exist when matching competitors' prices. If their price is based on the low cost of a large print run, it could be ruinous to equal it if your costs are significantly higher. Use competitive pricing only as an *indication* of the range in which you can price your book.

There are five major components to consider as you determine the retail price of your book. The first three are hard numbers, distinct and explicit: 1) your direct costs, 2) the discounts taken by your distribution partners and 3) the profit you expect to make. The other two are more intuitive: 4) the goals you have set for yourself and 5) the psychological impact your price has upon the prospective buyer. These five factors play upon and interact among themselves much like the ingredients of a recipe. The way you combine them (with a dash of intuition) determines your ultimate price, sales and profitability. Pricing is as much an art as a science because of the impact of your judgment upon the quantifiable ingredients of your pricing recipe.

In the Special Distribution sector, you must cover your discounts and production costs, which create your price floor. In this arena you also have less flexibility in pricing because your books will be on shelves of discount stores, nearby competitors' books, allowing immediate price/value comparisons.

But once you enter the Commercial Sales and Niche Markets sectors, price comparisons become much less immediate. Product managers at corporations are not so much concerned with the price, but with the cost of the item. They want to know the return on their investment. You may find that you can lower your price, and without having to consider a 65 per cent distribution fee, your revenue might actually increase. However, that does not mean that your profits will automatically increase because now you will be responsible for conducting all the activities your distributor once did—such as carrying inventory, shipping, handling returns and billing. You may need to maintain the higher price to cover these costs. There are pricing strategies that may be applied to both categories simultaneously (see Strategy # 32).

4. PROMOTION STRATEGIES (See Chapter Six). Promotion is the marketing function that makes people aware that your book exists, and communicates reasons why they need to buy it. There are four general promotional tools you can use at different times to accomplish these goals. These are all more useful and productive in nontraditional marketing.

A. PERSONAL SELLING occurs during person-to-person interaction. It is a persuasive selling tool because it allows two-way communication, giving you the ability to answer questions, overcome objections and close the sale at the same meeting. The major disadvantage is its high cost per contact.

B. ADVERTISING can be an expensive way to communicate to your audience. It rarely results in increased sales in the short run and is best used to generate long-term awareness and exposure. Co-op advertising may be the most efficient use of this tool. Also included in this category is direct mail, a highly targeted form of advertising. It is most efficient when you choose the right list, create compelling copy and mail your letters at the proper time.

C. SALES PROMOTION includes specialty items that may be given away or sold at a low cost. Typical examples include advertising specialties (matchbooks, key chains, pens), card packs, T-shirts, calendars, posters, business cards, a listing in *The Yellow Pages* (or other directories), coupons, premiums, refunds, rebates, sweepstakes and contests.

D. PUBLICITY is perhaps the most economical element of the promotional mix. It increases awareness and credibility through a third-party testimonial. On the other hand, you have no control over what is printed in a review or article about your book.

Most publishers define publicity as press releases and reviews. While these are important pieces of publicity, there is more to it. Good publicity positions your firm and titles appropriately. It creates positive awareness, informs, instructs, announces and can correct a mistaken perception. This may be accomplished through the use of letters to the editor, backgrounders, case histories, newsletters, bill stuffers and testimonials.

Endorsements from celebrities can give credibility to an unknown author. Once you know the segments to which you will market, approach well-known people in each to provide you with a testimonial. Prospective buyers may be swayed by a referral from someone they know locally, or who is a prominent person in their reference group. Serendipity can play a part. Mark Victor Hansen's endorsement of *Beyond the Bookstore* was obtained while the author sat next to him by chance on a flight following BEA.

The emphasis on each tool is reversed in special sales marketing compared to traditional marketing, shown here in relative order of importance:

Bookstore Marketing	Special Sales
Publicity	Personal Selling
Sales Promotion	Advertising
Advertising	Sales Promotion
Personal Selling	Publicity

The distribution, product and pricing choices you make dictate how you conduct your promotional tactics. Your distributor's sales efforts in Special Distribution require support, perhaps providing them with sales-promotional devices such as bookmarks, sales literature and additional covers. In the Commercial Sales and Niche Market sectors you perform the personal-selling activities, send direct-mail letters or conduct niche-advertising campaigns.

Product and pricing decisions also determine the text of your promotional copy. If you try to lower your costs by eliminating certain physical elements that are common to your competition, and you still charge a similar price, then your communication must demonstrate superior value to the readers, i.e., why they will still be better off buying and reading your book than those of your competitors.

Strategy # 16: Map Your Course to Special Sales Markets

After reading Chapter Two you know how to be more creative, but how can you apply this skill in your search for new markets? A technique called "market mapping" will help you. It is a two-step process that applies your creative powers to discover these lucrative, nontraditional market segments.

This approach combines the processes of creativity and mind mapping to demonstrate a two-step process for marketing books. The first step is to discover the new markets and the second step is to map how you are going to reach them.

STEP ONE

Begin market mapping with a creative session devoted to thinking of all the possible markets in which a particular title could be sold. The key word is *could*. Do not limit your thinking to markets in which you already sell books. Given no restrictions, how many different people *could* be interested in this title? Where might they congregate or look for products on your topic? You might come up with a chart that looks similar to that below.

Instead of writing the word *bookstores* in one circle, write the word *retail*. This is a larger niche in which bookstores compose only one segment. Given this broader definition, you might add new categories including gift stores, mass-merchandise clubs and specialty shops related to the title. For instance, a book on bicycling could be sold in country inns, an art book in craft stores and a book about dinosaurs in museums. Continue thinking of other retail venues. Could your title sell through book clubs or catalogs? What about home-shopping networks, or supermarkets?

Make a category for commercial sales. Businesses use books as premiums, gifts for clients and incentives for salespeople. Associations and foundations might consider your title as a candidate for a fundraiser or as a premium in a membership drive. What about sales to federal, state or local government agencies? Is it suitable for sale to the armed forces?

Always consider selling directly to consumers. This could be done in conjunction with personal presentations or media appearances. You may have your own web site or be able to link with others. Direct mail is always a possibility, particularly with a line of nonfiction titles.

The academic category leads to many subsets. Could your title be sold to elementary schools? What about high schools, colleges, or special-education and vocational schools? If you think it might sell to colleges, draw a line from the circle and write the word Colleges on it. Then think of all the places in which you could sell this title at colleges. For instance, most have their own bookstores and libraries. Could it be sold as a text or reference book? If it is sold as a textbook, is a teacher's manual required? Apply this thinking to each category until its map looks like this:

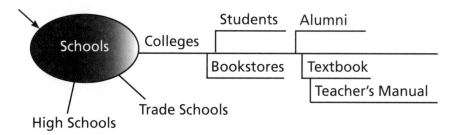

Have fun. Be creative and outlandish. Once you discover a market, dig deeper to find ways to develop it more fully. You will be surprised at the opportunities you uncover. Once you feel you have listed as many choices as possible, begin to apply judgment and eliminate those in which you have neither the desire nor the means to exploit. Refer to Strategy #12 for more tips on creativity.

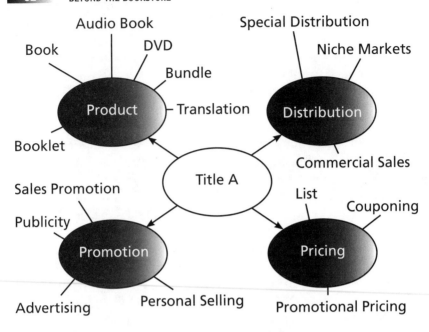

Where our work is, there let our joy be. TERTULLIAN

STEP TWO

Once you decide where you are going to sell your books, it is time to create another map showing how you are going to market them. Using the same rules and techniques you employed in step one, investigate possible forms the product could take and how it will be priced, distributed and promoted.

Use all these examples to stimulate your market-mapping sessions and you will find them to be an enjoyable yet strategic way to utilize your creativity and plan your marketing efforts for each of your titles. At the end of each session you will have flip chart pages full of circles and lines that define the markets in which you will participate and the ways you will distribute, price and promote your products in each. You can use this information to write your formal marketing plan, but keep the visuals posted as a reminder of actions you can take every day to increase your sales and profitability.

There are many paths, but only one journey. NAOMI JUDD

5

Develop Your Special-Sales Product Line Strategies

THE PRODUCT IN TRADITIONAL BOOK marketing is a given—it's a book. An author writes a manuscript based upon a topic with which he or she is familiar. It is typically published in a 6" x 9" format with a hard or soft cover. Once published, the book moves through the traditional book marketing distribution system, albeit sometimes at the speed of molasses flowing in the winter.

Once on the shelves, the books seem to find a permanent home, snuggled among friends, not willing to leave without a fight. But if the author promotes the title adequately, the buying public may succumb like a rock beneath the hammering assault of storm and sea.

Nontraditional book marketing is a more dynamic process. It rewards diversity. It recognizes that people want information, motivation or entertainment—not necessarily books. Special-sales marketing gives you the freedom to satisfy more customers' desires by producing a variety of products. This may be an audiocassette, a booklet, a spiral-bound book or a DVD. The emphasis is on the *content* of the product, not on its physical form, allowing you to transform your product line like an ice formation sculpted by and artisan.

Special-sales marketing creates options, which in turn generate opportunities. Of course, you can still sell books if that is all you want to produce. There are many non-bookstore prospects that will purchase them. But if you are open to providing the information in your books in a form desired by your ultimate consumers, then you are in a position to sell more units and increase your revenue and profits. This applies to fiction, too, as is demonstrated by the growth of audio books.

Serendipity also can play a part in your product development strategy. As reported in *Publishers Weekly*, B.K. Beckwith followed the chronicle of the famous racehorse Seabiscuit as it was unfolding in 1938. Then he wrote *Seabiscuit: The Saga of a Great Champion* based on his personal experience. Sixty-five years later, Bruce Franklin, publicity director for the University of Pennsylvania Press, learned that the title resided in the public domain and he turned it into a sixty-four-page coffee-table book. The title's publication coincided with the release of the movie *Seabiscuit*, giving it added momentum and saleability through racetrack gift shops.

The Benefits of Planning Your Product Strategy

A successful growth strategy is based on the premise that you cannot publish a title that is all things to all people. That title does not exist, except, perhaps, in the mind of the author. Titles must be written for—and marketed to—a defined segment of consumers. This presupposes that you have already recognized and defined your target markets per the instructions in Strategy # 8 in Chapter Two. Now your focus should turn to creating and marketing the products that you can sell to people in these niches profitably.

Product strategy is the armature around which you build your plans to add new titles, drop old ones or change the form of existing titles to make them more competitive and profitable. It is a planning tool used to translate your overall business strategy into a saleable, profitable product line. Product planning will help you drive sales into non-bookstore markets like a sheepdog herding its flock.

There are several reasons why you should consider planning a product line that is responsive to the needs of your target customers:

1) YOU WILL SELL MORE BOOKS AND BECOME MORE PROF-ITABLE if you develop products that are matched with what consumers want to buy. Publishers typically define their customers in terms of the people who purchase and read their books. Instead, define your books in terms of the people who could purchase and read them.

**2. YOU MAY BECOME KNOWN AS THE INNOVATING PUB-
LISHER IN YOUR SEGMENT, THE ONE THAT YOUR COM-
PETITORS IMITATE.** People remember and reward (with purchases)
the first publisher to develop a winning idea. For example, the *Dummies*
series helped IDG/Hungry Minds grow exponentially (and eventually be
sold) while it spawned "me-too" competitors.

3. INCREASE YOUR FIRM'S SHARE OF THE MARKET. Health
Communications was not a major factor in the publishing field until they
decided to take on two unknown authors and their idea for a book titled
Chicken Soup for the Soul. These books have sold over seventy million
copies, most of them outside of bookstores.

**4. REDUCE SEASONAL/CYCLICAL SLUMPS OR ECONOMIC
FLUCTUATIONS.** Sales in some categories have ups and downs, like
the marching succession of incoming waves at the shore. Adapting your
product line to consumers' needs can help you level your sales and revenue throughout the year. You may have a line of job-search books that
you would expect to decline in sales during a robust economy. But prudent product strategy would intervene, introducing a video tape about
job interviewing aimed at the 1.5 million college students graduating
annually who need employment regardless of economic conditions.

5. BALANCE YOUR PRODUCT PORTFOLIO. Your product mix
is constantly in a state of change and growth as you develop new titles,
extend promising titles or prune unprofitable ones. You can also nurture
titles that are rising stars, testing sales opportunities in different market
segments.

Strategy # 17: Develop a Product Strategy

How do you realize those benefits? Instead of thinking about publishing
and selling *books*, think in terms of *products*; not of *paper*, but of *people*.
The word *product* forces you to think of all the merchandise you can create that will satiate the needs of your prospects and customers.

   A product is the result of your *product strategy*. Only after the plan is
in place do you create the items you will sell. A strategy assumes a level
of forethought and planning based upon the needs and wants of your
potential customers. What is the information, or *content*, that they desire?
The strategic sequence looks something like this:

Need ⇨ Strategy ⇨ Product

First learn the needs of the consumers and then think about the formats in which they find the information easiest to use. If you are selling motivational information to which people could listen while driving, you might sell more products in the form of a CD or as an audio book. Information that is more visually oriented might be better communicated on a video or DVD.

He who puts . . . a product upon the market as it demands, controls that market. It is simply a survival of the fittest. GEORGE WASHINGTON CARVER, *U.S. chemist, educator*

A publisher that commissions an author to produce a manuscript based upon a proven need is traveling on this path. Even if the final product is a book, at least its form is the result of proven need. But as the old saw tells us, if the only tool you have is a hammer, you tend to see every problem as a nail. Sometimes, even with the best of intentions, the sequence ends up looking like this.

Need ⇨ Manuscript ⇨ Book ⇨ Bookstore

DEVELOPING A PRODUCT PLAN. Product strategy begins with an open mind. It asks the questions, *what do people want, and in what form do they want it? In what ways can I use that information to increase sales and profits?* This forces you to think about these decision alternatives:

1. SHOULD YOU CHANGE YOUR FUNDAMENTAL PRODUCT STRATEGY? You may choose to define yourself specifically as a book publisher. You can still do that and participate in special-sales marketing. But maybe it is time to revisit your core definition and think of yourself as a content provider. Then you might add books-on-tape, e-books, audiocassette programs or any medium with which you have a suitable comfort level.

2. COULD YOU MAINTAIN YOUR CURRENT PRODUCT LINE, BUT CHANGE THE STRATEGY? The intent of this discussion is not to overturn your entire business model. It is to point out new possibilities that could expand your potential while working within your comfort level. So, the short answer to the question is yes, you could continue publishing your current line of books and seek new markets in which to sell them.

Yet, there are decisions to make even if you decide to exclusively remain a printed-book publisher. You might begin by thinking about which of the two general product-line strategies will you adopt: a limited-line or a broad-line strategy.

In a limited line-strategy, the publisher attempts to cover one market with a single title or a limited line of titles. For example, Publishing Directions, LLC[6] addressed the need for training authors to perform on television and radio shows. It created a media-training package comprised of a video program (*You're on the Air*) and two books (*Perpetual Promotion* and *It's Show Time*).

Conversely, a broad-line strategy addresses multiple pockets of demand, each with distinct characteristics. In this case you would extend your line with different titles for deeper penetration into each segment. This system led Mark Victor Hansen and Jack Canfield to create many different *Chicken Soup for the Soul* titles such as *Chicken Soup for the Christian Soul, Chicken Soup for the Teenage Soul, Chicken Soup for the Pet Lover's Soul.*

A broad-line strategy is usually more successful because stronger titles support weaker ones, customer recognition spills over to the entire line, your books may experience greater presence on shelves in discount stores, airport stores and supermarkets, and your promotional costs are spread over more titles.

3. SHOULD YOU INTRODUCE NEW TITLES/PRODUCTS? One of the fundamental issues of special-sales marketing is that buyers are rarely concerned about whether the title is on the frontlist or backlist. Their emphasis is on the content of your material. If it is current and relevant to them, they will consider the purchase.

4. SHOULD YOU REPOSITION THE PRODUCT OR LINE? Sales of a viable title may decline even if the information contained within is still up to date. In this case, a makeover may be necessary to rejuvenate the title. This does not always require a new edition, but perhaps a new cover design, a new promotional concept, new markets and/or new uses.

The techniques described in the video program *You're on the Air* help authors get on and perform on television and radio shows, but the actual content applies to a variety of occupations. With a few changes, it will be repositioned as a media-training tool for any businessperson interested in marketing his or her firm, product or service on the air. The content will be repositioned for various segments such as Authors—*You're on the Air,* Design Engineers—*You're on the Air* or Small Business Owners—*You're on the Air.*

---

6. Publishing Directions, LLC, Box 715, Avon, CT 06001; (800) 562-4357; *OnAirNow@aol.com.*

5. WHEN SHOULD YOU ABANDON THE TITLE OR LINE? After a title has navigated its life cycle and reached its autumn years, its sales will eventually decline. There comes a time when you must consider cutting your loses and taking it out of print.

Eliminate weak titles as soon as you can. Unprofitable products tend to consume a disproportionate amount of your time, often require price reductions to sell, divert resources from more promising titles, can cause dissatisfaction among distribution partners and delay aggressive search for replacement products. These factors conspire to depress your profitability.

> Part of being a winner is knowing when enough is enough. Sometimes you have to give up the fight and walk away, and move on to something that's more productive. DONALD TRUMP

There is always the alternative of remaindering your books to recoup part of your investment, but do not choose that path too quickly. Instead, look for ways to leverage your investment. For example, think about creating a publicity event to give books away. This could help you establish contacts among people in the media, opening the door to future coverage. You can accomplish the same result by finding and donating your books to groups and organizations in need of them. These could include prison libraries, shelters, nursing homes or hospitals. The goodwill and contacts you create might be worth more than the money you would make through remaindering.

Strategy # 18: Form Follows Function

Remember that you are not selling products, you are selling content. You are selling what the information in your products can do for the readers, in the form requested by the user. If you decide to expand the definition of your company, this philosophy opens many opportunities for you since you are no longer limited to publishing and selling only books.

> The aim of marketing is to know and understand the customer so well the product or service fits him and sells itself. PETER DRUCKER

But what else can you do? The final form of the products you produce will be determined by their function. Provide the marketplace with the form in which it is desired. This may well be a book, but it could be a calendar, a television show or a party game based on your content. Do not wander too far from your base of expertise until you have performed enough research to make the venture worthwhile.

VIDEOS AND DVDS[7]

Even though videos and DVDs are different from books, the marketing process is similar. You produce the video, find a distributor to help you sell it to retailers and libraries, locate niche markets and then promote it in much the same ways as you would books. Unfortunately, the similarities do not end there. Videos are returnable, the distributors take a large percentage, payment is slow and large producers and retailers dominate the market at both ends.

But therein lies your opportunity. If you locate an underserved need in a niche market, you can produce and sell a video or DVD profitably. This can occur through libraries, schools, on the Internet, in gift shops, niche retail stores, to corporations and just about anywhere you can sell books. And you could market them in the same ways, too.

- Create a press kit much like the one you have for your books. It should include a press release, sales letter, testimonials, author bio, video sleeve, copies of reviews and relevant articles.
- Seek reviews in the major media.
- Conduct author signings at retail outlets.
- Get celebrity endorsements. But more important, have a celebrity in the video itself.
- Include a UPC.
- Sell seasonally, with the greatest revenues occurring in the fourth-quarter holiday period.
- Place a sample on your website. A short video clip functions much the same as a sample chapter.
- Attend the trade shows and read industry magazines for new marketing ideas and opportunities.
- Appear on television and radio to promote your products.

---

7. Wendy Brickman provided information about marketing videos. Contact her at 395 Del Monte Monterey, CA 93940; (800) 377-3739. Center # 250,

BOOKLETS[8]

Paulette Ensign has a mission in life. That is to convince publishers to "take a look at all the ways you can recycle what you've done once in as many different revenue-producing products as you can." She believes that you can use the information you have already created and published as a book and repurpose it in a different format. It could be a calendar, a poster or a booklet, which is the topic of this section.

Think of booklets as mini-books, useful to a target market for a variety of purposes. These can be used to recycle existing details about your topic, to disseminate new data, or as a marketing tool to promote yourself, your titles or your business. Booklets are smaller than books, so they can communicate your information in a less formidable package, making it easier to use, understand and perhaps reuse by your customers. And the attention span of people in general has been decreasing. Many in the general population initially want an overview of information to determine their interest level before investing more in information about a topic. Booklets can serve that purpose.

There are several reasons why you might want to create booklets. Primary among these is the fact that your target customers may prefer more bite-sized booklets rather than a more complete dissertation in a book. Booklets serve other purposes, too.

- **Sell booklets to your customers and prospects.** Other, non-competing companies serving your target markets may buy your booklets, insert their company's name on them and re-sell them, or choose to distribute them for free. They will get the credit for supplying valuable tips, and you get increased exposure and income. In some situations companies may buy your booklets on healthcare, motivation or safety and give them to their employees. They are likely to buy booklets—rather than books—for that purpose because of their lower cost.

- **Use your booklet to sell your books.** During your media performances you might offer to send one to each caller. People are more likely to ask for a free report than they are to order your book, and your reply delivers literature about it with the booklet. Also, leave some in the studio to give away in the future. As Paulette says, "the product varies, but the path to

8. Paulette Ensign, President of Tips Products International, contributed to the information on booklets found throughout *Beyond the Bookstore*; she can be reached at *Paulette@tipsbooklets.com*

the sale remains the same," and later adds, "the question is not necessarily one of *yes* or *no*, but *should I start with the book or the booklets?*"

- **Enhance your personal presentations**. People hiring you to speak to their company or organization may purchase your booklets in advance to give to each attendee. You can always bring your books and other products to sell at the back of the room after your presentation.

- **Allow magazines to excerpt from your booklet**. Writers are always looking for quick tips for their articles or to use in sidebars. Of course, you should receive full credit as the source of the material. Paulette Ensign benefited from publicity when an electrical manufacturing-representatives firm in San Juan, Puerto Rico, ran across a publicity excerpt about her booklet *110 Ideas for Organizing Your Business Life*. An executive from the company thought it would make a great holiday greeting and ordered 2,500 copies. An important consideration is that the company sent these booklets to their clients with Paulette's contact information included. "It was great to have another company pay to promote me," she says.

- **Build a complete product line**. If you are relatively new to an industry, a booklet can give you immediate credibility, exposure and income while you develop the rest of your product line. Build your first booklet into a continuity series, and then use that material to later create a full-length book, DVD or audiocassette package. There should be some similarity in the cover design if you are publishing a series of booklets.

  When Career Track, a public seminar company, came upon a publicity excerpt about Paulette's booklet, she said, "They came to me with an idea for an application I had never thought of." They wanted to use her booklet to clean their direct-mail mailing list. They bought over one thousand copies of *110 Ideas for Organizing Your Business Life* and offered it to people who reported receiving multiple copies of their seminar brochures. Prior to that, Career Track hired her to record an audiocassette program of the information in her booklet, creating another product sold by Career Track and by Paulette's company.

- **Use your booklet as a marketing tool for your business**. When properly written, booklets can promote your capabilities while providing information. You can use a booklet describing "101 tips for doing (whatever it is you do)" as an enticement to go to your website to download a free copy. Or, your prospect could send for a free report. Of course, your reply will contain your booklet as well as your collateral material. This gives you a mailing to your prime prospects at minimal cost. Under other circumstances you might give your booklets away as a reason to visit your exhibit at a trade show. Or, you could contact a company to buy your booklets to attract visitors to their exhibit.

Whatever your subject, condense it to a list of tips and hints, add some selling copy describing your services, and give it away for free or sell it. That exercise will force you to think more carefully about your subject. The process of coming up with a concise description of your services will serve you well in other areas, too.

- **Test a new idea for a book before going to the expense of publishing it**. If you have an idea and you are not sure of its market potential, create a booklet first to test the water. Booklets are less expensive to produce than are books so your financial exposure is reduced.
- **Tailor them to each customer**. Booklets can be produced quickly. Without changing the content, you can make your booklet appear to be the exclusive product of a company by placing its name and address on the cover. Of course, you want to maintain your identity, too.

You could also adapt the content to each customer, perhaps appropriately mentioning its name or product throughout. The job-search booklets created by Publishing Directions were favored by college students who wanted quick, useful job-search tactics, and by state unemployment offices seeking a low-cost way to disseminate practical information. Each booklet was rewritten to reflect the needs of the different target audiences.

- **Provide regular income**. If you sell to an organization, such as a college, that has repetitive need for your information, ask them to place a standing order each semester.
- **Use your booklet as a lead generation technique coupled with a sales letter**. According to Eric Gelb,[9] "A lead generation tool is a free item or a low-priced item that is designed to draw new

---

9. Eric Gelb, editor of *Publishing Gold* e-zine (www.PublishingGold.com).

customers to your business. Examples include booklets or chapter excerpts from your book. Last year, we created a booklet *157 Ways to Cut Your Grocery Bill*. Several newsletters reviewed the booklet and orders flooded in. In each envelope, we inserted a mail-merged sales letter inviting people to use the booklet as a premium and explaining all the benefits. We offer personalization and customization. One letter brought in an order for 500 copies. And, since we sold the booklet in the original offer, this entire campaign was very profitable. We are currently in discussion with a major magazine that is interested in using the Grocery booklet as a new subscriber bonus, and an online grocery shopping service that wants to use the booklet as a purchase bonus."

- **Workshop material**. If you conduct workshops or seminars, use booklets to augment your discussion material. Booklets are saddle-stitched which makes them lay flat more readily than would a bound book, making them easier to use during your presentation.

If you create a booklet to use during your presentations or workshops, you may want a larger sized booklet, even up to 8½" x 11." Although there is no "standard" size, there are certain sizes that are more economical than others to print. 5½" x 8½" is a typical size since it can be printed on an 8½" x 11" sheet and folded. The 3½" or 4" x 8½" is a good size to fit in a #10 business envelope.

Production Process

A booklet can be produced in almost any size and shape, but the primary considerations should be cost of production, ease of use and presentation of information. It should be convenient to carry and easy to read. A good size might be that which fits in a man's coat pocket or a woman's purse. If you keep it less than the size of a standard business envelope, your mailing costs for individual copies could be reduced. But in most cases you will be shipping your booklets in large quantities, not one at a time.

Cover. Your booklets will not be sold in bookstores, so a striking cover design is not mandatory. Neither is four-color production, embossing or other expensive techniques. You could even choose one color of ink with a different, complementary-colored card stock. If you are using your booklets to augment your workshops and speaking engagements your cover serves as an advertisement for you. Your name should be displayed in type larger than it would on a typical book cover.

The cover should not be too busy. Strive for clarity, and use white space to relieve visual clutter. If you offer a service to customize your booklets for your customers—which is a good idea—leave room on the front cover for their message or logo.

Since your booklets will be saddle-stitched, you do not need to create copy for its spine, but the rear cover should be treated as you would a standard book. There is no need for a barcode, but use this space for additional selling copy, particularly if used during your presentations. Leave enough blank space to be used for advertising by the large-quantity buyer.

Interior. Another consideration for saddle-stitched booklets is that they should not exceed thirty-two pages of text. This allows an even signature and makes it more likely that your booklet will lay flat. People buy booklets for quick tips or hints on some topic. Do not crowd the page with a lot of text. Use large type, white space and good layout techniques to make the information easily accessible.

You can utilize a variation of the print-on-demand concept by having your booklets printed to order. The unit cost will be higher at lower quantities, but that could also be reflected in your pricing (see Strategy # 32). Some of that higher price may be also be offset by the savings on storage space and not having to carry inventory.

Pricing

The dilemma with pricing booklets is that if the price becomes too high (relative to the price of a book), people will be less inclined to buy it. People expect "tips and hints" to be less expensive than a full-length book. Your booklets will usually be sold in large quantities so shipping is less of a factor (and the buyer will normally pay shipping costs). And there will be no distributors' discounts with which to contend. So try to keep your pricing at $4.95 or less.

If you are using your booklet only during your own workshops, you may price it higher and include it in the cost of the workshop. This also gives greater value to the overall experience.

The price of booklets is usually discounted based upon the quantity purchased. If you plan to have your booklets printed and shipped to order, check with your printer to get your cost at various quantities. If you intend to print in large quantities initially and ship from inventory, you will probably have a lower total unit cost and more pricing flexibility.

Price the lowest quantity high to encourage buyers to purchase in larger quantities. List your case quantities to encourage buying by the case. If your customers buy in large quantities (10,000 or more), or are interested in a non-English translation of your booklet, consider granting them a license to reprint the booklets themselves. Calculate the profit you would make on that sale, less the aggravation for putting it together each time and use that figure as the basis for the licensing agreement. Ask for royalties if your customer plans to resell your booklets; and in all cases make sure you retain the copyright.

With your costs and strategies firmly in hand, your price list for non-customized booklets might look something like this:

Table 4	
1–99	$4.95
100–499	$4.00
500–999	$3.50
1000–4999	$2.50
5000–9999	$1.50
10,000+	Priced to order

Add a premium for customization or other changes to your booklets. When you customize a project, ask for a 50 per cent deposit, or an amount that will at least cover your costs, because customized booklets are not saleable to other clients. It is standard to add 10 per cent of the invoice total for shipping and handling up to a certain volume, then add 5 per cent—or the shipping becomes exorbitant.

Strategy # 19: Preserve Product Quality

Product quality is a competitive marketing tool and a cost-saving strategy that has objective and subjective, tangible and intangible characteristics. Objective criteria are the obvious typographical errors, poor grammar, sloppy construction and damaged books.

Other criteria are more subjective and prone to personal bias. These include cover design and layout. In a marketing sense, instances of poor quality are also found in an inconsiderate telephone voice, inadequate or slow processing of complaints and not returning phone calls.

> Quality in a product or service is not what the supplier puts in. It is what the customer gets out and is willing to pay for. A product is not quality because it is hard to make and costs a lot of money, as manufacturers typically believe. PETER DRUCKER

THINK *POTENTIAL*

There is another way to think about quality from your customer's perspective. First, describe your book in terms of its generic function and what people expect of it. Then explain how you can augment their expectations by making a credible claim. This promise leads the reader to anticipate a potential payoff that no competitive product offers.

GENERIC CONFORMANCE. Certain elements are assumed to be included in every product. For a book sold to retail outlets, these include an ISBN, bar code, the price on the rear cover and the title on the spine. These features are not sale-breaking factors unless they are missing, especially when the item is being sold at retail.

EXPECTED PERFORMANCE. At the next higher level, your products are expected to adhere to minimum performance levels. Do they perform as expected? Not just functionally, but do they do what you promised them to do in your publicity? If your CD describing book-selling techniques is touted as having "everything a novice needs to sell millions of books," it should have a significant amount of information.

Your prospects and customers translate expected performance as *reliability*. From your distributor's perspective: do you publish your books when you say you will? Media producers worry if you will be the guest you purported to be. In general, it is better to underpromise and overdeliver.

Expectations are judged subjectively. Is your book easy to read? Is your booklet sized for convenience? Is its layout readable? Is the text in proper sequence? Is your table of contents easy to use? Is your video/DVD label descriptive of its contents? Disappointment caused by perceived inadequacy carries an opportunity cost expressed as negative word-of-mouth advertising.

AUGMENTED ATTRIBUTES. When you ordered a sandwich in a delicatessen, did it come with a pickle? You didn't order that, but it came anyway. What value-added, unexpected advantage can you give your prospects that they didn't expect (nor expect to pay for)? Michele Bledsoe's The *Doggy Bone Cookbook* comes with a cookie cutter in the shape of a dog bone. What added benefit can you provide that increases the perceived value of your product without increasing the price inordinately?

POTENTIAL BENEFITS. Product strategy at this final stage transcends the augmented attributes. It recognizes that people are willing to pay more if they perceive the extra quality worthy of the additional cost. A bundle containing a book and a video or CD, priced lower than the two items purchased separately, is a potential benefit. People are usually willing to part with additional funds for this added capacity.

For example, consider the title, *It's Show Time* about performing on radio and television. The *generic* product is a stack of trimmed, numbered pages, perfect bound and protected by a soft cover. People *expect* it to be a helpful, descriptive narrative about the techniques for performing successfully on the air. Most marketers stop here, promoting only these undifferentiated expectations.

Successful marketers take their message further by *augmenting* this expectation, offering prospective customers more than they envision receiving or have been accustomed to expect. In this case, *It's Show Time* promises practical advice about media performances based upon interviews with producers of top national television and radio shows. The *potential payoff* is that authors will perform successfully and sell more books when they appear on *The Oprah Winfrey Show.*

A book *is* what it *does* for each of its readers; the benefits they receive when reading it. Even though your title may be undifferentiable as a *generic* or *expected* product, you can still distinguish it from competitive offerings by means of value, brand identity, trade dress and promotion.

Strategy # 20: Conduct Test Marketing

New titles are like track-and-field athletes. Some may be sprinters, getting a quick start and setting a fast pace for a short time. Others may be long-distance runners, starting slowly and pacing themselves over a greater distance. Those lagging behind the pack may get a second breath and put on a last-minute kick to overtake the leaders.

Not every new-product idea you have will be a winner the first time out of the blocks, especially if you are unfamiliar with the competition and the track. Test marketing can be a risk-reduction factor by helping you learn the strengths and weaknesses of your stars.

Cover designs and text layout suitable for one market may not be appropriate to others. Test different combinations among knowledgeable people in your target market. John Kremer did that when preparing to print the second edition of his venerable title, *1001 Ways to Market Your Books.* He placed several cover designs on his website and asked people to vote on their favorite. Yielding to the results of the survey, he made a last-minute change overriding the choice that was about to be printed. The cover of *Beyond the Bookstore* was subjected to similar scrutiny among many book-industry experts.

The most important word in the vocabulary of advertising is TEST. If you pretest your product with consumers, and pretest your advertising, you will do well in the marketplace. DAVID OGILVY, *advertising executive*

Use your website to ask people in your target market to comment on your marketing plans. Ask your distributor, or query members of a listserve to which you belong. You could also accomplish this as an exhibitor at industry-specific or book-market trade shows. Seek informed advice on your physical product and its intended price, distribution and promotion tactics.

The major benefits of this strategy are that test marketing enables more accurate forecasting, makes it more likely that you will have a saleable product, allows you to identify and correct weaknesses, and not waste (or perhaps spend less of) any vital resources.

6

Promotion Strategies for Special Sales

I F YOU KNOW THE ANSWERS to two questions, you may sell thousands more of your books. First, how often do your potential customers think about your titles as they go about their daily routines? Second, how often do your prospects think about some problem *they* have? The answer to the first question is *probably never* because, at least initially, your title is unknown to them. The answer to the second question is *probably always* because their problems are very important to them. How can you use this rather obvious information to sell more books? The answer lies in your ability to describe the content of your book as a solution to their problem. How do you let them know that you can help them solve their problems? You do this by promoting your book with an integrated array of publicity, advertising, sales promotion, personal selling and direct marketing, with each message focused on the needs of that particular target market.

The best book ever written will never sell one copy—if people do not know it has been published. The function of the promotional element in your marketing strategy is to inform your prospective customers that 1) your book exists, 2) why it is important for them to have the information it contains, 3) how it is different from and better than other alternatives for obtaining the same information and 4) where they can buy it.

Strategy # 21: Promote Perpetually

The vast number of quick-fix products and services available today have led people to expect immediate results in almost all areas of their lives. But, there is no quick fix when it comes to selling books. People take their time making decisions about what they will buy. They must reach a certain comfort level before they will part with their money.

It is not enough for them to hear about your title one time. People have to be reminded about it by being exposed to your message repeatedly. And that takes time—at least ten times. They gradually become more comfortable with a product and need to have a reason to purchase it. They are more likely to make a purchase impulsively in a gift shop or an airport bookstore if they are familiar with your title. Here are the thoughts that might go through a consumer's mind after hearing your message regularly over a period of weeks:

Exposure	Reaction
First	"So what!"
Second	"What's in it for me?"
Third	"That's interesting."
Fourth	"What was that title again?"
Fifth	"I think I've heard of that book before."
Sixth	"I think I've heard of that author before."
Seventh	"My friend mentioned that book yesterday."
Eighth	"My friend read it and thought it was good."
Ninth	"I'll look for it when I'm at the book store."
Tenth	"I'll go out and buy it now."

This does not mean that you have to have a large budget for mass communications. It is more important to have a varied array of promotional channels. A "hit" on a person can come from hearing you on a radio show, listening to a friend talk about it, attending a personal presentation, reading a review in a favorite magazine or newspaper, or seeing your book on the Internet.

Advertising is like learning–a little is a dangerous thing. P. T. BARNUM

As potential customers hear about your book more frequently, they will recognize (and buy) it in an airport store, book club, mail-order catalog or supermarket. This process takes time to happen, but your efforts will succeed if you tell enough people frequently that your book is available and how it will help them. In the jargon of advertising people, this means you need *reach* (the number of people exposed to your message) and *frequency* (the number of times they are exposed to your message).

The obvious choice would be to reach all of the people all of the time. And with enough money, you could do that. However, few publishers have unlimited funds to spend on promotion. Given a limited budget you have the choice between two options: reaching more people less frequently or reaching less people more frequently.

The principle of segmentation comes to your aid again. By grouping people according to their need for your content you can reach this smaller group more frequently, with a message that is important to them, without spending a fortune.

A strategy of frequent communication reminds potential buyers that your book is available and the information in it will improve their lives in some way. It also gives you these benefits:

1. **You generate free exposure through media appearances**. Most shows do not charge you to be a guest, nor are you paid for your performance. But this free exposure can reap the equivalent of tens (if not hundreds) of thousands of dollars in publicity by informing people about your book.

   Potential customers in all markets can hear your message. Your media appearances will reach them, advancing your credibility, perhaps just as they are contemplating a large purchase of your books.

2. **You sell more books**. The more people you tell about the benefits of reading your books, the more likely it is that a significant number of them will buy them. Move consumers through the mental buying process rapidly through frequent repetition of your message and they will reach the conclusion to make the purchase.

3. **You tell people where to buy your book**. This may be directly through your toll-free number, your website, from local bookstores, at one of your library events or after one of your personal presentations.

4. **You create and maintain relationships**. Promotion enables you to network and make contacts. You will meet corporate buyers and media people who change jobs within the industry. Over the

years, your reputation will move with them. A book that was not right for their circumstances in the past may be perfect in their current position.

5. **You multiply your marketing effectiveness.** Increased exposure creates synergism among all your marketing efforts. As people see and hear your name more frequently, they begin to attribute increased credibility to your message.

6. **You create a promotional frame of mind.** As the results of your efforts begin to accrue, you will feel a sense of momentum, a belief that your big break will occur soon. You never know where or when it will appear, but you know that if you persist, something will happen to jump-start your sales.

7. **You receive an implied endorsement.** Media appearances and articles in print create an implied endorsement by the medium itself and by the show's host or newspaper's editors. Loyal followers may buy your book simply because their idol mentioned it. This is certainly the case when Oprah Winfrey mentions a title on her show.

8. **You create additional opportunities.** You never know who will see or hear your message. There could be a publisher looking for the rights to a book just like yours, a meeting planner seeking a keynote speaker, the regional buyer for a chain of airport stores, or the person who arranges guests for a national talk show.

9) **You grow professionally.** Most media appearances begin with a question by the host to establish your credentials. As your qualifications are repeated over and over again, you will rapidly become the expert to whom people will come for advice.

10) **You stimulate word of mouth advertising.** The more the public hears about your title, the more they will talk about it. People are more willing to buy if they get a "referral" from a trusted friend.

11) **You reap personal benefits.** As you objectively critique your communications, you can improve them next time. Subsequently, you will grow personally and professionally.

Strategy # 22: Promote with an Array of Devices and Media

Special-sales promotion is like being an archer with four arrows in your quiver. The likelihood of hitting the target is four times greater than it is with one arrow. The four arrows in the promoter's quiver are publicity, advertising, sales promotion and personal selling.

> If a billboard is posted announcing a circus, it's advertising
> If the billboard is put on an elephant, it's a promotion
> If the elephant walks into the mayor's flower garden, it's publicity
> If the mayor smiles, it's public relations
> AUTHOR UNKNOWN

THE PROMOTION MIX

You can use these four promotional tools together or at different times to accomplish your goals. Your job is to determine when and how to use each to optimize your sales. For example, suppose your author is about to conduct a tour making presentations to libraries. It will be more successful if you escort the events with an awareness campaign. This might include an enlargement of the book's cover featured in the library (sales promotion), press releases sent to the local media (publicity), postcards mailed to prospective customers (advertising) or media appearances promoting the occasion (personal selling).

PUBLICITY

Publicity can spread a message quickly and at low cost. Print and broadcast media can carry your message to a very targeted audience, too. This discussion is not intended to describe publicity in general terms, but only as it can be applied to special-sales marketing. Here are some ways in which you can use publicity to increase sales in nontraditional markets.

1. **Reposition a product.** Eric Kampmann's title *Tree of Life* is positioned as *a book of wisdom for men*. However, Eric uses publicity to reach women to inform them about the title and how it would be an excellent gift for the man in their lives. This opens up the possibility of a publicity campaign directed to gift-shop owners, too.
2. **Enter a new market.** Michael Heim has a series of travel guides written for specific areas in many states. These point out historical sites and points of interest along major highways. He rolls these out, state by state, with publicity targeted to places frequented by travelers. Examples include fast-food restaurants, tourism sites, bed-and-breakfasts, hotels, inns and resorts, guide services, chambers of commerce, local broadcast media, airports and aviation services, car rental companies, travel agencies, tour guides and operators, campgrounds and RV parks and gas station mini-marts.

3. **Introduce a new product.** Wendy Brickman suggests using publicity to market videos in the same way you would use it to promote books. She implores publishers to "use publicity wisely and frequently" to introduce a new video.

4. **Increase your reach and frequency to speed up the decision-making process.** Ellen Levine used publicity to repeatedly tell people about her title *Jewish Perspectives on Illness and Healing*. She regularly sent press releases to meditation centers, niche reviewers, as well as radio stations, television shows, magazines, newsletters and newspapers reaching the Jewish population.

5. **Extend a limited promotion budget.** Travel writers have a website to help them communicate their message to the media. It is *www.main.travelwriters.com* linking such diversified areas of the travel industry as travel writers, tour companies, public relations agencies, and travelers. Find a similar site for your subject and quickly reach PR firms, the media, syndicate your articles and reach editors and publishers.

6. **Build confidence among your distributors that you are promoting your book.** John Arnold wrote *Fallback Position* to help people better manage their careers. He frequently communicated with distributors and wholesalers to 1) convince them to carry his title and once they did, 2) to demonstrate that he was constantly promoting the title to support their sales efforts. He sent his releases to wholesalers for discount stores, warehouse clubs and libraries and directly to online career bookstores, online career catalogs, corporate librarians, book clubs for minorities in business, SOHO (small office/home office) book clubs, retail stores and chains, office supply stores and office supply wholesalers.

7. **Inform a target audience about the benefits of your titles.** Paul Krupin has a news-release distribution service that can help you reach target niches with a specific message. He can integrate your marketing and PR to create a custom targeted media list to meet your needs. Visit Paul's site at *www.imediafax.com* for great tips on using press releases and to subscribe to his free newsletter.

8. **Create company and brand identity.** Joan Stewart has an excellent site with information for using publicity to build brand identity as well as for many other reasons. Go to *www.publicityhound.com/* for her free newsletter, publicity tips, e-books, CDs, special reports and free articles.

9. **Publicize events and attract more people.** Brian Harvey, author of *Golf in Connecticut*, would attract attention to his in-store events

by publicizing his attempt to break the world's record for stacking golf balls, one on top of the other.

ADVERTISING

Advertising can reach many consumers simultaneously with the same message, with a relatively low cost per exposure. It can increase awareness of your titles and educate people about the benefits of buying them. In general, the return on your advertising expenditure is not immediate. One ad will rarely pay for itself, since the benefits of advertising accrue over time as readers are reminded repeatedly about your titles.

> If you make a product good enough . . . the public will make a path to your door, says the philosopher. But if you want the public in sufficient numbers, you would better construct a highway. Advertising is that highway. WILLIAM RANDOLPH HEARST, *U.S. newspaper publisher*

There are different types of advertising to consider. **Awareness advertising** alerts consumers that your title is available and directs them to book clubs to purchase it. **Direct-response advertising** provides a means to purchase your books directly. **Cooperative advertising** is a joint promotion that can reduce your costs, but it may reduce your exposure if you are one of 100 participants. For example, if you participate with other publishers to advertise your titles in a special insert in *Publishers Weekly* your cost is reduced but the impact of your message may also be diluted.

Advertising can be a strategic, supportive part of your promotional mix if it is implemented properly. The headline must be provocative and the layout attractive. Each promotional piece must be written with the needs of potential customers in mind, informing and reminding them of the benefits your title offers. Create copy that is applicable for each target market to which you are communicating. Librarians, bookstore buyers, distributors and ultimate readers all buy a book for different reasons.

SALES PROMOTION

Sales promotion includes useful items that serve as a constant, favorable reminder of your company and titles. Typical examples are bookmarks, giveaways (key chains, pens, etc.), brochures, games, point-of-purchase displays and coupons for generating awareness and stimulating demand through short-term price campaigns.

Sales Promotion Tools
Book signings
Counter or shelf displays
Self-syndicate your own column
Volunteer to be an expert
Sponsor a contest
Letter to the editor
Give something free (SASE)
Offer a guarantee
Special tie-ins (special month, day, holidays, natural events)
Cable television series
Letterhead with books listed
Ad specialties (matchbooks, key chains, etc.)
Card packs
Awards and honors
T-shirts
Calendars
Posters
Co-op advertising
Business cards
A listing in The Yellow Pages (or other directories)
Coupons, refunds, rebates, sweepstakes, contests
Distributor support
Bookmarks
Statement stuffers
Postcards with book covers
Create your own newsletter

Sales promotion techniques can be adapted to a variety of marketing objectives and can easily be tied in with other promotional tools. On the negative side, they usually have short-term impact, overuse of price-related offers may hurt your profits and competitors can easily copy effective promotions. Carefully plan each sales-promotional event or item using each to augment other marketing strategies. For instance, if your objective is to introduce a new title, you might consider placing a sample chapter on your web site, couponing, bundling with another proven item or offering a money-back guarantee to consumers. If your objective is to encourage repurchase you might consider bonus packs, contests, sweepstakes, coupons good on the next purchase or multiple-proof free premiums.

Helma Clark decided to learn about football because it was the only thing her son seemed willing to talk about as a young teenager. During the process, she fell in love with the game, and also realized it was an avenue of communication that wives, moms, and significant others could use with the men in their lives. So, she wrote *Snot Bubbles: A Football Guide for Wives, Moms & Significant Others*, a book geared to helping them understand the basics of the game. Helma promoted it with *Snot Bubbles* parties in stores. Then she sold it to school football teams and sororities for resale as a fundraiser. It was also picked up by the head coach of the Detroit Lions who purchased it as a gift for the wives of all of his coaches.

PERSONAL SELLING

Personal selling is probably the least favorite of all promotional techniques and is rarely performed in traditional bookstore marketing. At a minimum, author contact is with people at distributors, bookstores or the media. But in special-sales marketing you are heavily involved in selling directly to people with purchasing power. This may be a buyer at Wal-Mart or at a museum, a drug store, an association or a large company.

Personal selling occurs during person-to-person interaction when you are trying to convince someone to buy your products. It is a persuasive selling tool allowing two-way communication, giving you the ability to answer questions, overcome objections and close the sale at the same meeting. The major disadvantage is its high cost per contact.

Personal selling is setting yourself up to have some one-on-one contact with prospective buyers. This occurs at trade shows and booksignings, during personal presentations, networking at BEA or other association meetings and by participating in an online discussion group. Techniques for selling to corporate buyers are found in Chapter Fourteen.

Selling isn't a science. It's persuasion. And persuasion is an art.
WILLIAM BERNBACH, *U.S. advertising executive, copywriter*

Strategy # 23: Coordinate Your Promotion with Overall Marketing Strategy

A carpenter knows that the right tool applied in the proper situation gets the job done most effectively. Similarly, you should use the correct marketing tools when building a successful special-sales promotional campaign. This will be more likely if you match your activities to:

1. **The life-cycle stage of each title**. If your title is in its introductory stage, mass communication techniques should be emphasized. Initially, people need to know it is available. In the growth stage, they need to be reminded about why it is in their best interest to purchase it.

2. **The personality of your authors**. Authors who loathe media appearances might be better suited to a promotional mix heavy in direct mail, publicity and advertising. Others may thrive on national exposure and excel in performing on the air and in personal presentations.

3. **The nature of your product line**. A list heavy in fiction lends itself to a mix weighted toward sales promotion, publicity and advertising where mass communication's low cost per exposure stimulates demand most efficiently.
4. **The nature of your markets**. A nonfiction title destined for a tightly defined market niche profits from personal communication, perhaps augmented with a targeted campaign of direct mail, publicity and advertising.

You have many marketing strategies and actions at your disposal. These can be manipulated and applied in many different combinations with varying results. That is the good news. The bad news is that these can be manipulated and applied in different combinations with varying results. There is no one best promotional strategy that works all the time for everyone. Experiment with a variety of strategies and actions to determine what works best for you, for your unique product line at this particular time. Try different approaches, evaluate the result and make corrections as necessary. Then try something else. Eventually your efforts will pay off and you will go beyond the bookstore with trumpets blaring.

■ Strategy #24: Stop Selling Your Books

Charles Revson, then CEO of Revlon Company, was asked to describe what his company sold. He responded, "In the factory we make cosmetics, but in the stores we sell hope." He knew that people do not buy a product, they buy what the product does *for them*. This may be more important in non-bookstore marketing than it is in traditional marketing.

> Books have become products like cereal or perfume or deodorant.
> ALEXANDRA RIPLEY

Most products, including books, are combinations of tangible and intangible elements. People do not buy the tangible features of a book, i.e., the paper and ink that create it. They buy the intangible benefits they receive from reading fiction: a vicarious feeling of fantasy, romance, adventure or mystery. And when purchasing nonfiction they are buying information, motivation and help.

As a publisher, you will become more successful at marketing when you stop selling your products and begin selling what they *do for* the people who purchase them. That is the difference between marketing a *feature*, an *advantage* and a *benefit*. A *feature* is an attribute of your product. For a book, it could be its size, binding, title or number of pages. An *advantage* describes the purpose or function of a feature, and a *benefit* is the value the reader receives in exchange for purchasing your book. People buy value, not generic products.

One way of distinguishing among these three definitions is to use the "So What?" test. When thinking of a reason why someone would purchase your book, put yourself in the place of the prospective buyer and ask yourself, "So what?" Keep doing that until your imaginary customer says, "Oh. Now I understand." Then communicate that concept in your promotional literature and they will be more likely to buy.

Feature:	A four-color cookbook with a spiral binding. (*So what?*).
Advantage:	It will lay flat while you are preparing the meal, making it easy to read. (*So What?*)
Benefit:	It contains recipes that are easy to prepare and guaranteed to please your guests. You will have more time to socialize and enjoy yourself at your parties. (*Oh. Now I understand.*)

IMPACT ON SPECIAL-SALES STRATEGY

Just as individuals have a variety of reasons for purchasing your books, businesses also have diverse reasons for buying them. Just think about the companies in your channels of distribution.

People at each level of the distribution network have a unique reason for buying your books, and a plea to an incorrect appeal will not motivate them. The key to persuading each to carry your books is to show them why it is in their best interest to work with you. For example, when selling to the buyers at retail operations you could demonstrate that your superior promotional plan would bring more people into their stores, increasing their inventory turns and profitability. However, an appeal to profitability would not entice a librarian to purchase your book, nor would it persuade a college instructor to buy it as a textbook. The key is to match the appropriate benefit to each prospective customer's reason for wanting to own it.

To demonstrate this concept, assume you are selling a book containing information about child safety. Choose the benefit in the right column that corresponds to the customer in the left column.

1. Car manufacturer	A. Help patrons keep their families protected
2. Distributor	B. Use as a premium to sell more cars
3. Parent	C. Help students learn how to stay safe
4. Librarian	D. Your promotion will make their sales people more productive
5. School teacher	E. Keep children secure and feel like a good parent
	Answers: 1B, 2D, 3E, 4A, 5C

PRODUCTION

The process begins with the design of your book. To demonstrate this, think about its size. You may have designed it as 8½" x 11" so the readers will be able to use it as a workbook and make notes in the large margins. In this case you would not promote its size but the fact that the notes may be conveniently recorded and saved. If your leather-bound book is designed for a corporation to use as a gift, then spotlight the feel, smell and status of leather and not the information in the book.

PRICING

The *price* of your book is a feature. The *value* of your book is a benefit. Customers attach value to books in proportion to their perceived ability of it to help them solve their problems. If your book is more expensive than competitors' books, your promotional material must translate the price into value for the consumer. One way to do this is to describe the *incremental difference* and what the reader receives for it. If your $19.95 book is $5.00 more than the competition, demonstrate to the readers what they will gain in exchange for that amount. Or, you could appeal to their fear of making a wrong decision and how much they will lose by not spending the additional $5. In either case you will be more effective if you communicate the value your book offers your customers.

> He knows the price of everything and the value of nothing.
> OSCAR WILDE, *playwright, novelist*

You can also use a surrogate indicator, a cue that takes the place of a buying criterion, to demonstrate the benefits of your higher price. These cues include endorsements, guarantees and slogans. Even the way you write the price makes a difference. For example, which looks like a larger figure, $5 or $5.00? If you want to make a price look smaller do not include the numbers to the right of the decimal point. On the other hand, if you want to accentuate the difference, include the decimal point and zeroes.

PRACTICAL APPLICATION

Organize this information for everyday use by condensing it into a handy action guide that will regularly remind you of your item's benefits. To create this useful plan, align a page horizontally and divide it into four columns. In the left-hand column list the different market niches that are potential targets for your title. In the next column define the decision maker for this segment. Use column three to describe the benefits your title provides this group, the potential you should communicate. Column four lists the general promotion strategies you will implement to describe the respective benefits to each decision maker. The example below demonstrates this technique as it applies to *It's Show Time*, a book describing how to perform on television and radio shows.

Niche	Decision Maker	Benefits	General Promotion Strategy
Publishers	Director of Publicity	An author who is media trained will perform more effectively on the air, selling more books, making the publishing firm more profitable.	Communicate via direct mail, exhibit at PMA University and relevant seminars, advertise in *PMA's Newsletter*.
Writers, Groups & Associations	President	Use *It's Show Time* as a fundraiser, as a way to entice new members or as a gift for those who renew membership; this will increase membership and renewals, making the group more profitable.	Use direct mail followed by personal telephone calls, and personal sales calls.
Libraries	Acquisition Librarian	This unique book contains information sought by a large number of their patrons.	Cooperative marketing programs with Unique, Quality and B & T; Participate in co-op mailings

People do not buy features, they buy benefits. They buy what your book will do for them. Each decision maker has a unique reason for buying. Know what that is and communicate that benefit to him or her. Keep this in mind when you are creating your book or convincing people to buy it and you will sell more books, have fewer returns and become more profitable. (*Oh. Now I understand.*)

Many a small thing has been made large by the right kind of advertising. MARK TWAIN

Strategy # 25: Create an Unfair Advantage

Imagine the dilemma of prospective buyers seeking information from books. Of the entire selection facing them in a bookstore, airport store or discount store why should they choose your particular title? Or why choose a book at all if the information is available through other sources? These are important questions to ask yourself.

As Dan Poynter says, "The three critical stages of a title's life are writing, publishing and marketing (distribution and promotion)." The first two phases are responsible for producing a book that is needed by a significant number of people. But prospective buyers need to know why a particular title is different from and better than competitive ones. It is in the title's marketing phase that the reason to purchase it is communicated to the buyers.

Successful book marketing suggests that a book have one overwhelming reason—a unique selling proposition (USP)—why it is the best item in its category. This might be an exclusive benefit or performance quality. However, a customer-centric focus views the marketing process from a different perspective, i.e., the title should have a unique *buying* proposition (UBP) or a reason why that distinctive feature or performance quality will benefit the prospective customer.

The promotional campaign for each title must communicate its UBP to its target group of prospective customers. Perhaps to make things more difficult, the UBP may change for each segment. For instance, discount stores are interested in how your title will build store traffic or increase profitability. The fact that your title won a Ben Franklin Award will impress potential distributors but may have less bearing on consumers.

Your job is to find or create—through content or promotion—a meaningful and distinctive reason why your customers should choose your title over all the others. Not every difference is a differentiator. To be effective in motivating people to buy, the distinguishing characteristic(s) must be important to them, superior to similar titles, communicable, affordable and profitable.

There are several ways to create a difference that meets these criteria. The first is based on an attribute of your book. This may be its physical size, such as the position chosen by the publishers of *Life's Little Instruction Book*. It could be on the number of editions (such as Dan Poynter's *Self-Publishing Manual*) or copies in print or sold (i.e. *Chicken Soup for the Soul* series).

What if your title has no meaningful differentiating characteristics? Use your promotion to create one and distinguish yourself from competitors through some means that could be important. For instance, you could promote your title as having been written for a particular group of people (*Finance & Accounting for Nonfinancial Managers*), or that it is better than competitors (explain why), a leader in a particular category or the best value for the money. The UBP you communicate is important because it etches an image that occupies a meaningful and distinct competitive position in the minds of people in each of your target niches.

7

Organize Your Special-Sales Marketing Plan

IMAGINE YOURSELF AS THE head coach of a professional sports team, competing against one or more opponents in a week. You probably have a basic strategy but create a separate game plan based upon the strengths and weaknesses of each competitor. Then you will make adjustments as the game goes on to adapt to current circumstances. When coaches have only one strategy and apply it against each adversary uniformly, they limit their chances of success.

My Three Rules for coaching: 1) Surround yourself with people who can't live without football. 2) Recognize winners. They come in all forms. 3) Have a plan for everything. BEAR BRYANT, *U.S. football coach*

This same concept applies to special sales. The titles in your product line have unique strengths and weaknesses. A title's strength in one market (i.e., a spiral-bound cookbook sold through a catalog) may actually be a weakness in others (bookstores and libraries). Success in this environment depends on strategic flexibility, your ability to adapt to changing markets and conditions. But first you need a plan.

Strategy # 26: Look at the Word *Plan* As a Verb, not As a Noun

Your business plan is the statement of your basic strategy. It is the document that sets your company's overall purpose and direction, guides your thinking, and organizes your resources for maximum utilization. Your marketing plan is an integral part of your business plan, stating your marketing objectives and describing the marketing strategies and tactics you will implement to fulfill your company's mission. Your special-sales plan is a subset of your marketing plan, listing the strategies and tactics that you will execute in non-bookstore segments.

This may sound like too much work, but just for a moment, do not think of the word *plan* as a noun—a document created at the beginning of a fiscal period. Instead, think of it as a verb, a process to help you organize and direct your thinking so you can prepare your activities over the planning period.

Planning is a technique to help you focus on important issues and answer tough questions that you might have otherwise avoided. It allows you to take an objective, critical look at your business, product lines, markets and competition and create ways to improve your position in each segment.

Do not think of the word plan as a document. Instead, think of it as a process defining the parameters for the ways in which you do business. This will help you focus on the daily activities that fulfill your mission statement, and at the same time remain flexible enough to recognize potentially profitable, unanticipated opportunities as they present themselves.

The act of special-sales planning is simply making the decision to participate, and then creating the actions you must take to do it. Then ask yourself—and answer—questions that stimulate innovative ideas. *In what other markets could we sell our titles? At what price will they be sold in each? How will they be distributed in Special Distribution, Commercial Sales and Niche Market sectors? How can we use publicity, advertising, sales promotion and personal selling techniques to promote them in each segment? What will all this cost and how much can we expect to make at the end of the year? How will all that position us for future growth?* This is a creative process and you build your plan as you go through it.

Your plan is simply a written record of all the answers to your questions. In itself it has no worth. The value resides in the insight you get from creating the strategy and the results that occur from doing everything you said you would.

A written plan is not the preferred outcome of a planning session. The objective of the process is to define a course of action, a path rather than a document. Special-sales planning is simply the technique of evaluating the pros and cons of possible alternative actions and analyzing how each alternative will impact other aspects of your marketing programs.

A marketing plan is not so much a document to be written as it is a controlling device to be used daily. Writing a plan is like laying track for a railroad—it establishes a solid foundation, provides a path to your destination and controls deviation. But the track does not propel you forward, nor does your plan. Your passion and productive action provide the fuel for the engine taking you on your journey to success.

Planning Considerations for Bookstore vs. Special-Sales Marketing		
	Bookstore Winner	**Special-Sales Winner**
Market Appeal	Diverse market attraction; mass market appeal; wide acceptability	Product matched to the needs of a smaller segment
Availability	Broad availability through formal distribution channels	Available in one or more, narrow, but more interested audience segment(s)
Reliance on Economy	Sales dependent on general economic conditions	Less reliance on ups and downs of economy, or able to be repositioned to restore growth
Seasonal Variations	Sales increase during holiday selling periods	Less seasonal variations
Customer Dispersion	Customers widely dispersed	Customers congregated in geographical or demographical segments
Uniqueness	Requires a point of difference unique from competitive titles (not a me-too title)	Requires a unique point of difference based upon the item's ability to meet the needs of niche buyers; UBP changes with target market
Pricing	Priced competitively; produce at a marketable cost (not a lot of die-cutting, shrink-wrapping of components);	Less price competition; more value-based pricing; less impact of distribution discounts; (can charge more for die-cutting, shrink-wrapping of components);
Promotion	Reliance on uncontrollable PR, media appearances; broadcasting to reach target buyers among large populations	Pinpoint accuracy; narrowcasting to a small segment of interested buyers

Customer base	Saleable to present customers through existing distribution channels	Opportunity to find new customers
Break-Even Point	High BEP for unit sales due to distribution discounts, returns and delayed payments	Low BEP for unit sales due to few (if any) distribution discounts and returns
Author recognition/ history	More reliance on author name; difficult for "unknown" author to penetrate	Reliance on information and content
Publishing Process	Publishing process may be hurried to meet artificial deadlines, or to reach an imposed number of titles to publish annually	Emphasis on selling content, not publishing titles; eliminates the need for a frontlist and backlist
Life Cycle Planning	Interpretation of life cycle stage is left to others who decide if sales are sufficient to maintain market presence	Opportunity to extend growth stage with sales to new markets and buyers; more self-sufficiency
Publishing decisions	Literary decision dependent on quality of manuscript or fit with publishers line	Marketing decision based upon need for the information in the text
Forecasting	Sales dependent on uncontrollable factors, i.e., skills of distributors' reps, position on shelf, circulation of positive publicity	Forecasting dependent on more controllable aspects of marketing
Time perspective	Emphasis on short term perspective with need to show sales results quickly; minimum length of time for inclusion on frontlist	Emphasis on long term perspective; backlist as important as frontlist; concern more on relevancy of content than on year of copyright
Sales Reliance	Reliance on distribution channel for selling activities	Self-dependency, or contract marketing to other companies
Allocation of funds	Production phase can use funds previously designated for marketing	Buyers may contribute to cost of production; narrowcasting may require less promotional expense due to less wasted circulation

In preparing for battle I have always found that plans are useless, but planning is indispensable. DWIGHT D. EISENHOWER

Strategy # 27: Write Your Marketing Plan

Have you ever thought of the world's best idea at 3:00 A.M. only to forget it by the time you woke up? Had you taken the time to write it down, you would have had an indelible record of your innovation. Whether you write a formal plan or a series of actions, your new ideas will be burned out of your memory by the daily fires you face.

Unless you are submitting your plan to a financing source (in which case a professional and complete presentation is expected), the best form for a plan is that which works for you. Prepare it as an internal document, not to be seen by anyone who would judge its form instead of its content.

Terri Bowersock, author of *Success. It Can Be Yours: How to be a Millionaire by using Your Determination*, is dyslexic. So instead of writing a plan, she used pictures (not words) to organize her thinking, and she became extremely successful. Form follows function. Do not get so hung up on the way your plan looks that you forget what it is supposed to do. Your plan is a tool that guides, directs and reminds you of the actions you must take to achieve your goals.

Committing your ideas to paper creates a checklist, a reminder of what you should do next. Then when you find yourself with free time, you can consult your list and perform an action that you might have otherwise forgotten. Also, writing your plans serves to focus your attention on them, stimulating new ideas as you proceed.

At the same time, writing your plans stimulates passion for your efforts—the enthusiasm that comes from experiencing positive, forward progress. Some think that enthusiasm must come first, but this zest can be compared to the vigorous waves on a deep river, whipped up by a strong, yet temporary storm. Even though they are a potent force, the real power of the flow comes from the unceasing current, the essence of the river.

USE THE *MARKETING PLANNING* CD-ROM TO ASSIST IN YOUR PLANNING

A marketing plan is a document that outlines the ways in which your marketing activities will be implemented to reach your company's goals. The plan is typically divided into two sections. The first is descriptive. It sets your mission and objectives and describes the current market situation and lists important issues and opportunities. The second part describes the actions you will take to reach your goals and is comprised of a Strategic Plan (a statement of what you are going to do) and a Tactical Plan (which describes how you will do it). A general outline for a marketing plan can be found in Appendix A.

The Marketing Planning CD-ROM contains a template that you will find helpful. It is a step-by-step process for creating a condensed version of a complete a marketing plan. It instructs you on writing the most basic parts, those that are most useful in conducting profitable marketing activities.

For example, as you go to 1.1 Mission Statement you will find instructions for writing a mission statement. Then you will be asked to insert your copy for it in the right-hand column. As appropriate, the instructions refer you to the relevant strategy in *Beyond the Bookstore* where more information is available. Below is an example of how the instruction page will appear, when the text block is filled in with the mission statement for Book Marketing Works, LLC.

Your words are then transferred to a Word document (Marketing Plan—Ready to Print). When you are finished with the step-by-step instructions, your marketing plan will be complete and ready for printing. Your ready-to-print marketing plan will look like this:

1) MISSION STATEMENT. This section of your marketing plan should describe your special-sales mission, the reason why you are in business.	
1.1 Mission	Become the leading and most respected brand-name entity that provides high quality, pragmatic sales and marketing resources that continually enhance a publisher's efforts to generate more revenue and profits for its titles.
Your mission statement is a two or three-sentence answer to two questions. First, "What business are we in?" This may initially seem obvious because you are a producer and supplier of books.	
Instead, look more closely at what you are really providing. In special-sales marketing, the product is a variable through which you deliver your content to the appropriate market. What information do you convey? How do you want people to respond upon reading your content? How will their lives change as a result? This will give you greater understanding of your mission.	
Second, "Who are we trying to serve?" Create a profile of the people who are the ultimate beneficiaries of your content.	
See Strategy # 13 in *Beyond the Bookstore* for more instructions on writing your mission statement.	

Beyond the Bookstore is not meant to be an exhaustive description of strategic planning. The focus here is on creating a practical marketing plan that will help you sell more books and products into special-sales markets.

Begin with your strategies

Your marketing plan should list strategies that define how your product development, pricing, distribution and promotion decisions will interact. Then it should go on to describe the specific actions you can take to implement the strategies and reach your objective.

There may appear to be little difference between strategy and tactics, but each serves a dissimilar and necessary function. If your objective sets your overall destination, your strategies define the path you will take to get there. The tactics describe the steps you will take on the path. Strategies make sure you are headed in the right direction before you take action.

Strategies make you *effective* (doing the right things) and tactics make you *efficient* (doing things right).

Strategic planning recognizes that under certain conditions, sales of Title A may be more responsive to a heavy schedule of media performances while direct marketing might be more effective in stimulating sales of Title B. Tactical planning delineates the steps that should be taken to arrange the media appearances and the outline for implementing the direct mail campaigns. Most planners focus only on the tactical functions.

Here are six principles that will convince you to take the time to plan your strategy before you begin your journey to success:

1. Begin your plan with the right goal, or your strategy may be misplaced and ineffective. Poor strategic direction often results when goals are defined in terms of unit or dollar volume, with profits assumed to follow.
2. Your strategy must enable your firm to deliver a unique array of benefits for a particular set of customers. Strategic thinking defines how you will price, distribute and promote your titles to each target.
3. To establish a sustainable competitive advantage, you must perform different activities than rivals or perform similar activities in different ways. With uncoordinated activity you will end up performing most activities the same way everyone else does, making it hard to gain a unique advantage.

4. Marketing on a limited budget requires trade-offs. You may need to abandon some product features, services or activities in order to be unique at others. Trying to be all things to all customers almost guarantees that your product will lack a competitive advantage.
5. Strategy defines how all the elements of your marketing mix fit together. This involves making choices that are interdependent because your marketing activities must be mutually reinforcing. Your channels of distribution, for example, should reflect your target-market decisions. You would probably use different networks for selling to bookstores, libraries, mass merchandisers and academic markets.
6. Strategy creates consistency of performance. Frequent reinvention is usually a sign of poor strategic thinking and a sure route to mediocrity. Continuous improvement is a necessity; but it must always be guided by strategic direction.

Once you feel comfortable with your overall objectives, create the strategies that will direct your efforts to achieve them. Think of your strategies as statements of the general direction you will take in each of the four areas of marketing concentration (Product, Place, Price and Promotion) in order to reach your objectives.

STRATEGIES. Make a broad statement of the strategies you will take in each of the Four Ps.

1. Product mix. What will the makeup of your product line be? Do you intend to publish only books, or could audio and video programs fit into your mix?
2. Distribution. Will you distribute through the traditional network to, or directly to retail stores, libraries and your target markets? Or will you create a dual-distribution system?
3. Pricing. Will you invoke a penetration (low price), skimming (high price) or competitive pricing strategy, given your distribution, discounts, competition and costs?
4. Promotion. How will you combine sales promotion, publicity, advertising and personal selling to promote your titles?

Plan Your Specific Actions

Once your strategies are in place, start creating your tactics. Conduct a creative session and think of new things you can do to sell products. The examples below serve only as a starting point for your creative sessions and should not be considered an exhaustive list of possible activities.

Product Line Tactics

In what form will you introduce your products? To what target markets will they be directed? For instance, if you are publishing children's books, will you specialize in preschool picture books or nonfiction for young adults? What about cover designs and internal layout? Will you use four-color or black-and-white artwork, if any?

The packaging for one title may be different for various target segments. For instance, you may decide to release a title in hard cover for the library market, soft cover for book stores and in a small, 4" x 6" size for gift markets. The same title might also be customized for other prospects.

Distribution tactics

Will you utilize special distribution, direct distribution or some combination? Describe the idiosyncrasies of each channel. Will the wholesalers assess their usual 55 per cent discount (65 per cent or more for distributors) or will you bargain for other terms? Who will pay shipping? What fees will they charge for placement in their catalogs? In what time period will you be paid? What percent of sales will be returned? Under direct distribution, do you have the time and inclination to sell your products, and then ship them, invoice for them and collect the money due?

Some of the middlemen you employ will take your titles to bookstores, and others will take them to warehouse clubs, discount stores, libraries and supermarkets. Add to that your direct distribution activities and the question becomes one of how you will coordinate your marketing activities to optimize both networks?

Pricing Actions

The costs of production and distribution are two of the components to consider when pricing your books. In special sales, pricing is negotiated, usually based upon the quantity sold. And there are cases in which you can eliminate the distribution fees and the production costs when a buyer participates financially in the printing process. (See Strategy #32 for more information on pricing your books.)

Promotion Tactics

Divide your promotion plan into four sections: publicity, sales promotion, advertising and personal selling. *The Marketing Planning* CD-ROM helps you write all your tactics.

Strategy # 28: Create Your Special-Sales Action Plan

Unfortunately, once a plan is finished, most people see their job as complete and they go back to their habitual ways of dealing with the daily fires that overpower logic and control. The plan is filed away until the next planning period. Do not let this happen. Translate your overall special-sales plan into a series of action plans that you can keep with you.

Titles are like people in the sense that they will grow according to their heredity (planning) and environment (action). An action plan reduces your annual plan to a "To Do" list, a daily reminder that forces you to actively pursue your objectives. This process gives your annual plan a sense of relevance and flexibility, and gives you the chance to fine-tune your actions while responding to unforeseen opportunities.

Appendix E contains a tool that you will find helpful. It is template for a quarterly Special-Sales Action Plan. This is a single-page reminder of your strategies and actions that you keep with you and refer to as needed. List the actions that need to be performed in the first quarter and then assign each a start date. This automatically creates your monthly plans for the quarter. As you transfer that information into your weekly and daily plans, the information becomes more detailed. The right-hand column lists the next steps—and the follow-up—that must be performed.

An Example for Putting Your Plan into Action

The interaction of marketing planning and strategic thinking is demonstrated in the following example. If your objective is earn $100,000 in profit with a target profit margin of 10 per cent on sales, then you must set a goal of $1,000,000 in sales revenue. With an average list price of $14.95 on a book sold through a distributor discounting sales at 65 per cent, you would receive $5.23 per sale. Therefore, you would have to sell 191,205 books to generate $1,000,000 of revenue.

If last year you sold 145,000 books, then your unit sales would have to increase by 32%. With this in mind your goals would read:

- Achieve total sales revenue of $1,000,000 by 12/31/200X.
- Increase unit sales volume by 32 per cent to 191,205 in the same period.

Now the challenge becomes finding the way to reach these targets. This can be done through strategic thinking, the process of creating new approaches to implementing your marketing plan and matching them to your skills, resources and changing market opportunities. Such a practice is most easily accomplished by setting your direction in the four arenas of marketing.

1. **Product-Line Planning.** If you change the content of your product line, you can spread the unit sales projections out over more titles.
2. **Pricing.** Price your new products not as a function of cost, but as a result of the value they provide to the end users.
3. **Distribution.** Employ a dual distribution strategy to traditional and nontraditional markets.
4. **Promotion.** The promotion mix that you employ is influenced by your distribution choices and your decision to use a push or pull strategy. Push marketing is directed to the members of your distribution channel. Pull marketing drives readers to seek your titles in retail outlets.

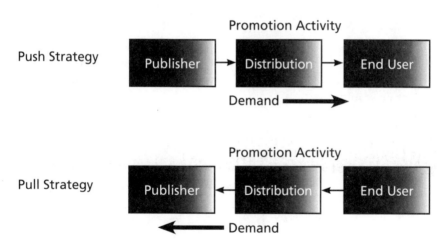

A balanced promotional mix should contain a combination of push and pull. For instance, you might provide your distributor's sales people with promotional devices or literature. You could also exhibit at BEA or at the Premium & Incentive show, informing retailers of your special offers (two-for-one deals, free shipping, etc.). At the same time, you could arrange print publicity and appear on television and radio shows to drive the general public to the outlets selling your books.

FIND A NEW PATH

Now that you have evaluated alternative ways to reach your objectives, it is time to organize all your strategic thinking into a proactive marketing plan. Your path to success might resemble this:

PRODUCT/PRICE DECISIONS. Additionally, publish one new title at $16.95, a video for $39.95 and a new line of booklets with a unit price of $4.95.

DISTRIBUTION DECISIONS. Segment your markets into niches according to their needs for your content. The resulting combined distribution network would reach the general public through bookstores, libraries and your Web site. Address other needs through book clubs, catalogs and sales to government and academic markets.

PROMOTION DECISIONS. Balance your promotional mix with both push and pull marketing activities. First, schedule appearances on television and radio shows to drive people to bookstores, libraries and your web site. Then contact prospective buyers in other niches through direct marketing and personal presentations.

Although the total revenue goal remains firm, your path to it has changed. With your new average selling price of $15.95 (one title at $14.95 and one at $16.95 nets $5.58 per sale after a discount of 65%) you could actually sell fewer books than last year to reach the same revenue. In addition, plan to sell 5000 books to the academic segment, 4000 videos to corporations and 30,000 booklets to state governments. Then your new objective would read:

- Achieve total sales revenue of $1,000,000 by 12/31/200X by reaching these unit sales volume targets:

110,000 books	@ $ 5.58	=	$613,800
5,000 books	@ $15.95	=	79,750
4,000 videos	@ $39.95	=	159,800
30,000 booklets	@ $ 4.95	=	148,500
149,000 units			$1,001,850

This strategy offers many benefits, including a broader base for generating revenue in terms of product selection and customer segments. In addition, it will reduce your reliance on bookstore sales. Profit as a percentage of sales increases since many direct and special-sales customers pay in thirty days, rarely return books and generally pay shipping expenses. Your product-development techniques will become well entrenched and your new strategic-thinking abilities will help you in all areas of your business.

Publishing a book successfully is not easy. However, the process will be less difficult if you begin with a topic that has proven demand and then communicate its unique point of difference to a targeted, receptive audience. Adequately forecast the title's most likely sales volume and promote it early and often. Give it the time and attention it needs to prosper and do not be too quick to replace it with a new title. Do not yield to artificial pressures that can subvert the process, force shortcuts and result in decreased sales.

Finally, create a plan for your company and for each title. Decide where you want to go and how you will get there. Write your plan and then implement it. Regularly evaluate your relative progress toward the attainment of your objectives and make changes as you proceed. Make the time to take your time, focus on the opportunity and not the process, and the results will be extraordinarily superior to that which you have done in the past. The Special-Sales Planning Stimulator found in Appendix F may help you, and the remainder of *Beyond the Bookstore* shows you how to plan and implement your actions successfully.

The best business plans are straightforward documents that spell out the "who, what, where, why, and how much."
PAULA NELSON, *U.S. economist*

8

Prioritize Your Prospect List and Forecast Your Sales

THERE ARE SEVERAL WAYS in which you can create a list of prospective special-sales buyers for your title. One is to search online. Others are to purchase mailing lists or a *Book Market Map™* directory[10]. But these lists typically include names of *suspects*, people who may or may not be interested in your subject matter or genre. The people are not necessarily ranked in order of their desire to buy *your particular titles*. Save time and money by ranking your prospects according to the various criteria described below.

Special Sales Strategy # 29: Qualify and Prioritize Your Prospects

A logical first step in finding likely buyers is to *qualify* your suspects according to several criteria. The first of these is the need the buyer feels for your subject matter, and then, your specific title. Your research will help to discover the level of need, and your promotional activity can stimulate preference for your title.

---

10. This is a list of non-bookstore buyers customized to a specific title: *www.bookmarketingworks.com*

Marketing activities with a relatively long time from start to results
Advertising
Book Reviews
Placing articles in print media
Exhibits at trade shows
Direct mail campaigns
Sales to book clubs and catalogs
Distribution to discount stores
Distribution to warehouse clubs
Distribution to airport stores
Sales-promotional tools
Selling books as premiums to companies
Distribution to libraries
Contacting associations
Networking

Another way to prioritize your prospects is by the length of the selling process, which is not the same for each prospect or segment. In general, you will find that the larger the potential order, the longer the selling process will take. People in the Commercial Sales sector may purchase tens of thousands of books at a time but it might take a year or more to consummate the sale.

As the list to the left illustrates, book clubs require long lead times, and many catalogs are seasonal, requiring submission six or more months before they are actually mailed. In addition, the process of submitting articles to magazines and newsletters must be started months before they appear. And it could take three or more months for a book review to be written and published. Then there may be an additional period before people read them and make a purchasing decision.

Once you tender your material to these venues you cannot simply sit around and wait for sales to occur. There are many interim prospects on which you could call for more immediate income.

Rank your prospects according to the length of the decision-making process, first contacting those with a longer cycle. Then, as that process unfurls, call on those with a shorter buying period to generate revenue in the meantime.

As another rule of thumb, the more you contact people directly via telephone and email, the faster the process will be. Mail campaigns, press releases, networking and exhibits at trade shows all make valuable contributions to your sales efforts, but they take longer to motivate people to buy your books.

If you like to use the telephone as a sales tool, you may find it to be the most efficient means by which you can personally reach the largest number of people in the shortest period of time. And using the telephone will shorten the purchasing process. It also serves other purposes, only one of which is actually selling. For example, you can use the telephone to *qualify your prospects* by determining their relative need for your title.

Then you can spend more time following up on those with the greatest likelihood of buying.

Another use of the telephone is to *perform research*. You can learn why people in a particular niche are interested in your title. Then you can feed this back to them in your promotional material. You can also call people at magazines to learn their guidelines for submitting articles about your book's subject matter. The same concept is true with people at airport stores, military exchanges and even reviewers. This will help you avoid having your book returned unopened because you did not follow their procedures.

Promotion activities with a relatively short time from start to results
Contacting prospects in niche markets
Placing articles in ezines
Participation in communities and forums
Press releases on current topics
Telephone calls to prospective customers · Targeted emailing to prospective customers · Personal visits to prospective customer
Viral marketing
Selling after speaking engagements
Broadcast media appearances

GET A *FASTART*™ CHECKLIST

Below is a series of steps you can take to help you start implementing your special-sales marketing efforts more quickly. It guides you through a process you can take to reach certain high-priority prospects. It recognizes that some people take longer to make decisions than others, and that certain opportunities require a longer lead-time. Become familiar with your prospective customers, organize and contact them according to the suggested process and then use the *Fastart*™ checklist in Appendix B to measure your progress.

All prospects are not equal in their ability to purchase from you profitably. Some will have little interest in your titles while others may have an immediate need. Most will be somewhere in between. But given a limited time for creating new customers, first prioritize your prospects according to what you believe is their ability to meet your (and their) objectives.

Start by listing potential customers by market segment. Every contact within each segment may be further categorized since not every one is at the same stage in the purchasing process, and some people represent a more significant opportunity for revenue. Go through each of your groupings and rank them according to some priority system. You might use something like this:

A PRIORITY. Prospects who are most likely to purchase your books, have a short buying cycle and could possibly order in large quantities.

List your top ten A Prospects

1. _____
2. _____
3. _____
4. _____
5. _____
6. _____
7. _____
8. _____
9. _____
10. _____

B PRIORITY. Potential customers who may buy a few books or have less need for—or are unaware of—your title.

List your top ten B Prospects

1. _____
2. _____
3. _____
4. _____
5. _____
6. _____
7. _____
8. _____
9. _____
10. _____

C PRIORITY. These people may say they have no budget now, but "call me in six months." Or, they may have recently purchased a quantity of similar books. Remember that C prospects may turn into A-priority people in the future. If they have no need for your title, remove them from your active prospect list.

List your top ten C Prospects

1. _____

2. _____

3. _____

4. _____

5. _____

6. _____

7. _____

8. _____

9. _____

10. _____

...do the things that need to be done according to priority.
ELEANOR ROOSEVELT

Spend time every day with A and B prospects. Work frequently with the As to close the sale. Explain your topic to the Bs, persuading them to increase their order size or get them to buy more quickly. Revisit your C list periodically to remind them that you will be around when they are ready to buy. Contact them periodically to keep your name before them. Use ACT or some other contact-management software to keep good records of each contact and immediately plan when our next contact will occur.

How can you tell if a suspect is an A, B or C prospect? Here are several ways to organize them according to their ability to buy your books. As you complete the listing in each section you will begin to pinpoint the A prospects while at the same time choosing those who will take more time to cultivate. Qualify and prioritize your prospects...

1. **By size of opportunity.** Not all prospects are created equal in terms of their ability to buy your books. Online bookstores may display your title on their website and purchase from you as sales are made. Orders will come in for a book or two at a time until sales warrant stocking larger quantities. On the other hand, a company buying

your books to use as a premium may purchase thousands at a time, but the sales process may take a year or longer.

> **STRATEGY HINT.** *Contact those likely to purchase quickly and easily so you will receive revenue while you are working on the longer-term sales.*

List and contact ten prospects likely to buy your books quickly

1. _____

2. _____

3. _____

4. _____

5. _____

6. _____

7. _____

8. _____

9. _____

10. _____

2. **By the people involved in the decision.** When you contact a gift shop, the owner of the store may give you a small order on the spot. But buyers in the Corporate Sales sector will probably buy in much larger quantities. In the latter case there are two groups of people involved in the book-buying decision process: the people who actually make the purchasing decisions and those who influence them. You have to reach both in order to complete a large sale. The decision *influencer* may not be a person. It may be articles in newspapers and magazines, reviews, advertising and your media appearances.

> **STRATEGY HINT.** *Submit articles to printed magazines that may have deadlines 3–6 months before publication date. Then do the same for online magazines and ezines, since they typically have shorter lead times. Provide them with a free article if they mention your ordering information in it. Contact all the print media to have them publish reviews of your title.*

List ten magazines and e-zines and send an article to each

1. _____

2. _____

3. _____

4. _____

5. _____

6. _____

7. _____

8. _____

9. _____

10. _____

3. **By your familiarity with the market.** You probably know more about some potential markets than others, particularly those in the Special-Distribution sector. These mirror the traditional distribution with which you are familiar, so you are likely to close a sale more quickly.

> **STRATEGY HINT.** *Contact those with whom you are more familiar, while learning the buying habits and purchasing nuances of people in other segments. Read Strategy # 53 to learn how and why people in corporations buy and use books as premiums, incentives and sales promotional tools.*

List ten prospects with which you are most familiar

1. _____

2. _____

3. _____

4. _____

5. _____

6. _____

7. _____

8. _____

9. _____

10. _____

4. **By benefit (to them).** People buy for their reasons, not yours. And they all have different reasons for doing so. For instance, supermarket buyers seek quick inventory turns in limited shelf space, webmasters look for increased traffic to their sites, editors want greater subscriptions and readership. Show these people how your title can benefit them and meet their needs.

> **STRATEGY HINT:** _There is a difference between marketing a feature, an advantage and a benefit. A feature is an attribute of your book. It could be its size, binding, title or number of pages. An advantage describes the purpose or function of a feature, and a benefit is the value the reader receives in exchange for purchasing your book. People buy value. See Strategy # 24 for more details on this topic._

In motivating people, you've got to engage their minds and their hearts.
RUPERT MURDOCH

List three benefits of your titles for buyers in the Special Distribution category

1. _____

2. _____

3. _____

List three benefits of your titles for buyers in the Commercial Sales sector

1. _____

2. _____

3. _____

List three benefits of your titles for buyers in the Niche Market segment

1. _____

2. _____

3. _____

> **STRATEGY HINT.** *Create a one-page letter describing all the features and benefits of your title. Then focus on one target segment at a time and think about the reasons why your title will be important to people in it. Then create a segment-specific sales piece to match the needs of each, and send it to the respective audiences. Create a text version of your literature to send as part of the email text. Many people will not open an attachment for fear of contracting a virus.*

5. **By means of communication.** Some people prefer to be contacted by telephone and others by e-mail; some by direct mail and others by personal visit. Find out how people want to learn about new titles and accommodate their desires.

> **STRATEGY HINT.** *Organize your day so that you spend an hour or so each morning making telephone calls. Then spend time sending and responding to emails. Next, write and send letters. If there are prospective customers nearby—and the opportunity warrants significant use of your time—visit them personally. Vary the way you spend your time so you do not get burned-out on one technique, particularly if you don't like doing it.*

6. **By their awareness of your topic.** People move through a series of stages before buying a product such as a book. First they are unaware that it exists. Once they learn about it they may not understand its benefit to them. After a series of exposures to your message they may (or may not) decide to buy it. Unfortunately, people are at various points along this continuum at any given point.

> **STRATEGY HINT.** *Group people by their knowledge of your topic and title and give them the information they need to move closer to a favorable purchasing decision.*

Once you have ranked your potential customers, it is time to begin contacting them. Focus on one target market and direct your attention to it. Call, e-mail, fax or send people information about your books. Use contact-management software to keep records of the date on which you contacted the prospect, his or her name, and the results of the discussion. Continue to follow up until you receive a positive or negative answer.

If the answer is positive, send the requested information or a copy of one of your books. Then follow up again. If the answer is negative, add the respondent's name to a list of C prospects to reach again in three, six or nine months.

■■■■ Strategy # 30: Calculate Your Sales Forecast

How do you plan for the future? How many books should you print? What income might you anticipate in the next year? From which customers will this revenue be derived? Wouldn't it be great to know the answers before you commit to a print run, calculate your annual budget or plan your marketing strategies?

Proper forecasting can help you resolve these issues and run a more profitable publishing company. Predicting sales can also help you better control your inventory costs, time the introduction of new titles, exploit areas of opportunity, decide when to harvest ailing titles, predict the timing and amount of cash flow, control your expenditures and adapt with new marketing strategies.

The most reliable way to forecast the future is to try to understand the present. JOHN NAISBITT

Your forecast will be more accurate if you prepare a series of monthly plans instead of making a lump-sum prediction of the total number of books you expect to sell in a year. When in doubt about expected sales, be conservative in your estimate. It is better to be pleasantly surprised than discouraged by an overly optimistic approximation.

STEP ONE: Calculate Your Unit Sales Forecast

Begin by estimating the unit sales resulting from each marketing action you listed in your plan. For example, determine how many books you might sell as a result of sending out review copies. According to a rule of thumb you should receive one review per ten copies you send, and sell twenty books for each review. Therefore, if you send one hundred galleys out for review you *could* stimulate two hundred sales. Similarly, if you decide to make one personal presentation per week to groups of one hundred people, and you generally sell books to half of the people in the audience, you could forecast two hundred copies per month from your presentations.

STEP TWO: Create Your Dollar Forecast

Next translate your unit-sales forecast to a dollar amount in a Cash Flow Statement. This technique not only points out the number of books you might sell, but it shows you the customers most likely to buy them in existing and new markets. And if you perform these calculations quarterly you will have a more accurate picture of the timing of your cash flow so you can adjust your plans and forecast.

The Sales Forecasting Table			
Sales—Last Period	Backlist	Frontlist	Total
Current Bookstore Customers			
Distributor A	$30,000 30%	$15,000 15%	**$45,000 45%**
Wholesaler A	$10,000 10%	$ 5,000 5%	**$15,000 15%**
Online Bookstore A	$10,000 10%	$ 5,000 5%	**$15,000 15%**
Non-Bookstore Customers Library Wholesaler	$15,000 15%	$10,000 10%	**$25,000 25%**
TOTAL	**$65,000 65%**	**$35,000 35%**	**$100,000 100%**

STEP THREE: Calculate Your Existing Sales to Current Customers by Title.

This step has several advantages. First, it will point out your strong and weak titles. It will also allow you to review activities in which you may have engaged so you can see what worked and didn't work. Further analysis may lead you to learn why they worked or why they didn't, providing additional information to prepare future marketing strategies.

	Backlist			Frontlist		
	Title A	Title B	Title C	Title D	Title E	Title F
Current Bookstore Customers Distributor A Wholesaler A Online Bookstore A	$5,000	$5,000 $10,000	$20,000 $10,000	$5,000 $5,000	$10,000 $5,000	
Non-Bookstore Customers Library Wholesaler	$15,000			$5,000	$5,000	
Total	**$20,000**	**$15,000**	**$30,000**	**$15,000**	**$20,000**	

Some publishers might stop the forecasting process here and begin implementing their new marketing plans. For example, in the table above they might increase their bookstore promotion for Title C as they decrease its support in library markets. They might also decide to take Title F out of print. These same publishers may even create next period's forecast simply by increasing last period's total sales by a given percentage, and then allocating that figure among the remaining titles and customers. However, if you add two more steps to the process you may see a different, and perhaps more profitable picture.

STEP FOUR: Discover New Sources of Revenue.

This next step adds a fresh dimension to your forecasting. Instead of trying to market your existing titles to the same people you did last year, evaluate new markets in which your titles may be sold. Creatively search for other prospective customers who could possibly use the information in your books.

Use the same process you did in Step One to estimate the likely sales in each quadrant. If this is your first entrée into special-sales marketing, avoid the temptation to be overly optimistic. Many of these markets take months, if not years, to develop.

The beauty of nonbookstore marketing is that your backlist gains new strength as many potential customers seek valid information regardless of the year of publication, and frontlist titles with little potential in bookstores may create a new source of revenue.

	Backlist	Frontlist	Total
Forecast—Bookstore Customers Distributor A Wholesaler A Online Bookstore A	$40,000	$15,000	**$55,000**
Forecast—Non-Bookstore Customers Libraries Gift Shops Book clubs Catalogs Museums Airport Stores	$75,000	$70,000	**$145,000**
Total	**$115,000**	**$85,000**	**$200,000**

STEP FIVE: Determine Your New Sales Forecast.

If this is your first time through this process, you will find the term "accurate forecasting" an oxymoron. Foretelling sales is more an art than a science, a skill honed through trial and error. But you have to start somewhere. In this example the publisher is doubling its total sales while reducing its reliance on sales through bookstores.

Your forecast may be more accurate if you prepare a series of monthly or quarterly plans, and then add these together to calculate the total number of books you expect to sell in a year. Make sure you factor in a percentage for returned books, particularly among bookstores and mass merchandisers.

	Backlist			Frontlist		
	Title A	Title B	Title C	Title D	Title E	Title F

**Forecast—
Bookstore**
Customers
  Distributor A
  Wholesaler A
  Online Bookstore A
	$5,000	$5,000
		
		$5,000
			$20,000
			$5,000
				$5,000
				$2,500
					$2,500
					$2,500
					$2,500	

Total Bookstores	$5,000	$10,000	$25,000	$7,500	$7,500	
	Backlist			Frontlist		
	Title A	Title B	Title C	Title D	Title E	Title F
Forecast—Special Sales						
Libraries					$5,000	
Wholesaler A	$15,000			$5,000	$2,500	
Customer A			$2,500			
Gift Shops						
Customer A	$2,500				$5,000	$2,500
Customer B	$2,500					
Book clubs						
Customer A	$2,500		$7,500	$2,500	$5,000	$2,500
Customer B			$2,500			$2,500
Catalogs						
Customer A		$2,500	$10,000		$5,000	$2,500
Customer B			$10,000	$5,000		$5,000
Museums						
Customer A	$2,500		$2,500			$2,500
Customer B	$2,500		$2,500	$5,000		$2,500
Airport Stores						
Customer A			$2,500	$2,500		$2,500
Customer B	$2,500		$2,500	$2,500		$2,500
Total Forecast—Special Sales	$30,000	$2,500	$42,500	$22,500	$22,500	$25,000

This forecast points out a different set of circumstances. Title F, which earlier was a candidate for deletion, now appears to be a strong contender in special-sales markets. Title B seems to be destined for sales only through bookstores, and your earlier decision to put more promotion behind Title C is reinforced. This analysis also points out that even though some niches might be good for increased sales (such as gift shops or book clubs), some may be more deserving of your marketing support than others.

> The rule on staying alive as a forecaster is to give 'em a number or give 'em a date, but never give 'em both at once.
> JANE BRYANT QUINN, *U.S. journalist*

You can easily go back through this sequence of events to refigure your estimates if the bottom line does not meet your expectations. This does not suggest that you should simply increase the number of books sold from each tactic, because any increase in sales probably has a concomitant increase in expense.

Once you complete your sales forecast, go back over your marketing plan. Manipulate your promotional strategies to see how you might increase sales by trying different tactics. How would your sales change if you put more effort and money behind Title B in the college market and reduced the effort behind Title C among bookstores? What if you sold Title A directly to corporations instead of through wholesalers? What would happen if, instead of mailing a flyer to acquisition librarians in February, you waited until May when their fiscal year is about to expire? Could you stimulate sales of Title D by offering a price discount? When you finish reviewing your marketing plan, recalculate your marketing budget based upon these revised tactics.

Forecasting should not be done in a vacuum and it is important to confer with your distribution partners about your plans. Discuss your marketing tactics with them, and talk about how you can best promote your titles. Work with them to prepare a suitable forecast and agree on how you can best support their sales efforts.

Forecasting must also be congruous with marketing planning. An aggressive forecast demands equally vigorous promotion. Use your sales figures to create a cash-flow analysis (see Strategy #33) to determine if you have the funds available to support the marketing efforts necessary for success.

Proper planning and forecasting will enable you to better control your business and not just "wait to see what happens." It will also help you analyze and trim your product line, work more effectively with your distribution partners, prepare creative marketing strategies, find new customers and markets, resolve potential problems before they become calamitous, discover fresh product opportunities and plan your expected revenue and expenses on a more timely basis. And it may allow your entire business to flourish and become more profitable.

However well organized the foundations of life may be, life must always be full of risks. HAVELOCK ELLIS, *English psychologist*

9

Capitalize Your Special-Sales Efforts Sufficiently and Price Your Books Profitably

TOPICS DISCUSSED IN THIS CHAPTER . . .

STRATEGY # 31: Use Marketing Planning to Improve Financial Results
STRATEGY # 32: Price Your Books Profitably
STRATEGY # 33: Prepare Your Cash-Flow Projection

YOUR DESIRE TO SELL MORE BOOKS into special sales markets should result in better-looking financial statements with bottom-line numbers in black ink. Special-sales marketing can increase your revenue and profits more quickly than perhaps any other business strategy. You have already taken a great step toward making this happen by purchasing, reading and applying the information in *Beyond the Bookstore* and *The Marketing Planning* CD-ROM.

The Sales Continuum below depicts the range of financial possibilities open to an independent publisher. Your business is at some point on it.

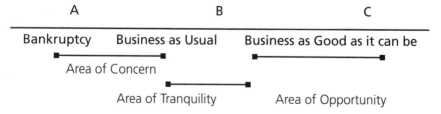

The area between Points A and B is the Area of Concern, the territory where many publishers focus their attention. They try to move away from Point A or toward Point B to establish some equilibrium in their business.

Most attempt to reside in the Area of Tranquility where little financial pressure looms. Here, business is okay, you are paying your bills and you have enough revenue to publish your next frontlist. Life is good.

There is comfort in the familiarity with this territory. The annual additions to the frontlist are produced, distributed to bookstores and promoted in much the same ways as all previous books. Publishers' desire to remain in the relative tranquility at Point B leads them on a quest for new manuscripts to publish. Once these are released, the publishers lean on traditional means of distribution and promotion to steer them back to their comfort zone, which now looks as welcoming as a safe harbor does to sailors seeking refuge from a storm.

This area between Points B and C—the Area of Opportunity—is the world of special sales, the place where you have the freedom to make your business grow and thrive. This non-traditional market -- with its broad, varied, new and potentially lucrative pockets of opportunity – gives you the chance to take your business to a higher level. Here you can creatively find new markets for existing titles, develop new titles to bring to current markets, choose different distribution channels, design unique ways to offer price incentives while maintaining your margins, and innovate ways to promote your titles above the ever-increasing clutter of competitive advertising, sales promotions and publicity.

Risks exist, but they are manageable if you plan for them. Financial planning in tandem with marketing planning helps you maximize your return on special sales. For example, a publisher may contemplate conducting certain marketing activities for which he or she thinks there is a reasonable likelihood of success. Let's say this is a direct-marketing campaign aimed at a niche market. If analysis of current funds determines that there is not enough money to pay for it the plan may be abandoned. But if that same publisher found that the campaign could be funded from future revenue, he or she might proceed.

And the trouble is, if you do not risk anything, you risk even more.
ERICA JONG, *author, poet*

Strategy # 31: Use Marketing Planning to Improve Financial Results

Marketing and financial planning epitomize a chicken-and-egg relationship. It takes money to implement the marketing activities that will help you sail toward and through the Area of Opportunity. However, you won't have the money to invest in promotion, to put the wind in your sails, until the title becomes successful. If you do not have sufficient funds on hand, what do you do?

> I find the great thing in this world is not so much where we stand, as in what direction we are moving—we must sail sometimes with the wind and sometimes against it—but we must sail, and not drift, nor lie at anchor.
> OLIVER WENDELL HOLMES JR. *Former Justice to the U.S. Supreme Court*

Look for the marketing activities that do not require out-of-pocket expenditures, starting with distribution strategies. Marketing through Special Distribution channels will cost you about the same in discounts as distributing to bookstores. And it costs you nothing to set these up. In some cases your traditional distributor may already be calling on discount stores and airport stores.

One of your initial distribution strategies would be to talk with your existing distributor. If nothing else, this will help you avoid contractual conflicts. If you do not have coverage in, or prohibitions excluding special-sales marketing, contact AMS, Anderson News or one of the other middlemen to sell your books to mass merchandisers, supermarkets and/or drug stores, as appropriate (see Chapter Eleven for contact information).

The Distribution Profitability Calculator in *The Marketing Planning* CD-ROM helps you calculate the optimum combination of distribution activities that will yield the greatest net profit, before considering promotional expenses. Use it to experiment with various combinations of distribution strategies to determine the most lucrative system for you by changing the quantities sold in each row. The form in *The Marketing Planning* CD-ROM looks like that shown below, for an inventory of one thousand books.

Next, divide your total market into smaller segments in which you can promote more efficiently. Review the priority lists you created in Chapter Eight. Where are there niche opportunities that could stimulate short-term proceeds? Are there gift stores, military outlets, government

Distribution Channel	Bookstore Distributor	Library Wholesaler	Direct	Discount Stores	Total Sales	Net
Distributor only	1,000				1,000	$732
Wholesaler only		1,000			1,000	$2,228
Direct only			1,000		1,000	$7,460
Maximum discount				1,000	1,000	–$15
Alternative A	250	500		250	1,000	$1,293
Alternative B			500	500	1,000	$3,723
Alternative C		500	250	250	1,000	$2,975
Alternative D	500		500		1,000	$4,096

agencies, retail stores or Internet opportunities to which you could sell and generate immediate earnings? Go through the *Fastart*™ Checklist in Appendix B looking for other ways to fuel income. Do not disregard long-run income by ignoring the Commercial Sales sector. Simply delay activity there until your revenue stream reverses course and begins to flow inward.

> What earthly good is it to know the cost if it tells you cannot manufacture at a price at which the item can be sold? HENRY FORD

Place more attention on prepublication publicity to hit the ground running when your title is published. This will usually cost less than using advertising, sales promotion or personal selling as your springboard. Create and send review copies and press releases to centers of influence. Contact the broadcast media to arrange interviews on the air, and the print media to place articles about your new titles. Review Chapter Six for additional hints to publicize your titles.

Pricing your book properly is an important decision, one with perhaps the most impact on your financial performance. This marketing strategy will be discussed next.

Strategy # 32: Price Your Books Profitably

The price you choose for your books will determine your sales, profits and the time it takes to traverse the Area of Opportunity. It also has psychological connotations, creating an image of relative quality and worth. If your price is too low, people may perceive your book as not capable of providing the value they need. If it is too high it may be perceived as not worth the money you are asking for it, especially if there are similar competitive books from which to choose.

PINNACLE PRICING

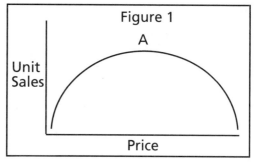

Figure 1

These concepts are illustrated in Figure 1, demonstrating the impact pricing has upon sales. This chart shows that sales will increase as the price increases to the point where the money asked is greater than the perceived value. Then sales will plummet. Your objective should be to determine and maintain a price at point "A," the peak level of sales. A lower or higher price will have a negative impact on revenue.

PRICING AND FINANCIAL PLANNING

This feat may be easier said than done, but one way to achieve it is to view the price of your book as part of your overall marketing strategy and not to simply multiply your printing cost by eight to determine your price.

Suppose your unit printing cost is $1.87. Eight times this amount would yield a list price of $14.95. This covers your distributors percentage (70 per cent), and even with a marketing budget of $1.00 per book you could still make over $1.62 per sale. At that rate you would need to sell 619 books to generate $1,000 of net income. That seems doable at first glance.

However, what if your competition is selling a relatively similar book for only $11.95? If you matched that price and maintained the same cost structure you would only net $ .72 per sale. Now you will have to sell almost 1,400 books (a 126 per cent increase in sales) to reach $1,000 of contribution. A simple chart demonstrates this situation.

List Price	$14.95	$11.95
Distribution @ 70%	$10.47	$8.37
Production	$1.87	$1.87
Promotion cost	$1.00	$1.00
Total costs	$13.34	$11.24
Net Income	$1.62	$0.72
Books per $1000 of revenue	619	1399

What should you do? There are at least three alternatives from which you may choose:

Option 1: Price at $11.95 without changing the cost structure.

In this case there is not enough margin to apply against overhead and still yield a sufficient profit. But this would not be a consideration if your strategy were to use this title as a break-even venture to establish a presence in a new market. You could sell to special-sales niches, avoiding some of the distribution discounts, but this does not all drop to the bottom line. Your promotion costs will escalate, as will the time necessary to perform the sales function.

Option 2: Price at $11.95 and apply creative and strategic thinking to reduce your costs.

Look back to Chapters Five and Six to review product development and promotion strategies you might apply. See where you can save money in production, without sacrificing quality. Focus on reducing your unit costs by eliminating high-cost, low-return features that will not reduce your sales. If you must have four-color photos in the interior of your book, can you group them in sections instead of dispersing them throughout the text? You could print a higher quantity initially, but consider the impact of carrying costs. An alternative strategy might be to print 10,000 of your book's four-color cover, but only assemble 2000 books. This will reduce the cost of the most expensive part of the printing process and allow you to quickly supply additional copies in the future.

You might consider increasing your promotion expenditures to move more books (rather than cutting promotion costs to save money). Keep in mind that increased spending on communication does not automatically increase sales. Poor strategy or implementation might have you communicating the right message to the wrong market, or vice versa.

With these strategies as examples, if you price your book at $11.95, reduce your production costs and increase promotion you could make 267% more money by selling one-third fewer books:

List Price	$11.95
Distribution @ 55%	$6.57
Production	$1.25
Promotion cost	$1.50
Total costs	$9.32
Gross Income	$2.63
Books per $1000 of revenue	381

Option 3: Price at $14.95.

You might decide to go with the higher price and implement all the cost-saving actions stated above. At first glance this appears to be the strategy that would pour the most money into your coffers. But if you provide a premium-priced book that is seemingly identical to that offered by competition, most people would opt for the lower-priced one.

All is not lost because you can still apply creative marketing strategy. Make your communications prove your title's superiority over competition. Tell prospective readers how much money your ideas will save them.

Eliminate price comparisons by avoiding bookstores and selling directly to the Commercial Sales and Niche Market sectors. Here the buyers do not have ready access to substitute titles and will view yours only in relation to how well it helps them solve their problems.

Your higher price gives you more leeway to maintain a higher *price* while reducing the *cost* to the buyer. You can do this by offering discounts or promotional and discriminatory prices that you cannot do in the traditional marketplace.

> *Discounts.* Consider *cash discounts* to reward buyers who pay their bills promptly (2/10, net 30) or quantity discounts to those who purchase in large volumes (in the Commercial Sales and Niche Market sectors).
>
> *Promotional pricing.* A money-back guarantee is one example of promotional pricing, as is seasonal pricing, i.e., offering a discount for purchases made during the winter months for a book about sailing techniques. A reduced price for this day only is an example of special-event pricing. Bundling is another example of promotional pricing.
>
> *Discriminatory pricing* is exemplified by customer-segment pricing. *Product-form pricing* (hard vs. softcover, library edition) and *location* (geographical) *pricing* are also valid approaches.

Now, what should you do? The answer lies in your ability and willingness to apply creative strategy to your marketing efforts. Choose the option that suits your particular skills and the time you have available to implement your strategies. Also keep in mind that there are book-marketing consultants who can help you plan and implement a successful marketing program.[11]

---

11. Visit *www.bookmarketingworks.com* for help in marketing your books to special-sales segments.

Strategy # 33: Prepare Your Cash-Flow Projection

As you have seen, financial planning working in tandem with marketing planning can impact the timing and amount of projected income. This in turn has a great bearing on your ultimate success in penetrating the Area of Opportunity. How can you plan and track your journey to Point C? Create a cash-flow statement.

A cash-flow statement is a document that projects how revenue and expenses flow over time. It records when your forecasted revenue should appear, and predicts the amount and timing of expenses so you can make marketing decisions that keep you moving ahead. It also points out the possible need for—and the amount and timing of—external financing. And when prepared properly it takes into consideration distributor discounts and the impact of returns on your earnings.

There are three sections to a cash-flow statement. The first shows your expected revenue, the income you anticipate receiving, by month, over a twelve-month period. The second section lists your selling, administrative and operating expenses. These are also predicted by month, over twelve months. The third section keeps a running total of the projected monthly beginning and ending balances. It quickly points out any shortfall that must be made up with external funds.

REVENUE

The earnings for each month represent the aggregate sales (for all titles) you forecast for that period, multiplied by the selling price of each book, less distribution discounts and returns. The beginning cash balance for January represents the cash with which you start. The beginning cash balance for every consecutive month is the previous month's ending balance.

As you determine the revenue for each book, consider the deductions that are assigned to it. For instance, if you are distributing Title A to bookstores through a distributor, you must calculate the discount (perhaps 65 per cent) with payment received 90–120 days after the sale.

Use the illustration below as a template for creating an Excel spreadsheet. Start with the revenue portion of your cash flow statement. Column N shows the totals of rows for each month. Limit your initial cash-flow statement to one year. Create other plans for Years Two and Three. Years Four and Five need only have revenue and expenses planned on a quarterly basis since monthly figures would probably not be forecasted accurately at this point.

A	B	C	D	E	F	G	H	I	J	K	L	M	N
1													
2	Jan	Feb	Mar	April	May	Jun	July	Aug	Sep	Oct	Nov	Dec	Total
3 **Revenue**													0
4 **Bookstores**													0
5 Distributor A (65%)													0
6 Wholesaler A (55%)													0
7 Online Bookstore (45%)													0
8 Returns (25%)													0
9 Total Bookstore													0
10 **Special Distribution**													0
11 Library Wholesaler A													0
12 Library Direct													0
13 Gift Shops													0
14 Book Clubs													0
15 Catalogs													0
16 Airport Stores													0
17 Total Special Distribution													0
18 **Commercial Sales**													0
19 Company A													0
20 Total Commercial Sales													0
21 **Niche Markets**													0
22 Museums													0
23 Total Niche Markets													0
24 **Total**	0	0	0	0	0	0	0	0	0	0	0	0	0

Use your cash-on-hand balance as beginning total in Month One. Add to that the first period's total revenue, and then deduct its total expenses to compute the Monthly Total. This figure becomes the Beginning Balance for the next period.

	A	B	C	D	E	F	G	H	I	J	K	L	M	N
		Jan	Feb	Mar	April	May	Jun	July	Aug	Sep	Oct	Nov	Dec	Total
1	**Expenses**													0
2	Rent													0
13	Utilities													0
14	Outside Services													0
15	Salaries													0
16	Benefits													0
17	Withholding													0
18	Telephone													0
19	General S&A													0
20	Postage													0
21	Printing—General													0
22	Printing—Books													0
23	Royalties													0
24	Interest													0
25	Design and Layout													0
26	Editing													0
27	Miscellaneous													0
28	Insurance													0
29	Taxes													0
30	Professional													0
31	Trade Shows / BEA													0
32	T&E													0
33	Meals													0
34	Other													0
35	Other													0
36	Total Expenses													
37														
38	Beginning Total													
39	Revenue													
40	Expenses													
41	Monthly Total													

WHAT DOES THIS SHOW?

1. Shortfalls in revenue and the months in which they occur.
2. Revenue and expenses for a year-at-a-glance.
3. Months in which you may need to borrow funds to make up a shortfall.
4. How revenue from certain promotional activities could pay for their expenses.

Once you have your cash-flow document finished, begin evaluating your strategy. Appraise each line item with the thought of eliminating it, reducing it, moving it to a different time period or leaving it as is. Of course, any changes in marketing expenses should be reflected in the amount and timing of your revenue. For instance, if you postpone an ad in the *Radio-Television Interview Report*,[12] to what extent would sales also be delayed? Similarly, you could put off the $2,000 for your direct-marketing campaign in February, but what negative impact would that have on your income in March?

Question every line item. Can you arrange ninety-day payment terms with your printer? Could you delay the direct-mail campaign or send out half of the letters one month and half the next? What if you used an existing display instead of buying a new one for this year's BEA exhibit? What if you printed your brochure in two colors instead of four? What would be the impact on earnings if you performed more frequently on television and radio? Is your contemplated price reduction absolutely required to stimulate sales? What if you delayed production of a sales-promotional item?

This analysis is a circular process requiring frequent analysis. If you need to increase your revenue, go back to your marketing plan to see how this can be done. Then recalculate your sales forecast and the resulting impact on your cash-flow statement.

---

12. *The Radio Television Interview Report* is published by Bradley Communications, Lansdowne, PA. Reach them at *www.rtir.com*, or (800) 989-1400.

Manipulate your revenue and expenses:

1. You may be able to delay some expenses to make up for a cash shortfall in one particular month.
2. Consider payment periods. You may not receive money for books sold through distributors in 90-120 days, as your contract requires.
3. There may be a month in which expenses exceed revenue. Resist the temptation to simply increase the sales figures to eliminate a negative balance in one particular period. Any increase in sales must be rooted in market need and have its cost allocated as an expense. Also, if more books are sold, inventory may be depleted, requiring an expense for additional printing. Use this pro-forma statement to reveal the changes in revenue that will occur as you make adjustments in your marketing strategy.
4. You may also be tempted to increase your forecast for non-bookstore sales, thus reducing or eliminating distributor discounts and returns. While this may be true, the onus (and costs) for promotion—as well as administrative and handling costs—falls upon you.

Go through your document repeatedly until you have a strategic, coordinated and profitable program in place. This will give you a more accurate reflection of your potential sales and the marketing effort required to generate them. The result is a synergistic plan with which to guide your actions, evaluate your performance and run your business more profitably.

You can measure opportunity with the same yardstick that measures the risk involved. They go together. EARL NIGHTINGALE

10

Energize Your Implementation

MARKETING BOOKS IS LIKE TENDING a garden. Once you plant the seeds, you nurture them and revel in their growth. But if the plants are not properly treated, they wither. Similarly, if your marketing activities do not support and sustain continuous growth for your titles, they, too, will languish.

The preparation phase of the special-sales marketing process is now complete and it's time to being putting your plan into action. The steps you have taken so far are like preparing an item to be painted. You are eager to begin painting, because that is where the results of your efforts are most visible. But the actual painting looks better, lasts longer and goes more quickly and smoothly if the preparation is done properly. The planning you did will help the implementation of your plan go more efficiently and effectively.

Just as your planning was different for each of the three segments in which you can market your books—Special Distribution, Commercial Sales and Niche Markets—so is your implementation. The discussion over the next four chapters shows how to reach each most effectively and efficiently. Regardless of the segment to which you are selling, remember that people are not interested in your physical product as much as they are about how its content will help them in some way

Below is a list to help execute your plan as you journey toward successful special-sales marketing. Use it to continue achieving positive results. Apply your efforts to the actions that accomplish results, keeping your business moving forward constantly in the Area of Opportunity described in Chapter Nine.

Strategy # 34: Act Effectively

Success occurs when you become effective (doing the right things) rather than efficient (doing things right). You can become very busy doing the wrong things right, leading you toward point A in the Area of Concern. Remember, action is not the same as accomplishment. Like the revving engine of a car stuck in traffic, you can be busy working without moving ahead.

Stop worrying about time management and think in terms of time utilization. Proponents of time management would have you allocate two hours one day to make telephone calls to arrange media appearances. But with wrong numbers and voice mail, you could call for two hours and never talk to one human being.

On the other hand, a philosophy of time *utilization* would have you continue calling within a reasonable period until you arranged meetings with a specific number of gift shops within a fifty-mile radius. Here, the emphasis is on results rather than on the activity of making calls. So, instead of blocking off chunks of time to conduct certain tasks, make a list of what you want to accomplish in that same time period. Then perform the work that will accomplish your goals.

Strategy # 35: Act Strategically

Special-sales marketing effectiveness means performing activities better than rivals perform them, while building a separate identity for your business. You can outperform rivals only to the extent you can establish a customer-oriented difference that you can preserve. You must deliver greater value to your customers or create comparable value at lower cost, or do both. The arithmetic of superior profitability then follows: delivering greater value allows you to charge higher average unit prices; greater effectiveness results in lower average unit costs.

Strategy # 36: Act Productively

The mantra of the publishing business is "What have you done for me lately?" Your customers expect more from you today than they did yesterday, and you must work diligently to meet their expectations and stay ahead of your competition.

Strategy # 37: Act Intelligently

Intelligent action is based on the understanding that knowledge is different from wisdom. Knowledge is information, but intelligence is the prudent application of knowledge earned through experience. It is the good judgment that prevents mishaps from recurring or enables you to act differently when they do.

You apply intelligence when you learn from a mistake. As Ben Franklin said, "a cat once burned by jumping on a hot stove will never jump on a hot stove again... or a cold one." Evaluate your results and understand how your actions caused them. If the desired outcome occurred, repeat those actions under the same circumstances in the future. If your progress is not goal-directed, analyze it and take appropriate action to rectify the situation and return your motion toward success.

Use the information from your evaluation as you would the details from traffic reports when traveling. This information alerts you to potential obstructions and gives you time to decide upon an alternative route. Informed feedback will help you redirect your forward motion around obstacles and keep you operating in the Area of Opportunity.

Intelligent action is also the result of continuing education, which is a neverending process. Continue your education by registering for book-marketing seminars and PMA-University. Attend BEA and other publishing conventions to talk with the exhibitors and network with your colleagues. Read *Publishers Weekly* and other sources of information about the book business. Go online to *www.bookmarketing.com*, *www.pma-online.org*, *www.bookmarketingworks.com* or other informative sites for answers to your questions. Join PMA (Publishers Marketing Association) and read its monthly newsletter. The publishing business is changing rapidly and you have to keep up with it to remain competitive.

Intelligent action also depends on the ability to do what is necessary, not only what you like to do. The difference becomes evident with a simple exercise. Make two lists, one containing the tasks required to keep your business operating in the Area of Opportunity, the other a record of what you enjoy doing, and do, every day. Now compare the two lists to see if you are doing what needs to be done or what you like to do. Hopefully, the lists are identical. Incongruence does not mean you must stop doing what you enjoy; it simply points out where you may need to apply yourself.

Strategy # 38: Act Creatively

Some people think that intelligent thinking is different from creative thinking. However, these two processes are similar in the sense that creativity helps you discover and implement imaginative ways of apply-ing your wisdom. Innovation is the same as resourcefulness, the ability to look at a task and find new ways to perform it. It is a playful way of looking at ordinary events, stimulating your thinking and inventing new ways to accomplish results. Creative thinking is productive and fun. Like wearing glasses, it improves your vision.

> Creativity is a force. It is not a result; it is a cause. It is not a product; it produces. It is a power, like money or steam or electricity. LEE IACOCCA

Strategy # 39: Act Boldly

You may encounter opposition in your journey to special-sales success because some people are wary of untested concepts. New ideas are neither right nor wrong—they are simply different. They are round pegs that do not fit into square holes. Evaluate your marketing plans and cash-flow statements, then trust your intuition, make strategic choices and imple-ment them courageously. This does not mean that you should throw all caution to the wind and advance blindly. Bold action is informed, planned work implemented with passion.

Many people have an unrealistic approach to special sales. They in-variably invoke the fatal conjunction "if" as a condition: "I would do it if I had more money or more time." Set a goal and make it happen. Trust your instincts and take yourself by surprise.

▮▮ Strategy # 40: Act Passionately

Negativity happens. Discount stores might return books. Levy and AMS may reject all your submissions. Problems conspire to erode your enthusiasm and make it more difficult to remain passionate about your special-sales business and your future. Yet the axiom for success in any business is to do what you love and love what you do. When you have reached this state, a sparkling effervescence exudes in everything you do and say. You will remain focused on achievement, excited about your circumstances and confident of your future. Believe in your ability to create sales in non-bookstore markets, and attack each challenge enthusiastically.

A sense of enthusiastic expectation is your most valuable asset. Without passion, in your voice and actions, your pursuit of success will be more difficult. Invest in your attitude regularly, build interest in it and protect it from depreciation as you would any other asset.

▮▮ Strategy # 41: Act Persistently

Passion begets persistence. If you believe in what you are doing it is easier to perform all the activities that, in spite of everyday obstacles, will propel you forward.

Persistence is tenacity in the face of obstacles, determination to succeed, perseverance in conducting marketing activities and perpetual promotion in spite of resistance, rejection and returns. This resolution is supported by the knowledge that ultimate achievement is not immediate, and the fact that you start your journey anyway and do what is necessary to reach your objectives.

▮▮ Strategy # 42: Act Cooperatively

None of us is as smart as all of us. People interacting with people make success happen. This requires an understanding of yourself and your limitations as much as it involves finding people who can help you accomplish what you cannot do alone. For example, you may be a person who is good at implementing details but cannot metaphorically rise to thirty-thousand feet for a view of the big picture. If so, ally yourself with the strategic thinker who may be poor at details. Your sea-level strengths are just a valuable to the high-flying strategist as his or hers are to you.

Strategy # 43: Act Responsively

Cooperative action permits everyone to be responsive to the needs of the people upon whom they depend for success. Remember, your suppliers, distribution partners and special-sales customers need you as much as you need them. Understand and respond to their needs, and your journey through the Area of Opportunity will be abbreviated.

Find out how you are performing in terms of customer service. You may need to improve it by returning telephone calls the same day, shipping your products promptly, packing them carefully to reduce damage in transit, training employees to speak professionally on the telephone, handling returns quickly and always doing what you promise. Make it a habit to underpromise and overdeliver.

Strategy # 44: Act Ethically

A trek through the Area of Opportunity keeps publishers busy, sometimes so busy that they neglect to perform some necessary tasks. This does not mean they are irresponsible, but that they need to be more vigilant. Responsible action is just that—observant, dependable and conscientious diligence. It means doing what is ethically and morally right to build or maintain a reputation of integrity.

If you have integrity, nothing else matters. If you do not have integrity, nothing else matters.

11

Special Distribution Markets

WHERE IS THE BEST PLACE to sell books? It is where people go to shop for items of interest to *them*. Think about where consumers *could* buy your products, and that is where you should sell them. In this way you could reach them in discount stores, supermarkets, drug stores and libraries. This tactic could eliminate your competition and make you the sole supplier in your niche. The beauty of nontraditional book marketing is that there are a variety of options available to you to create a distribution network that meets the needs of your topics, titles and target segments.

Special-sales distribution systems are like snowflakes—no two are exactly alike. Your challenge, opportunity and responsibility is to choose from among the various alternatives and sculpt one that makes it easy for people to obtain your books. When Michelangelo was asked how he could create such a magnificent statue as David, he replied, "All I did was chip away everything that wasn't David." Just as he knew that in every block of stone there lurks a perfect form, the perfect distribution system for your product line awaits your discovery.

Strategy # 45: Arrange Special Distribution

Familiarity breeds sales. That is what most publishers must think, because they typically launch their special-sales marketing efforts in the Special Distribution sector. It is a logical decision because supplying your titles to nonbookstore retailers is almost identical to the time-honored book-store-marketing channels. In both networks, publishers use distributors and wholesalers to distribute their books to retailers. These middlemen take their fee from the sale of your book, and there may be returns. The retailers rarely buy directly from the publisher and payment periods may be drawn out to ninety days or more.

There are also positive reasons to distribute your books in this fashion. Your current distributor may already be representing your titles to discount stores and warehouse clubs. It will sell your titles through their sales people or rep groups, giving you instant national representation. The middlemen with whom you partner will also perform the functions of shipping, billing and collecting, freeing more of your time to do what you do best—publishing and marketing.

There are four factors to consider before deciding whether or not to use Special Distribution: the title's content, the author/publisher, and the customer and industry practices.

1. **The topic itself may dictate your decision.** Special Distribution is a logical alternative for fiction or nonfiction books applicable to large groups of readers. Mass merchandisers, supermarkets and airport stores overwhelmingly carry titles of interest to large, varied audiences.

   There are situations that may need more select distribution. If your book is written for a non-English-speaking audience and you are not familiar with the buying habits of people in this group, it would be in your best interest to market through distribution partners who are familiar with that market.

2. **The skills and desires of the author or publisher.** Self-published authors and small publishers may not have the time, proficiency or inclination to contact buyers, negotiate contracts, ship, bill and collect for books sold. Nor might they want to bask in the spotlight as is necessary to successfully promote their titles. In these cases it would be well worth their time to have a company do it for them.[13]

---

13. Visit *www.bookmarketingworks.com* for assistance in contacting non-bookstore markets

3. **The customers' buying habits.** The slogan "write it and they will come" does not apply to special-sales distribution. Make your products available where your customers seek them. If they purchase via direct mail, in drug stores or on the Internet, then that is where your books must be accessible.

4. **The purchasing practices of the industry.** Discount stores, warehouse clubs, supermarkets, drug stores and libraries prefer to buy from middlemen, not directly from publishers. Distributors, wholesalers, sales-rep groups and fulfillment services are more likely to take on an unproven title, if it is backed by a solid marketing plan (see Appendix A). Find out what you need to do to sell more books and make it happen.

CHANNEL DESIGN

Most large retailers prefer to buy through a wholesaler than directly from the publisher, although they will buy directly in some cases. When limited-line publishers call the buyers at Wal-Mart, Costco, Kroger or Safeway they are given the names of the appropriate wholesaler to contact. So, it may behoove you to team up with a distribution company right from the start. There are established companies and relatively standard distribution discounts and agreements that can make life easier for independent publishers.

It may be necessary to create a different distribution arrangement for each of your titles, or for the same title. Depending on your market opportunities, you might choose AMS or Anderson Merchandisers for distribution to discount stores and warehouse clubs, or Anderson News or News Group West for supermarkets and drug stores. A key to optimal profitability is to customize a nontraditional network that is best for your marketing objectives, distribution strategies, product lines, target markets and selling skills.

HOW TO CONTACT DISTRIBUTORS

Once you have compiled your list of potential distributors, approach them as you would any other marketing partner. Start by calling to learn the name of the person to whom you should send your proposal. The package you send them should include the following information:

A **cover letter, describing what the book is about.** If it is in a competitive category, explain how it is different (and better) than the others. Include information about the size of the market, and any geographical pockets of opportunity, if applicable. What is the source of your information? Is the title based on personal experience? If not, describe the research that was performed to back up any major or controversial claims made. A retailer such as a drug store will be particularly wary of a title on a health-related topic unless you can substantiate all of your assertions.

The author's resume. The purpose of the resume is to establish the author's credentials for being the best person to write a book on this subject. Do not list all his or her education and work experience, but only that which establishes credibility. What are his or her qualifications to write the book? What previous titles has he or she written?

A sample of the book. Discount stores, supermarkets and warehouse clubs thrive on rapid inventory turns. Therefore, the cover of your book is as critical to selling it in the Special Distribution sector as it is in bookstores. If you send a galley, send one with a completed cover, perhaps wearing a flag stating that it is an "Advance Reading Copy," or "Unedited Proof."

According to Eric Kampmann, president of Midpoint Trade Books, "Why does the book jacket matter? The obvious answer is that it is the best and cheapest advertising vehicle you will have for your book. But the obvious answer is not the right answer. Here, I am thinking about the competitive factor. Does a good book jacket help get the book into stores initially? The answer is a definitive *yes*. The reason is clear to those who sell everyday because we get to see the stacks and stacks of book jackets sitting on the buyer's desk ready to be accepted or rejected. The problem is that your book is in the same stack as the Random House title or the Putnam or Harper Collins title, all professionally produced. If your cover design does not measure up to the best, then the likelihood of that title ending up in the rejection heap increases dramatically. So you need to have a good designer and you often have to get them to produce more than one design concept; and you need to talk to your distributor's sales people early in the process so that mistakes are minimized."

A fact sheet listing statistical information. Include one page that lists all the pertinent statistical data. This should contain the author's name, the title of the book, its publication date, price, number of pages, trim size, number of illustrations, type of binding, ISBN, publisher, publisher's contact information, copyright date, Library of Congress Catalog Card Number (when submitting to library wholesalers) and the names of your editor and graphic designers. Also list any celebrity endorsements and note if any notable industry person wrote the foreword. When sending your proposal to a wholesaler for mass merchandisers, Steve Linville of News Group West suggests that you "include a color photo of any floor or counter displays you have to offer."

A **list of bullet points** summarizing the top ten reasons why people would want to buy your product. These benefits will aid the distributor's salespeople and will probably be used in their catalog. Write these from the consumer's standpoint, not from yours. Include testimonials. Mitch Rogatz of Triumph Books says, "Buyers do not care if the author says it is *the best book on the subject.* However, these same words will have impact if taken from a major review, or if said by a celebrity or industry notable."

A **summary marketing plan.** Antoinette Kuritz will not even consider taking on a client without a marketing plan. She advises publishers to "describe your promotional plans and tell what your budget is for advertising, direct mail, personal presentations, tours or any other activities you intend to perform." This plan and your cover are the two most important parts of your proposal. A weak book with a strong promotional campaign will almost always outsell a well-written book that is not promoted heavily. An example of a summary marketing plan is found in Appendix C.

The resellers' choice of titles they wish to carry is a marketing decision, not a literary decision. A title that has a good track record, is on a "hot topic," or is supported by an aggressive promotional campaign will usually get an affirmative nod over one that may be better written, but is not as saleable.

Tips for Selecting a Distribution Partner

Apply the same due diligence in the decision process that you would when selecting a distributor in traditional marketing. Compare discounts and terms. Are you paid in ninety days? For sales or collections? Is there an escrow for returned books? What return rates do they experience? Do they carry competitive titles? How many salespeople will represent your titles? If you are evaluating sales rep groups, make sure you have adequate geographical coverage.

Working with Your Distributor/Wholesaler

If you work closely with your partners in any distribution network you are more likely to establish a long-term, mutually profitable relationship. Here are several tips for creating and maintaining a professional relationship.

1. **Communicate frequently.** Meet with your distribution partners—at least your local sales representatives—and get to know the people behind the company. You can do this at BEA or by visiting their offices. If you send out a regular newsletter about your title or subject matter, make sure they are on your mailing list.

2, **Share marketing programs.** Show your marketing plans to your distribution partners and keep them updated on your promotional activities. Monthly, send them a list of the personal presentations and media appearances you have scheduled and a list of what you accomplished during the previous month. Tell them well in advance of your major media appearances so their sales people can stock their customers' shelves sufficiently. Send them samples of all your promotional material, such as literature, advertising and direct-mail letters. Take advantage of any cooperative marketing plans that are consistent with your strategies and meet your objectives.

3. **Meet their deadlines.** Distributors' deadlines for catalogs and promotional material may be months before their salespeople go out on their rounds. Eric Kampmann tells us, "Is it important to meet a certain deadline for publishing your book? The answer is, yes, sometimes it is important to get a book into the marketplace to coincide with a particular event. For example, a Christmas book must be in bookstores sometime in October at the latest. Or a gift book for graduation should be out there by April. There are many examples where timing is critical for a proper launch of your title."

4. **Support their sales efforts.** Once you commit to work with a distributor, let it do its work. Do not duplicate its sales efforts by calling on major-account buyers. Find out where they do not call and fill in those gaps yourself.

5. **Help them control your inventory.** Distributors do not buy books from you; they take them on consignment. You still own them. Have your distributor send damaged copies to you so you may use them to send to producers of radio shows. If you receive orders from special-sales customers not covered under your contract, have the books shipped directly from your distributor rather than reprinting an additional supply. Careful management can help you minimize

the money you have tied up in inventory while minimizing the fulfillment time for major orders.

6. **Keep your perspective.** Books are not sold by the distributor, wholesaler, sales person, gift shop, airport store, supermarket or bookstore. The publisher and author sell them. The distribution channel simply delivers them to appropriate level in the network in response to the demand you create. Books are returned because they are not sold, which could be the result of ineffective or nonexistent promotion. If your returns increase, change your marketing strategies to keep them sold.

Each segment in the Special Distribution sector has it own players and nuances. As a case in point for one title, you may choose Bookazine to take your title to airport stores, select Anderson News for distribution to supermarkets and drug stores, and pick AMS to approach the top discount stores. There are also ways for you to participate in promoting your titles to augment your distributors' sales efforts. The discussion below gives you an understanding of your options and opportunities.

Strategy # 46: Selling to Discount Stores and Warehouse Clubs[14]

Publishing events in mid-2003 signaled the growing power of discount stores and warehouse clubs in book-selling channels. It was then that these outlets accounted for almost half of the record-breaking sales of three titles: *Harry Potter and the Order of the Phoenix*, *Living History* by Hilary Rodham Clinton and John Steinbeck's *East of Eden*.[15]

Discount stores (Wal-Mart, Target, K-Mart, Best Buy, Toys "R" Us) and warehouse clubs (Sam's Club, Costco, BJ's Clubs) are becoming formidable players for selling books. Since 1992, the share of sales through bookstores has fallen to 38 per cent from 50 per cent of total book sales, according to research conducted by Ipsos-NPD Group. During that same period, the combined share of book sales through the discounters and price clubs increased to 13 per cent from 9 per cent. This expansion has been much stronger than the retail industry (6.0 per cent), general merchandise stores (6.4 per cent) and food stores (3.2 per cent).

14. Contributions to this section were made by Carla Ruff, Publishing Consultant, *carlainsf@aol.com*, and Chuck Williams of AMS.

15. "Book Buyers Stay Busy but Forsake Bookstores;" David Kirkpatrick; *New York Times*, June 30, 2003

Warehouse clubs sell billions of dollars worth of books, tapes and CDs every year ($4.029 billion in 2002) primarily because of the low prices they offer customers. This fact was indelibly etched on the minds of many independent booksellers when they replenished their depleted stocks of *Harry Potter* by purchasing books from nearby clubs and reselling them profitably in their stores.

Discount stores and warehouse clubs rarely buy directly from publishers. Although they will entertain submissions directly from publishers, they typically forward that information to distributors or wholesalers. The top middlemen include:

Ms. Debra McKirdy; Book Purchasing Department, Anderson Merchandisers, 421 East 34th Street, Amarillo, TX 79103 (buys for Wal-Mart); (806) 376-6251 ext. 4489

Advanced Marketing Services (AMS), 5880 Oberlin Drive, #400, San Diego, CA 92122-9653; (858) 457-2500, Fax (858) 452-2167 (mass merchandisers and wholesale clubs), *www.advmkt.com*

Levy Home Entertainment; Book Buyer, 4201 Raymond Drive, Hillside, IL 60162-1786; (708) 547-4400 (warehouse clubs, supermarkets, drugstores)

The Chas. Levy Circulating Company operates the largest magazine and book distribution center in the mass market, grocery, and drug class of trade chains. It only focuses on distributing magazines and books. Affiliated with Levy Home Entertainment; 1200 N North Branch Street, Chicago, IL, 60622; (312) 440-4400, Fax: (312) 440-4434; *www.chasevy.com*

The Handleman Company, (Music and videos), 500 Kirts Boulevard. Troy, MI 48084-4142; (248) 362-4400.

Contact these companies with the same approach as you would use for a bookstore distributor. Demonstrate why it is in their best interests to carry your title. How do you do that? First, call to find out the name of the proper buyer for your topic. In most cases you will receive a voice-mail message with this information, along with their submission guidelines. Usually you will be asked to send a cover letter with a sample of your book, your terms, a press kit, a fact sheet and a one-page marketing plan. Most have submission guidelines, and you can learn these from their websites.

Use this opportunity to prove that you are a professional book marketer by demonstrating how you intend to promote your books to help make their sales job easier and make more money. Share your sales projections with them and your plans for reaching them.

Your marketing plan should be 50 per cent what you plan to do and 50 per cent about what you have done. Anyone can make grandiose statements about their intentions. If you submit a plan with the statement that your sole promotional tactic is to get on *The Oprah Winfrey Show*, you will immediately label yourself as someone who is not realistic in his or her expectations. But if you can prove that you have done something similar in the past, your plans are more believable. Your previous actions give your statements credibility, and demonstrate that you are experienced and a realist.

Provide them with a list of the media appearances you will conduct (other than Oprah), or the direct-mail campaigns you intend to send or the publicity you expect to generate. Tell your potential distribution partners how you plan to support their sales representatives with sales-promotional tools. Convince them about your intention to communicate with them on a regular basis and to give them advance notice of your promotions, appearances and publicity programs.

Appendix C shows a format you can use to organize your submission package. It describes your plans in all four areas of the marketing mix as well as providing much of the information they need to make a favorable decision.

SELL YOUR CONTENT TO A WAREHOUSE CLUB

There may be a side door to marketing to warehouse clubs, and that is to sell them your content. Let's say you published a cookbook and were unable to locate a distributor willing to carry it. There is a technique you could try in order to get your recipes to consumers: cooperate with the manufacturers of ingredients in your recipes and get Costco to be your publisher.

This is not as farfetched as it may first appear. According to *Publishers Weekly*[16], Costco entered the publishing business by printing 100,000 copies of its cookbook, *Entertaining the Costco Way*. Costco controlled every aspect of production, acting as publisher, distributor, packager and retailer. Manufacturers funded the production of the book, and in return for sponsor payments, products from those manufacturers were included in the recipes. Dave Fuller, editor of Costco's monthly publication, The *Costco Connection*, oversaw the cookbook project. Fuller said, "We do not see ourselves as a book publisher at all. What we're trying to do is provide a good cookbook for our members to use with all the great food products they're buying from us."

---

16. *Publishers Weekly*, November 18, 2002.

THINK OUTSIDE "THE BOX"

Mass merchandisers offer an enormous opportunity, but it may not be wise for all publishers to sell to this segment. Jen Linck of Biblio Distribution offers a cautionary perspective. According to Jen, "many more customers are buying their books from the "big box" and club stores. The space for books in these stores is very limited and they focus on the bestsellers and books that target at least 75 per cent of their customers. Also, because they have extensive and strict inventory demands, most small presses are unable to risk working with them (and endure the possibility of returns) even if they are lucky enough to get the opportunity.

"For example, if Target agrees to put your book into a *planogram* for their stores (which means it's being supported by the wholesaler, Levy, that sells to Target) then the publisher is expected to stay in stock during the promotion month(s). They may order ten thousand copies up front and expect you to be able to provide ten thousand more on demand. So, you have twenty thousand printed and warehoused with Biblio. If the book doesn't sell through and they return them, you're left with twenty thousand copies on your hands.

"I recommend that independent publishers focus on consumer promotion and on their niche markets getting nonreturnable sales through special, non-bookstore opportunities (gift shops, catalogs, etc.) and not look to the clubs or "big box" stores for sales. It's best, for now anyway, to leave those risks to the big houses that can afford it."

All business success rests on something labeled a sale, which at least momentarily weds company and customer.
TOM PETERS, *consultant, author*

CONTACT INFORMATION FOR MAJOR DISCOUNT STORES AND WAREHOUSE CLUBS

Wal-Mart Stores Inc. is the largest retailer in the U.S. with 1,736 stores, 888 Super Centers and 475 Sam's Clubs. Sales are discounted heavily, addressing a target audience with low-income demographics. Books are not a high priority, typically grouped with paper products. Topics that do well here are romance, mystery, juvenile and cooking. Bibles also sell well in most Wal-Mart locations. The hot buttons with Wal-Mart buyers are price and inventory turns. Wal-Mart purchases through Charles Levy (550 stores) and through Anderson Merchandisers for

Anderson = 1 - 800 - 999 - 0904

the remaining stores. Your submission package should report your promotional activities that will increase store traffic. Publishers are encouraged to contact local stores with regional titles. The contact information is: 702 SW Eighth Street, Bentonville, Arkansas 72716; (501) 273-4000 Fax: (501) 273-1917. For a Supplier Proposal Package go to: *www.walmartstores.com/wmstore/wmstore/homepage.jsp.*

Target Corp. has more than 1,400 stores in forty-seven states, with twenty-two distribution centers. It projects an image as the "middle-class discount store" so its demographics skew more upscale than are those for Wal-Mart's customers and lean toward women with families. Target buyers are more "book friendly" than most discounters due to a corporate commitment to reading and learning. Mailing address is 777 Nicollet Mall, Minneapolis, MN 55402; (612) 304-6073 *www.targetcorp.com.*

Best Buy has over 475 stores, with a goal of 550 by the end of 2004. It buys books primarily from Charles Levy. 60 to 70 per cent of their sales are fiction and nonfiction bestsellers, and the remaining sales are comprised of juvenile, craft and reference titles. An affiliate program is available. The products sold through Best Buy stores attract more of a male than female audience. Corporate Headquarters is located at P.O. Box 9312, Minneapolis, MN, 55440-9312; (612) 291-1000.

Toys "R" Us Inc. has approximately 1,580 stores in the U.S., with another 491 located internationally. Buyers purchase from publishers and from Charles Levy. Stores average up to thirty-two linear feet of shelf space for books, considerably more than the average of all mass merchandisers of eight to twelve linear feet. Toy "R" Us fills these shelves with 300 to 400 titles for kids of all age groups. The top one hundred titles account for almost 85 per cent of their sales. The sell-through rate is higher than others at 75–85 per cent, so returns are generally lower than competitors. Your book should be priced at less than $9.00 (softcover and board books) to sell well in Toys "R" Us stores. The mailing address is 225 Summit Avenue, Montvale, NJ, 07645; (201) 262-7800, *www.toysrus.com*, James Feldt, Executive Vice President, Merchandising.

Sam's Club is the nation's largest members-only warehouse with forty-six million members; the address is 608 Southwest 8th Street, Bentonville, AR 72716; *www.samsclub.com.* Sam's Club's sales of books, tapes and CDs in 2002 were $1,743,000,000.

Costco had fewer stores (412) than did Sam's (591) at the beginning of 2003, but its sales of books, tapes and CDs in 2002 was the highest of the top three clubs, amounting to $2,030,000,000, half of the industry total. Prospective vendors of books, tapes, DVDs and CDs can contact the corporate office at 999 Lake Drive, Issaquah, WA 98027; Costco also sells books and DVDs online at *www.costco.com*.

BJ's is an east coast membership wholesale club and the smallest of the big three with 140 stores at the beginning of 2003; BJ's main office is located at P.O. Box 9601, Natick, MA 01760. Its website is *www.bjs.com*, and sales of books, tapes and CDs in 2002 were $257,000,000.

There are other clubs that participate in industry sales of books, tapes, DVDs and CDs. These are Smart & Final, Cost-U-Less and PriceSmart.

Smart & Final has 235 non-membership warehouse grocery stores in four states: Arizona, California, Florida, Nevada, Mexico. Although it has two-thirds more stores than BJ's, Smart & Final's total sales are less than half those of BJ's. Smart & Final Inc.'s home office is at 600 Citadel Drive, Commerce, CA 90040; contact Randall Oliver at (323) 869-7607; Fax; (323) 869-7865; *www.smartandfinal.com*.

Cost-U-Less operates warehouse-style stores in offshore island communities. Corporate Headquarters is located at 8160 304th Avenue S.E., Building 3, Suite A, Preston, WA. 98050; (425) 222-5022, Fax: (425) 222-0044; *www.costuless.com*.

PriceSmart is a volume-driven, membership merchandise and services provider serving the rapidly emerging market in Latin America, the Caribbean and Asia. With the recent addition of a third location in Mexico and the first in Jamaica, PriceSmart now operates thirty-one warehouse clubs in twelve countries and two U.S. territories. PriceSmart also licenses eleven warehouses in China and one in Saipan, Micronesia. Headquarters is located at 4649 Morena Boulevard. San Diego, CA 92117; (858) 581-4530; Thomas D. Martin is the Executive Vice President-Merchandising, and their website is *www.pricesmart.com*.

▇▇▇ Strategy # 47: Fly High with Sales to Airport Stores[17]

All major airports have at least one bookstore, surrounded by a captive audience of weary travelers looking for something to do to help pass time. What better way to while away the hours than by reading a good

---

17. Part of this information about selling to airport bookstores was provided by Kathleen Willoughby, Bookazine.

book? Apparently many travelers seek that option because "a major store in a large airport will sell between $1 and $2 million of books each year" says Kathleen Willoughby of Bookazine.

Bookstores in small airports have space constraints limiting the titles they stock to only the top fiction and nonfiction titles as well as the popular classics. Among the bestsellers are popular annuals such as *Best American Short Stories* and *Best American Essays*.

But a title does not have to be a bestseller to find its way into the stores in large airports. These shops will carry titles by local and regional authors, as well as books pertaining to its specific locale and destination points. For example, the title *Fenway: A Biography in Words and Pictures* by Dan Shaughnessy and Stan Grossfeld, can be found in bookstores in Boston's Logan Airport.

Titles for children tend to do well in these outlets, as do titles for business travelers who spend a good amount of time in airports. Also titles on management, investment, economics, business biography, personal finance and health work well in the airport setting.

Summertime is the peak travel period, and as you would expect, it is also the peak bookselling period. There is a bump in sales in the fourth-quarter holiday season, too. Softcover books seem to sell more units than casebound, and the typical size is 6" x 9". Your book must have an ISBN, EAN bar code and its price printed on the rear cover, although some exceptions are made for nonbook items.

The major airport bookstore chains are listed below. You can reach buyers for these stores directly by sending them a complete package of marketing material and a sample of your book. Include contact information for your distributor or wholesaler since airport stores place their orders through them, using them as both suppliers and warehousers. Call to learn their specific submission guidelines before sending your package.

HMS Host, Book Buyer; 6600 Rockledge Drive, Bethesda, MD 20817; (866) 467-4671.

Paradies Shops operates over one hundred airport stores. Contact the National Book Buyer, 5950 Fulton Industrial Boulevard SW, P. O. Box 43485, Atlanta GA 30336; (404) 344-7905; Fax: (404) 349-7539; *www.theparadiesshop.com*. left message 4.13.07

W.H. Smith operates or owns 255 airport shops and 421 hotel stores under the names of WHSmith, WHSmith Booksellers, Waterstone's Booksellers, *WHSmith Books.com* and Benjamin Books. In late 2003, The Hudson Group purchased 180 WH Smith airport stores, including a number of Waterstone's Booksellers Outlets. Contact the

National Book Buyer, 3200 Windy Hill Road #1500 W, Atlanta, GA 30339; (770) 952-0705; Fax: (770) 951-1352.

Many traditional distributors and wholesalers will sell your books to airport stores. When you send your material to them, describe the number of books per carton and how many units were published. Also include information about who is providing sales, marketing and distribution services on your behalf.

You can generally expect to be paid 50 per cent of the amount due you in 90 days and the balance in 180 days. The 50 percent unpaid balance is held as a reserve against returns. Once your book "takes off" you can usually negotiate different terms. Bookazine and Anderson News are two of the larger wholesalers to airport stores.

New Vendor Development Coordinator, Bookazine Co. Inc., 75 Hook Road, Bayonne, NJ 07002. Complete submission guidelines for Bookazine may be found at *www.bookazine.com/customer_service/ instructions.shtml.*

Anderson News Co. (Knoxville, TN), Purchasing Division; 6016 Brookvale Lane, Suite 151, Knoxville, TN 37919; Tel: (865) 584-9765; Fax: (865)584-9400. ~left message 4-13-07

When you submit your material to these buyers, send them a complete package giving them everything they need to make a favorable decision. "The more the better," says Randy Yarbrough of Anderson News. "Include a copy of your book, your terms, a summary marketing plan, reviews, sales history and newspaper articles.

The buyer will review your material to determine if there is a market for your title. If they deem that your title might be appropriate, you will be asked to complete a vendor questionnaire. Since most books are displayed cover out, the front cover design is critical to the title's success. Airport stores rarely discount the books, so your list price is important, too. Sales are made on a returnable basis and standard wholesale terms are expected.

■■■ Strategy # 48: Selling to Supermarkets and Drug Stores[18]

There are tens of thousands of supermarkets and drug stores of all sizes around the country. Many of these sell books, booklets and videos. Some of the larger supermarket chain stores—such as Kroger—actually have a

---

18. John Styron and Randy Yarbrough of Anderson News contributed to this section.

bookstore, rather than a book section. The means of marketing to these two segments is similar, so they will be discussed together.

In the past, most of the sales through these outlets were mass-market paperbacks, but today's super stores carry a wide variety of books, cards and magazines. That is why the middlemen distributing to this market usually stock the shelves with both books and magazines.

"This is one area in which fiction outsells nonfiction," says John Styron of Anderson News, a sister company to Anderson Merchandisers and one of the wholesalers reaching this niche. Other titles that sell well are those by local and regional authors and those about local and regional topics. There is less opportunity for hardcover titles in supermarkets particularly.

Randy Yarbrough believes that sales to this segment "are very likely" for independent publishers. "We sell their titles all the time," he notes. Steve Linville of The News Group holds an opposing view, saying, "There is not a lot of shelf space dedicated to the category." He continues with, "It can be frustrating for a small publisher to break into the market, given the returns, discounts and dating required."

Steve recounts the tale of one author who showed many retailers his book and asked how many they might purchase. Their responses added up to over thirty-thousand copies, so that is how many he printed. Unfortunately, when it came time to actually place the orders the numbers were significantly lower.

Randy and Steve agree that "supermarkets discount the list price up to 25 per cent, so your pricing must allow for that to occur profitably." The list price on books sold in drugstores should be $15.95 or lower, with a price below $10.00 the norm in supermarkets. However, the price could go up to $20.00 or more for a hardcover book sold in a supermarket. They also concur "that cookbooks, travel books and regional titles do well in supermarkets, but health-related topics move better in drugstores, particularly in the form of booklets." Steve adds, "Children's titles also seem to do well in supermarkets. Fiction remains the mainstay in these outlets."

Authors may conduct booksignings at supermarkets and drugstores in which their books are being sold. "One of our authors recently sold five-hundred copies of her book during a recent booksigning at a Ralph's Supermarket in California," says Mr. Yarbrough. Steve Linville cautions, "Cross-merchandising is not as easy as it may seem, because several different buyers may be involved."

Author and consultant Eric Gelb[19] has sold successfully to supermarkets. Eric said, "Some years back, I sold several hundred copies of

---

19. Reach Eric at *ericgelb@aol.com*.

my book, the *Personal Budget Planner* to a nearby supermarket chain. The company managed the bookracks in the supermarket. The sale was final and the exposure was valuable. Several months ago, our local Mail Boxes, Etc., store took copies of our *Mastering Communication through Technology* on consignment. While small, this effort was profitable, and the store marketed no other books at that time. Once, we located a consumer buying service that purchased a quantity of our personal finance books to give away as a new member bonus."

The competition in this segment is stiff, due to the limited shelfspace granted to books. The hot button for these stores is "profit per square foot." If you can demonstrate that your promotional activities will help bring in new customers, you will get their attention. You may submit your book and marketing package directly to the major supermarket chains, but they normally direct you to their wholesalers. Three major supermarket chains are:

Kroger Co. 1014 Vine Street, Cincinnati, OH 45202-1100; (513) 762-4000; *www.Kroger.com, customers@kroger.com.*

Safeway Inc., Judy Russell—Book Buyer, 5918 Stoneridge Mall Road, Pleasanton, CA 94588-3229; (925) 520-8000, (877) 723-3929; Fax: (925) 467-3321; *www.safeway.com.*

Stop and Shop Companies Inc., 1385 Hancock Street, Quincy, MA 02169-5510; Book Buyer: (617) 770-8743; *www.stopandshop.com.*

DISTRIBUTORS TO SUPERMARKETS INCLUDE:

Anderson News Co. (Knoxville, TN), 6016 Brookvale Lane, Suite 151, Knoxville, TN 37919; (865) 584-9765; Fax: (865) 584-9400. Magazines, books, videos and music to supermarkets, drugstores, airport stores and military exchanges.

Hudson News Co., 1 Meadowlands Piz. Suite 902, East Rutherford, NJ, 07073; (201) 939-5050, (800) 326-7711; Fax: (201)939-6652; Willard Goldberger—Vice President, Merchandising; *www.hudsongroupusa.com.*

The News Group West services major retail chains in the west, with a dominant share of the Washington, Oregon and Alaska markets; 3400 D Industry Drive East, Fife, WA 98424; (253) 922-8011; Fax: (253) 896-5027; *www.thenewsgroup.com.*

When you submit a title to these distributors, include a color sell sheet with all the pertinent information on your title. Include the price, author, case quantities, and a photo of any floor displays you could provide. See Appendix C for a form you might use with your submission.

It is interesting to note that these buyers do not always wait for publishers to contact them. If they, or their sales people note your title in a local news story, in *Publishers Weekly* or at a trade show, they may seek it out according to its applicability. Again, it behooves you to seek as much exposure as possible for your titles.

Strategy # 49: Selling to Libraries[20]

Marketing to libraries has changed dramatically in the past few years. The number of titles available, the move toward electronic ordering, increasing market segmentation, a more demanding base of patrons and an increasingly value-added distribution system have all created a more sophisticated book-marketing opportunity. These changes can all work in your favor with an understanding of how to work under these evolving conditions.

The number of libraries in each category (United States)[21]		
Public libraries		9,074
Academic Libraries		
Less than four year	1,438	
Four year and above	2,220	3,658
School Libraries		
Public school	76,807	
Private schools	17,054	93,861
Special Libraries		9,170
Armed Forces Libraries		1,326
Total		**117,418**

Libraries represent a target market of 117,418 locations, divided into many submarkets. In addition to the 9,074 public libraries, there are libraries in colleges as well as public and private schools. Libraries serve governmental agencies (i.e., prisons) and the armed forces personnel. And there is a category for special libraries including corporate, medical, law and religious libraries.

---

20. Martin Warzala of Baker & Taylor contributed significantly to this information on marketing to libraries.

21. Source: U.S. Department of Education, National Center for Education Statistics.

> The library is the temple of learning, and learning has liberated more
> people than all the wars in history.
> CARL ROWAN, *U.S. columnist, journalist*

MARKETING TO PUBLIC LIBRARIES

Although there are 9,074 public libraries in the U.S., these represent 16,300 book-selling opportunities including central locations and branches. That translates into an excellent opportunity for book sales since the main library may purchase copies of your book for all locations.

Public librarians have an obligation to meet the education, information, entertainment and recreational reading needs of the people who visit their institutions—their patrons. These needs can vary dramatically geographically. But in most cases, the acquisitions librarian is presented with a dual responsibility, and that is to satisfy the local needs while administering to their broader needs. He or she does this by manipulating the library's collection in two categories.

1. **A credible core collection.** A library must anticipate the information needs of its patron through its compilation of *generally* nonfiction titles. These include reference books and titles of national importance. Current events drive this assortment, as do reviews of new titles. Of course, this includes some fiction, too, but primarily that of nationally known authors.

2. **A patron-driven collection.** Typically, library purchases depend upon the nature of the community being served. Most libraries have a Selection/Collection Development Librarian who evaluates the available books with regard to local economic conditions and the needs and interests of their patrons. This might include large-print editions for the visually handicapped or Spanish translations for a nearby Hispanic population. Librarians continually seek new titles that better serve their patrons, not necessarily what is reviewed. This category has a tendency toward fiction, and local authors may have an advantage.

In many libraries, this process is conducted in two steps. Once the Collection Development Librarian has decided upon the selections, the Acquisitions Librarian actually purchases them. He or she will search for the best source and price, and negotiate contracts with suppliers. The need for multi-tasking in smaller libraries places both these functions in the hands of one person.

There are several factors common to both of these collections that will help you market to libraries more effectively and efficiently.

1. **Demonstrate the credibility of the author.** A nationally known author has a credibility factor that gives him or her an advantage in the selection process. Yet all is not lost for the less-known author. Many librarians rely on the wholesalers' sales representatives to alert them to new or particularly applicable titles. The choice of the proper wholesaler automatically gives you a "credibility stamp." In this case it would be to your advantage to sell through one of the top library-distribution firms.

   A professional presentation of your material will also enhance your credibility. A black-and-white Xerox copy will not create the desired image as quickly as a colorful package comprised of the cover of your book, a sample table of contents, and a cover letter describing your title's fit with their collection. Make it simple for them to order by providing an easy-to-use order form, perhaps even partially completed before sending it.

   Develop literature especially for libraries including a description of the author's credentials. If the author has qualifications that make him or her particularly suited to writing the book, be sure that is included.

2. **Produce a quality product.** The quality of your book may be its most important factor. If it is not properly designed and produced, it doesn't matter how well you communicate its benefits to librarians.

   A quality book has all the proper registration information, including a Library of Congress Catalog Number as well as an ISBN. A LCCN is easily obtained online, and it is free. The Cataloging In Publication (CIP) program preassigns cataloging information. Provide the CIP office with details about your book (go to *www.cip.loc.gov/cip* for more information). Make sure the information you send them is complete and accurate. If they incorrectly catalog your title, it will be misfiled in every library across the country.

   Librarians do not like fill-in-the-blank books because the first patrons to use them may fill in the blanks. They also appreciate a book with a glossary, bibliography and index. Editions with special library bindings or acid-free paper may receive high marks, too. Children's books must be especially durable to withstand the (friendly) abuse to which they are subjected.

Quality is also sought in the content of the book. A nonfiction text must be well written and accurately documented. Fiction must be written in an entertaining fashion. Historical fiction must be accurate in its detail, too. Reviews quickly point out any shortcomings in quality writing. A well-written text with content relevant to the consumer is the first step to getting a good review.

It costs a lot to build bad products.
NORMAN AUGUSTINE, *author, business executive*

---

3. **Get positive reviews.** The process of creating a collection is disposed to positive reviews in the major library review media such as *Booklist, Choice, Kirkus Reviews, Library Journal, Publishers Weekly,* and *School Library Journal* as well as in the general review media upon which librarians rely (such as the *New York Times Book Review*). For a list of niche reviewers, go to *www.bookmarketing.com/reviewers.* For a directory of book reviews on the web, go to *www.acqweb.library.vanderbilt.edu/acqweb/bookrev.html.*
4. **Promote.** Acquisition librarians must be aware of your title before they can order it. Therefore, promotion to the library market is as critical as it is to others. Author appearances drive patron interest as much as they do through retail stores. And since librarians pay particular attention to their patrons, your media performances can stimulate word-of-mouth advertising among them.

Trade shows are an excellent place to introduce your book to librarians. There are national (American Library Association), regional (New England Library Association) and local (Connecticut Library Association) shows at which you can exhibit your books. Dates for all these conventions can be found at *www.ala.org/Template.cfm?Section=Events1.* See Chapter Fourteen for more information on attending and exhibiting at trade shows.

There are cooperative mailings (packages comprised of many flyers from different publishers) that can help you reach librarians economically. Publishers Marketing Association offers co-op mailing programs to libraries. It conducts individual mailings dedicated to titles on fiction, poetry, business, children, health, travel and multicultural topics, among others. They also mail to public, academic and corporate libraries. If you are marketing through a wholesaler, be sure to include its ordering information on your literature.

PMA also has a co-op mailing program on Books for Review. This is a color catalog sent to newspaper, magazine and media book reviewers. It features the front cover of your book and ordering information. For more information on all their co-op programs, go to *www.pma-online.org/ programs.cfm.*

In all the literature that you design make it easy for the librarians to order your books. Provide them with information that demonstrates the benefits of your books for their patrons, as well as its price. Also, describe the durability of your books, if that is the case. Inform the librarians of the upcoming publication date and let them know if it is part of a continuing series. Typically libraries do not return books unless the books are defective or if the orders for them were processed incorrectly.

5. **Give librarians advance notice of titles.** The composition of each library's collected works changes over time, and librarians are aware of the number of collection turns that occur, just as a retailer watches its inventory turns. They must have a sufficient number of desired books on hand as their patrons' needs transform. Librarians need information as efficiently as possible and rely on advance notice or automatic ordering processes.

You may be thinking that this capability is the province of large publishers, but that is not necessarily the case. Independent publishers can use their distribution partners as a surrogate for credibility and communications. For example, Baker & Taylor has a specialized collection program called *Automatically Yours™* that automatically delivers to a library the latest books by the top authors as soon as they are released.

Baker & Taylor also provides librarians with *B&T Express Wired*, a source for prepublication book information. As available, this service lists the title, author, ISBN, publisher, publication date, list price, binding, book type (fiction or nonfiction), print run and ad budget.

6. **Sell to niches within niches.** Individual libraries may have diversity within their individual collections. For example, there could be a different person responsible for purchasing children's titles than reference books. Find out who the decision maker is for your subject matter and reach that person with the reasons why your title meets his or her needs better than competitive titles.

As an example of subniche marketing within libraries, Baker & Taylor has a program called *CATS* (Children's and Teen Services). Here, B&T provides libraries with a free, monthly, comprehensive guide to juvenile selections featuring titles appropriate for all interest levels from toddlers through young adult.

7. **Use timing to your advantage.** Librarians want to appear up to date to their patrons, so they quickly seek titles related to current events. In fact, there are situations where timing may be the over-riding selection criterion. For example, if, in mid-2003, you had a title on communicable diseases, and you could relate it to SARS or Monkey Pox, you might have sold a large quantity of books since people swiftly sought information on these conditions.

Be a little careful about your library. Do you foresee what you will do with it? Very little to be sure. But the real question is, What it will do with you? RALPH WALDO EMERSON, *philosopher, poet, essayist*

---

8. **Recognize your competition.** In 2002 there were 150,000 titles published in the United States. You are competing with many of them for limited space on the libraries' shelves just as you are in bookstores. Your title has to have a "knock-off" factor to replace an existing title in a library's collection.

However, the competition for shelf space in libraries may actually be more severe than it is in bookstores. In libraries, you are competing with other sources of information or entertainment. Reference material is increasingly available in electronic form, making it easier to retrieve. And libraries supply their collections in many formats, including e-books, spoken-word books, audiocassettes, DVDs and video programs. The needs of the local patrons dictate the form in which the information will be provided.

These circumstances can work in your favor. The library marketplace is changing with the needs of its patrons, and new-product opportunities abound for the creative publisher. You can level the playing field when competing with large publishers by offering packages with combined media. For instance, you could provide a DVD with text, sound and full-motion video. Expand your thinking and you may broaden your sales opportunities at the same time. Revisit the creative techniques described in Chapter Two and investigate new ways in which you can provide the information in your titles and improve your competitive position.

9. **Work with a wholesaler.** Even though it is possible to sell directly to libraries, it is generally not a good idea. Your distribution partner can help you in many ways, in addition to those described above. They have sales people who know the library market, what the librarians are looking for and when they want it. You can take ad-

vantage of these relationships, and at the same time create instant national coverage for your titles.

Your distribution partner can help you more if you communicate with it regularly. Let your account person know about upcoming titles, changes to old titles (pricing, binding) and details about your promotional plans. Look into advertising in their magazines or newsletters, if they offer such an opportunity.

These middlemen also offer the libraries value-added services such as cataloging and processing. For instance, Baker & Taylor makes the purchasing process more efficient for the library by sending their orders already processed, cataloged and ready for shelving and circulation.

Furthermore, wholesalers give you a third-party credibility factor that is important to librarians. You can reach them directly, or through one of the wholesalers listed below. However, it is preferred that you have a wholesaler, even if you contact the librarians directly. This will help streamline their ordering and payment procedures.

Ambassador Book Service, 42 Chasner Street, Hempstead, NY 11550, (516) 489-4011; Fax: (516) 489-5661; *www.absbook.com, ambas sador@absbooks.com.*

Baker & Taylor is a leading full-line distributor of books, videos and music products to libraries and retailers. It maintains one of the largest combined in-stock book, video and music inventories in the United States. Baker & Taylor provides its customers with value-added services, proprietary data products, customized management and outsourcing. Contact Sally Neher; Director, Publisher Relations; nehers@btol.com, P.O. Box 6885; Bridgewater, NJ 08807-0885; (908) 541-7460; *www.btol.com.*

Book Wholesalers, Inc. is a full-service children's and young adult book vendor servicing public libraries. They are located at 1847 Mercer Road, Lexington, KY 40511; (800) 888-4478, (859) 231-9789; Fax: (800) 888-6319, (859) 225-6700, *www.bwibooks.com/ index.php.*

Emery-Pratt Company Book Distributors are book distributors to academic, public and hospital libraries; 1966 West Main Street, Owosso, MI 48867-1372; (517) 723-5291, 1-800-248-3887: 517-723-4677, 1-800-563-6379; *custserv@emery-pratt.com, www.emery-pratt.com.*

JAMCO Distribution Company distributes to public, private, corporate, school and medical libraries. They also cover shipments to gift stores, and businesses. Contact Al McClendon, 1401 Lakeway Drive,

Lewisville, TX 75057; (972) 353-1287, (800) 538-1287; Fax: (972) 353-1303; www.jamcodist.com, jamco@majors.com.

Matthews Medical Book Company, 11559 Rock Island Court, Maryland Heights, MO 63043; (314) 432-1400, 1-800-633-2665; Fax: (314) 432-7044, 1-800-421-8816; *www.mattmccoy.com.*

Quality Books Inc. is a distributor of small press books, special-interest videos, audiotapes, CDs, CD-ROMs and DVDs on subject matters ranging from ethnic and environmental issues to health, fitness and business. Contact Carolyn Olson, Manager, Publisher Relations Department; 1003 West Pines Road, Oregon, IL 61061-9680; (800) 323-4241; Fax: (815) 732-4499; *www.qualitybooks.com.*

Rittenhouse Book Distributors - Health Science Book Professionals, 511 Feheley Drive, King of Prussia, PA 19406; (800) 345-6425; Fax: (800) 223-7488, 610-277-0390 Email: *www.rittenhouse.com, customer.service@rittenhouse.com.*

Unique Books a library distributor of book, videos and audios published by small and independent presses. It carries more than 12,000 titles from over 1,600 publishers and specializes in popular reading adult and juvenile nonfiction. Titles are chosen for the timeliness of their content, as well as their accessibility. Only about one out of every five titles that publishers submit to Unique Books is chosen to offer to libraries. Unique Books offers a full range of processing and cataloging for the outsourcing library. 5010 Kemper Avenue, St. Louis, MO 63139; (314) 776-6695 (800) 533-5446; *www.uniquebooks.com.*

University Park Media is a full-service library book vendor that specializes in high-interest, difficult-to-acquire reference materials. It offers "superior discounts and unparalleled commitment to customer service." PO Box 177, State College, PA 16804; (800) 752-8498; Fax: (814) 364-2902; *www.uparkmedia.com.*

Opportunity: Libraries are in desperate need of credible, high-quality non-English and bilingual titles in most genres.

SCHOOL LIBRARIES

The general category of school libraries includes those in kindergarten through twelfth grade. The critical factor determining the selection of a title for a school library is the credibility of the title in relation to the school's curriculum. And just as the composition of patrons varies from public library to public library, the curriculum varies dramatically from state to state.

Titles that work for the public libraries may not work for school libraries, so the process of marketing to them is different. Schools may purchase independently or their school system may have a centralized purchasing system. You have to find out the proper procedures for each school system making it even more beneficial to market through distribution partners to school libraries.

There are independent sales representatives for the school-library market. However, these may not be as effective as marketing through a wholesaler because buyers do not have time to meet too many people. Baker & Taylor is one of the wholesalers with which you could work, or you might choose one of these:

Follett Library Resources is a leading supplier of books to K-12 schools. It is located at 1340 Ridgeview Drive, McHenry, IL 60050; (888) 511-5114, (815) 759-1700; Fax: (800) 852-5458, (815) 759-9831; *www.flr.follett.com/ customerservice@flr.follett.com* or (800)-435-6170

Brodart Books is a full-service library supply company selling everything from furniture to electronic ordering systems. 500 Arch Street, Williamsport, PA 17705; (800) 233-8467, (international) (570) 326-2461; Fax: (570) 326-1479; *www.brodart.com. bookinfo@brodart.com.*

For an exhaustive list of library vendors, go to *www.acqweb.library. vanderbuilt.edu/acqweb/pubr/vendor.html.*

ACADEMIC LIBRARIES

Libraries servicing colleges and universities fall into the category of academic libraries. While curriculum is a major consideration here, entertainment and research are also criteria. Titles must be current and related to the students' needs. But titles pertaining to research may be applicable to the teachers who may need the data for their publishing requirements.

An added dimension is the field of distance education. These students may also purchase text and titles related to the courses offered. In general, the same wholesalers servicing the public and schools libraries also supply academic libraries. Distributors to the academic market include:

YBP Library Services (a Baker & Taylor Company) provides books and supporting collection management and technical services to academic, research and special libraries around the world. They are located at 999 Maple Street, Contcoocook, NH 03229; (603) 746-3102, (800) 258-3774; Fax: (603) 746-5628; *www.ybp.com.*

Blackwell North America Inc., 6024 SW Jean Road, Building G, Lake Oswego, OR 97035; (503) 684-1140, (800) 547-6426; Fax: (503) 639-2481; *www.blackwell.com, custserv@blackwell.com.*

J.A. Majors Company, 4004 Tradeport Boulevard, Atlanta, GA 30354; (404) 608-2660, (800) 241-6551; Fax: (404) 608-2656; www.majors.com. They also publish "A Major Report" newsletter to medical librarians.

MARKETING SERVICES PERFORMED BY WHOLESALERS

Library wholesalers offer many services to public and school libraries, such as those described below. If you decide to market directly to libraries, they might expect the same capabilities from you. In most cases, an individual publisher will not be able to provide them, so it again behooves you to market through a wholesaler.

1. **Opening-Day Collection Service.** Many wholesalers will recommend an opening-day collection list for elementary, middle, and high schools based on discussions with library media specialists and national review sources.

2. **Automated Cataloging and Processing.** Your wholesaler should complete the details of cataloging and processing. A range of processing options provides shelf-ready books or loose components for new material processing at the library.

3. **Machine-Readable Cataloging.** Some wholesalers provide MARC records for books shipped in a variety of formats compatible with the library's management software. MARC is the acronym for Machine-Readable Cataloging. It provides the mechanism by which computers exchange, use and interpret bibliographic information and its data elements make up the foundation of most library catalogs used today. MARC became USMARC in the 1980s and MARC 21 in the late 1990s. (CAN/MARC is the Canadian MARC.)

4. **On-line services.** On-line ordering is fairly common, and the system should allow librarians to search for title information and check status and availability.

5. **Electronic Data Services.** An order could be entered with as little

as an ISBN and the quantity. The wholesaler's title database should normally be updated to reflect the most recent changes in title status and availability.

6. **Collection Development.** Wholesalers can assist schools with core-collection development and curriculum support since they have greater access to award and best-books lists and review sources. Once the library provides the selection criteria, the wholesaler can provide a customized selection list based on their requirements.

7. **Title Suggestions for New Schools.** Opening a new school library is a time-consuming process that involves a number of complex tasks. Wholesalers can help a librarian get through every step of the process by suggesting a complete selection of titles.

INTERNET ASSISTANCE FOR SELLING TO LIBRARIES

For information on finding local libraries in the United States, including the address, phone, operating expenditures, go to: *www.nces.ed.gov/surveys/libraries/liblocator/library.asp* and follow the instructions. This site will tell you the size of the library's collection, services offered and other facts. For similar data on libraries in Europe, go to *www.portico.bl.uk/gabriel/index.html*, or for libraries in other parts of the world go to *www.ifla.org/II/natlibs.htm*.

There is a downloadable report (pdf format) that provides a statistical profile of state library agencies in the fifty states and the District of Columbia. It includes information on staff, income, expenditures, services to libraries and systems, public service hours, service outlets, service and development transactions, collections, allied operations, and electronic services. The data was collected through the State Library Agencies Survey conducted by the National Center for Education Statistics (NCES). Download this document at *www.nces.ed.gov/pubsearch/pubsinfo.asp?pubid=2002302*.

There are many journals and newsletters of interest to acquisitions and collection development librarians. If you want to learn more about them go to *www.acqweb.library.vanderbuilt.edu/acqweb/journals.html*. This site lists those that have free Web access to either their full contents, partial contents or a complete table of contents. It also links to the archives of appropriate e-mail discussion groups (such as listserves) and usenet newsgroups.

You may find it helpful to learn more about associations and organizations of interest to collection development and acquisitions librarians. For a comprehensive list of local, state, national and international associations related to library services, go to *www.acqweb.library.vanderbilt.edu/acqweb/assn.html*.

If you have a garden and a library, you have everything you need.
MARCUS TULLIUS CICERO, *Roman statesman, scholar, orator*

CONDUCT A PROFITABLE LIBRARY BOOK TOUR
by Jerry Labriola

One of the least appreciated ways to sell books and gain crucial exposure at the same time is to conduct a regional library tour. This might include most libraries in your state if it's small. If too large for that, confine your visits to a manageable geographical area. The idea is to arrive at the library, make your presentation, have the book signing and be back home within two or three hours.

Among the benefits of such visits is the possibility of receiving requests for further speaking engagements. It isn't unusual, for example, for program directors of service clubs (e.g., Rotary, Lions) to be in the audience. Libraries tend to promote such events heavily, so even if the number of attendees is low, your name and the title of your book may be published in local newspapers or mentioned on radio. Multiply this by the number of visits you plan on making, and you will have a sense of your potential media coverage.

Some individuals may attend the program with your book already in hand. This is still favorable for you because they may have made the purchase in anticipation of your appearance and are there primarily to hear what you have to say and obtain your signature.

Tour Characteristics

My tour took me to 120 libraries throughout Connecticut. Each program lasted about an hour. I spoke for fifteen minutes, took questions (most dealt with details of criminal cases) and concluded with the signing session. My book, *Famous Crimes Revisited* (Strong Books), which I co-authored with Dr. Henry Lee, lent itself to such a format, but tailor your program to the book's subject matter. For example, in initial remarks, you might incorporate a reading from your novel or collection of poems, or in the case of nonfiction, take questions about the book's information or the advice you've advanced.

The number of attendees ranged from a handful to several hundred with an average of fifty to sixty. About one-third purchased books, but the number often represented two-thirds of the audience because spouses would attend and the couple would buy a single copy. Sometimes a person would buy several books to give as gifts.

Steps to Schedule a Tour

Obtain a list of all the libraries in your state or region. Make sure it contains vital information about each library such as address, phone number, names of staff and its operating budget if available. Also find out if it has meeting rooms and, most importantly, a *Friends of the Library* organization or its equivalent. *The Friends* are proud of their work and will usually put more time into rounding up attendees than will the library staff, which has other responsibilities. All of this should be taken into consideration when choosing which ones to contact. Be selective.

Make your own phone calls. Ask for the program director or reference librarian. Indicate what you have to offer and that you charge no fee as long as you may bring books along for signing and purchase. Some provide an honorarium; either accept it or offer to donate it back. Others might indicate they do not allow the transfer of money in the library, but that you're welcome to put on your program. Do honor the invitation and do show up. Stress that you'll bring your own supply of books.

Send promotional materials. Mention you'll arrange for a media kit to be mailed to them along with a complimentary copy of the book. My kit contains a news release, bio, photo, and several reviews and newspaper articles.

Pick the right time. I've found the ideal time for the program is weeknights or, occasionally, Sundays, but you also have to be guided by the preferences of the library. For confirmation, call the library a few days before your scheduled appearance. Ask for a podium if you need one. Inquire about any interest in the program to date so you have an idea of the attendance. Some have sign-up sheets, others do not.

Procedure for the Big Day

Arrive about a half hour early to set up. My only props are an aluminum collapsible easel and a poster blow-up of the book cover. I also bring bottled water, an extra pen for purchasers and business cards, which I spread on a table. These help obtain other talk invitations and media interviews.

Arrange for a proper introduction. Be sure the introducer will not wing it; he or she should read from the bio you previously sent or from one in your book. Leave the room and return just before start time and sit unobtrusively in the back of the room. After the introduction is made, walk to the front from that location (a bit theatrical!).

If it's convenient for you, stand, do not sit, during your talk. I always request a podium even though I never speak from notes. It provides something to drape my arm over from time to time. If the library anticipates a large turnout or the room is large, a microphone will usually be available.

Even if the room is small, stand—unless the turnout is also small (like four or five people). In that case, do not run home. Often, they're more embarrassed than you are, so you must put them at ease. Here's how to handle it: Pull up a chair and say something like, "Last week, I was in Hartford and two hundred people showed up. The next night, Stratford, and there was only a handful. Last night, New Haven and eighty or ninety came. Tonight? A handful. One can never tell. But it makes no difference. Let's start; maybe others will join us."

Book Signing Recommendations

Write a brief inscription over your signature. Keep all receipts unless an agreement has been made to donate a portion to the library (in my case, 20 per cent). Take only cash or check. Collect it yourself and allow the money to lie on the table, off to the side. Bring small bills to make change and make the transaction from the table, not from your purse or wallet. Round off to the nearest dollar amount. And, to repeat, if a person arrives with your book in hand, that's OK. Sign it with a smile. It still represents a sale.

Follow Up

Send the library a thank-you note the following week. State that you look forward to a similar presentation with another book in the future. This helps establish a network you can count on.

Finally, keep brief notes. I have a card for each library with a notation like 80/24. That means eighty people showed up and twenty-four books were sold. I'll contact that library again for my next book. If the notation reads 7/2, I might not.

Jerry Labriola, a physician, author and past president of the Connecticut Authors and Publishers Association. His second mystery, *Murders at Brent Institute* (Strong Books), was released in October 2002. Website: *www.jerrylabriola.com*. Jerry's latest novel, *The Maltese Murders*, will be published in 2004.

Strategy # 50: Become a Star on Home Shopping Networks

Home shopping networks reach millions of people every day with information in a wide variety of products, including books. Before you try to reach these buyers, consider your products' salability on television. Does it meet their criteria? Does it:

Demonstrate well in eight minutes of airtime? That is not a lot of time to sell your product, so it must have unique and demonstrable benefits that are easily and quickly communicated.

Solve a common problem or make life easier? This gets back to the need for which you created your product in the first place.

Appeal to a broad audience? Titles of interest to a small group of people will not make it past the first decision-making round.

Have unique features and benefits? How is your product different from and better than competition?

Relate to a topical or timely subject? If your product is associated with a current event it is more likely to be selected than one that is not.

Pitch your product from the perspective of what is important to the viewer. Exclusive product launches and unique products offered for the first time are always of interest to them. Typically, programming is thematic; part of the product selection criteria is based upon how they will fit within existing programs.

QVC's viewing audience is idiosyncratic to the topic of the show. For instance, *Make Life Easier* is for people who are "looking to save time, work and money around the house so that you can enjoy life to its fullest. It features cleaning solutions, electronics and appliances, even self-help books and health-related products. *Now You're Cooking* presents "cookware, kitchen gadgets, gourmet foods, cookbooks, small appliances and more, for everyone from the occasional cook to the gourmet chef." *For Race Fans Only®*, airing every Friday evening during race season, draws a primarily male audience. QVC continually strives to expand its appeal to an ever-broadening customer base by increasing the variety of products available to their audience of over eighty-four million homes.

To have your product evaluated for possible airing on a home shopping network you typically must submit completed Product Information Sheets with a photo or brochure of your product. Each network has its own forms, so go to each site and follow their directions.

For an example on how to submit your information to QVC, go to *www.qvcproductsearch.com*. Here you will find the QVC Product Submittal forms. Print out each completed page, attach a color photo or brochure and mail it to: QVC Studio Park, Vendor Relations, 1200 Wilson Drive, Mail Stop #128, West Chester, PA 19380-4262. From time to time, QVC goes out on the road to meet entrepreneurs from around the country and evaluate their products. This is called a Regional Product Search.

A network Product Specialist will review your submission. You will receive notification of the status of your submission within approximately three weeks of their receipt of your package.

If your product is of interest to the network, it will move to the next level of evaluation. At this stage a sample will be requested and will be evaluated against rigorous Quality Assurance requirements. If a sample has been approved, your buyer will work with you to create a sales strategy for your product, a purchase order will be written and you will ship your goods to a designated warehouse.

Minimum initial purchase orders are usually not less than $20,000 to $25,000 per individual item at its wholesale cost. QVC prefers to air products with a selling price of $15.00 or higher so you might consider bundling several titles or products to build the price of the package.

QVC does not sell products in the following categories: guns, furs, tobacco and all related products, subscriptions, 900-number phone programs, service-related products, and products with bounce backs or consumer solicitations such as sweepstakes, questionnaires, etc.

The major home shopping networks are:

Deborah Wooley, Shop at Home, 5388 Hickory Hollow Parkway, Antioch, TN 37013; Book submission forms at *www.ishopathome.com*.

Home Shopping Network, New Business Development, 1 HSN Drive, St. Petersburg, FL 33729; download book submission forms at *www.hsn.com*.

QVC, Vendor Relations, QVC Studio Park #0128, West Chester, PA 19380-4262; www.qvc.com, book submission forms are found at *www.vendor.studiopark.com*.

Shop NBC, Attn: Customer Service, 6740 Shady Oak Road, Eden Prairie, MN 55344, (800) 676-5523; *www.shopnbc.com*.

Television Shopping Network (TVSN) - Australian shopping channel, *www.itvsn.com.au*.

No one should negotiate their dreams. Dreams must be free to flee and fly high. JESSE JACKSON, *civil rights leader, minister*

▦ Strategy # 51: Selling Through Book Fairs

Books Are Fun, Ltd. (A Reader's Digest Company) is a leading display marketer of books and gifts. They offer hardcover books, gifts, and educational products at up to 80 per cent off retail prices. Their book fairs and book displays supply innovative, premium quality products to corporations, schools, hospitals and early learning centers throughout the United States and Canada.

The Books Are Fun formula is simple. They buy huge, non-returnable quantities of books and gifts directly from publishers and manufacturers, and sell those products at deep discounts directly to end users through display marketing events. They typically donate a percentage of the proceeds in books or cash to the sponsoring organization or to a designated charity.

Books Are Fun serves over sixty-thousand schools, twelve-thousand corporations, twenty-thousand early learning centers, and many hospitals, universities, government offices and nonprofit organizations in the United States and Canada through a variety of programs:

Corporate Book Fair Programs are one- to three-day events held at large corporations and hospitals once or twice a year, offering a selection of hundreds of different titles to employees.

The Business Fair Program is comprised of one- to two-day events held in medium sized office buildings, hospitals, nursing homes and churches, offering employees a wide selection of titles.

The School Program includes displays of twenty-five to thirty different titles and gifts are placed in the faculty lounges and media centers of schools every six weeks. Teachers and staff members can order the books for their own personal use and enjoyment.

In the Early Childhood Development (ECD) Program, book displays are placed in daycare centers, churches, preschools and Headstart centers. Staff and parents can evaluate and purchase the books.

In the Business Display Program book displays of ten to fourteen titles are placed in small businesses for employees to look over and order at their leisure.

The Art Fair Division holds one- to two-day events at hospitals and corporations offering gallery-quality framed art to employees and the community.

Books submitted to Books Are Fun will not be returned. For questions regarding book submissions, e-mail *baf_submissions@booksarefun.com*. Book submissions can be sent to: Books Are Fun Attn: Submissions Department, 1680 Highway 1 North, Fairfield, IA 52556.

"Book sold through Books Are Fun have to sell themselves," says Charlene Costanzo, author of *The Twelve Gifts of Birth*. Charlene should know; she sold 225,000 copies of her book through Books Are Fun display functions before selling its rights to Harper Collins. "Quality of production, cover design and interior layout are critical to the sale because there are no salespeople at the events," she adds.

Since the topic and quality of the book are so important, the path to placing books with Books Are Fun can be arduous. Charlene's journey began with the idea that book fairs could be a great place to sell her book. So, she made a cold call to a buyer who showed interest immediately. "She was not a high-level person," says Charlene, "but she was very helpful. There is no need to go right to the top. Authors need to know that. It will make it easier for them to make the first call."

Charlene sent a package via overnight mail. It included a copy of her book, a cover letter a press kit and a page detailing the sales history for *The Twelve Gifts of Birth*.

The very next day, the buyer called Charlene, interested in the book. The buyer described the process, which always begins with a limited test market. She ordered four hundred copies and told Charlene that if the test went well, they would place an order for a minimum of ten-thousand to thirty-thousand books. During one particular successful period, the supply of books sold out and the Books Are Fun representative needed more copies to sell. "It was nearby, so my husband loaded the car and delivered the books to the sales representative," Charlene said. "The sales rep was very impressed," she added with a knowing smile.

The market test exceeded all expectations and the president of Books Are Fun called Charlene personally to negotiate terms for a larger purchase. The suggested conditions were not to her liking, so she did some investigation among others who had dealt with the company and made a counteroffer. After further discussions, they agreed on a sale of "cost plus about $1.50" for a large quantity. At first it didn't seem like a lot of money for all the work Charlene had put into the effort. "But then I looked at the sale not as a discounted book, but as a great way to advertise. And they were going to pay me to do it," she exclaimed.

That is a good way to view such a sale. Her costs were covered, someone else did all the selling and Charlene made approximately $1.50 per sale. "There was no cannibalization of bookstore sales, either," said Charlene, "because sales through other outlets (distributed through Midpoint Trade Books) actually increased. Book-fair buyers liked *The Twelve Gifts of Birth* so much that they wanted more copies for gifts to other people, and they went to the bookstores and gift shops to buy them."

12

Selling to the
Commercial-Sales Segment

SOME BUSINESSES PREFER TO PURCHASE directly from the publisher and not through a middleman. These companies are included in the Commercial Sales sector. These prospects include buyers in corporations, associations, schools and government agencies related to your titles' topics.

The good news about marketing directly to those prospects is that there are few discounts (unless you choose to offer them) and returns are usually limited to damaged copies. On the other hand, you have to perform all the functions otherwise provided by the distribution companies. Without middlemen to execute certain tasks, you are now responsible to stock, sell, ship, bill and collect for your sales. Your selling and administrative costs will be higher, eating into the savings you experience by not contending with distribution discounts.

Even though selling to corporations, the armed forces, and schools have common tasks, there are certain marketing functions idiosyncratic to each segment.

Strategy # 52: Conduct Direct Distribution

Content is king in the Commercial-Sales sector. Companies and associations want to use the information in your books to help them sell more of the products or services they offer. Your content is repurposed as a premium, as a fundraiser or as another device. In the case of schools, your content could help the teachers improve the education they provide their students. Government agencies purchase books, but they also seek publishers to create and deliver content that does not exist in the form in which they currently need it. The opportunity to increase your revenue and profits is limited only by your creativity.

> Since new developments are the products of a creative mind, we must therefore stimulate and encourage that type of mind in every way possible. GEORGE WASHINGTON CARVER

The general theme throughout *Beyond the Bookstore* is that you are not selling books, but the benefits people get from them. The form of the product is of less consequence than is the content. This is particularly relevant when marketing your titles in the Commercial-Sales sector. Indeed, one of the greatest benefits of marketing to this area is that all your titles are frontlist—there is no such thing as a backlist. You only have a now-list of information that is needed presently, and a no-list of titles that are not applicable at this time.

Frank Fochetta, vice president, Director of Special Sales and Custom Publishing at Simon & Schuster, agrees. According to Mr. Fochetta, "There is only one way to increase your sales, revenue and profits in the commercial segment. That is, *sell content.*" Businesses are less concerned about the place your title holds in your frontlist or backlist. They want to know, "how can the information contained in your product line help my business more than that of some other marketing tool?"

Frank goes on to say, "the primary reason companies are interested in using a book as a marketing tool is to repurpose its content. And there are three areas in which they look for this opportunity."

1. **Value for the customer.** Books can be of value to your customers in two ways. First, the content must be important. Your customers should be able to use the information in your titles to help them improve, educate or entertain *their* customers in some way. Second, books have a high-perceived value. People generally hold books

in high esteem and are reluctant to throw them away. They keep books, giving them a long shelf life in the customers' homes and offices. Fortunately, your customers can purchase books relatively inexpensively relative to their perceived value.

2. **Repackaged content.** When selling to a business, the starting place for your negotiations is the content that you can provide. If your prospect decides that your content has value, then you settle on the form in which the content will be disseminated. This may be as a book, booklet or DVD. Even if you choose a book as the final form, it can still be customized by 1) changing its size (an abridged or miniature book packed inside a box of cereal), 2) reducing the weight of its paper to lower shipping cost, 3) creating a custom version using the client's product as the hero of the story, or 4) publishing it in softcover if it is only available case bound, or vice versa.

3. **Brand association.** A book should have the same image as the item with which it is associated. A book provided as a premium at Dollar Stores will be much different than the one offered with a $200 suede coat at Eddie Bauer.

Frank suggests that instead of categorizing your titles as frontlist or backlist, divide them into categories according to the benefits of the information they contain. Your category headings should be target groups instead of publication date.

In the example below, two titles have different meanings for various types of people. Regardless of publication date, the information in *Coping with Unemployment* is probably not salable to college students, but it could be sold to churches, career counselors or marriage counselors for an older audience. The title *Job Search 101* could be sold to colleges, but with a different sales pitch than that used to sell it to reemployment groups such as Forty Plus.

Title	College Students	Mid-Career Adults
Title 1: *Coping With Unemployment*	Not Applicable	How to deal with negative emotions while unemployed with a family, mortgage, etc.
Title 2: *Job Search 101*	Creative ways to find employment opportunities while seeking one's first job	How to become reemployed when experience and age may be a negative factor

Your title's content is important for another reason. If a brand name is mentioned in it, the owner of that brand becomes a likely prospect. The concept of *product placement* functions as much and as well in the publishing industry as it does in television shows or movies. The capabilities of print-on-demand publishing make it easier to change the name of the product, if necessary, to sell to a different buyer.

Orders for products sold in the Commercial-Sales segment can be large and are placed directly with the publisher, not with a distributor. Sales are generally made on a nonreturnable basis, and discounting is based upon the volume sold. Payment is usually received in thirty to sixty days, and governments must actually pay you interest if they are at fault for delaying payment for more than thirty days for an uncontested invoice. These points make the Commercial Sales segment an attractive market.

You know your product better than anyone else, so it is up to you to make the sale. Make appointments with, and call upon buyers in government agencies, at corporations and at associations. This requires a lot of telephone work, networking at trade shows and association meetings, and personal visits wherever possible. The pricing is negotiated, so you must have an accurate knowledge of all your costs.

If you do not like (or do not feel you are skilled at) the selling process, all is not lost. There are premium and incentive agencies, telemarketing firms, fundraising companies and book-marketing consultants[22] that will represent your titles to businesses. Their fees reduce your profits, but if you view their sales as incremental revenue you are still better of with them than without.

Strategy # 53: Sell to Businesses[23]

Businesses comprise a unique position in the Commercial Sales arena. They can purchase products, or re-purpose content, to use as sales promotional tools with customers and prospects, offer as motivational or educational devices to employees or to resell in company stores.

Buyers in this market may need to be educated about the value of books to their business. Those who have used premiums and incentives in the past probably used lower-priced items (key chains, pencils) as giveaways. They must be informed on how books can play in increasing their sales.

---

22. One such company is Book Marketing Works, LLC at (800) 562-4357, *www.bookmarketingworks.com.*

23. Mark Resnick, partner in FRW Company, a premium agency, was particularly helpful in contributing information used in this section; *markresnick@earthlink.net.*

For instance, while hotels provide free pens and pads in each room (with the hotel name on each item), they may not think about purchasing your books as gifts for frequent guests or as items to sell in the hotels' gift shops—that is, until you tell them. Your creativity will be a valuable asset here as you suggest ways in which your books can help your prospects meet their goals.

Art is making something out of nothing and selling it.
FRANK ZAPPA, *singer, guitarist, philosopher, actor*

Why a Company Might Use a Book As a Marketing Tool

- Books do not have the liability that some products carry. Some toys and products oriented to children may come apart or be swallowed, leading to negative publicity and legal problems.
- Books are tasteful. "Their high-perceived value does not demean the sender or recipient. In a way, a book defines the taste of the giver," says Mark Resnick, partner in FRW Company. "People like a premium that flatters their intelligence, and books do that."
- A title may be coordinated with a season or holiday. For example, Nestle's, Betty Crocker or Pillsbury might seek a book as a premium offering recipes for Christmas cookies. Independent publishers may have an edge over larger publishers in the sense that a company may not want a bestseller as a premium. If *everybody* already has it, it would be less desirable as a sales promotional tool. A less known, but equally applicable title, may be preferred. For similar reasons, your prospect may want an exclusive on your title. It will not want to waste its promotion dollars if someone else is offering the same title in a promotion.
- A book can be personalized to the recipient. You might place the company's name on the cover of the book, or replace the cover with one of leather.
  "Most companies won't advance the money to pay for the production of a customized book. Be prepared to front the money yourself," Mr. Resnick notes. Then he adds, "Small publishers may be required to put some money in escrow to guarantee that they will fulfill the contract for the books as agreed."
- Additional books can be supplied quickly.
- CD/DVDs do not have the "feel" of a book; they do not elicit the same emotions a book does.

IT EVEN WORKS WITH
PRINT-ON-DEMAND (POD) TITLES

According to John Harnish[24], "arrangements are well under way for major drug companies to make monthly volume purchases of Jane M. Martin's book[25] and then distribute them through their many contacts in the health care community. Because this is a POD title, corporate sponsors have the option of inserting a page with their own message. The sponsorship page can be changed quickly and easily tailored to the various groups receiving these books. As few as one hundred books can be personalized with a unique sponsorship page, and since books are produced on demand, they can be printed and shipped to the site of a conference in a matter of days.

"This new POD approach to special sales is cost-effective and budget-friendly to sponsors, and books are always current with the most recent updated material. With POD books, sponsors are assured of always getting the most up-to-date book in the exact quantity desired, and delivered when and where the books are needed."

FICTION AS A PREMIUM?

Fiction is more difficult to sell as a sales promotional tool because it is a more elusive commodity. Its success as a premium depends on the taste of the recipient. When selling such books as a premium, drive home the fact that fiction is almost timeless—not like many nonfiction titles written about current trends.

> A classic is a book that has never finished saying what it has to say.
> ITALO CALVINO, *Italian journalist, short-story writer, novelist*

HOW COMPANIES USE BOOKS

Sales to corporations can be large in terms of unit sales and revenue. The buyers with whom you will be negotiating are skilled professionals, used to dealing with knowledgeable, competent sales people. You cannot simply wander into a buyer's office and ask them how they use books as premiums. Most probably has never done so. But if you have conducted research and can provide them with some examples, you can

---

[24] John is the Special Projects Director, Infinity Publishing. *john@infinitypublishing.com*

[25] *Breathe Better, Live in Wellness: Winning Your Battle Over Shortness of Breath*, (Infinity Publishing, 2003).

collaboratively plan innovative ways to use your content to help your prospect sell more of their products or services.

Below are suggestions to fuel your discussion. Do not assume this list is all-inclusive. Use it as a conversation starter to get the prospect talking about how he or she might use your titles.

1. **Human Resource Planning.** If you have a concept that would help employees plan for their retirement, ask people in the Human Resources department if they could use your titles in their retirement planning programs. They might also consider titles that would help them implement other parts of their benefit programs. Demonstrate that your content could help them save money on insurance premiums by showing employees how to improve their health and you may make a profitable sale.

   Do not try to sell the entire package at one time. Proceed step by step. Once you agree that your concept could be beneficial, then continue asking questions that get your prospects to 1) sell themselves on the original idea and 2) come up with new ways in which your content could help.

Those convinced against their will are of the same opinion still.
BRIAN TRACY

But those convinced by what they say will sell themselves and stay that way. BRIAN JUD

   A title on finding a job could be a hit with HR people, too. Show them how they can use your titles to ease their released employees' transition into the job market. The company could save money by using your titles as an alternative to providing outplacement services. Once you have set this hook, talk about the form the product might take. It could be a book, or perhaps it could be a series of booklets.

   Remember that companies look not at the price of your book, but what the item will cost them. If you can prove to your customer that it will *save them* more than your product costs, or help them *make* more than it costs, you are likely to make a sale.

2. **Training and Motivation.** According to Frank Fochetta, "Companies such as Herbal Life and Amway buy motivational and business books to resell to their distributors." In many other businesses, managers regularly seek new ways to train and motivate their

employees, too. Content on leadership, motivation, self-help, selling techniques or new business topics could be useful to these executives. Salespeople and other employees need to be informed or motivated periodically. If your title suits this need, it may be invaluable to the company as a training tool for the people who work there.

3. **Sell Through Their Stores.** If companies have stores for employees, either on the premises or online, they may purchase your books for resale. Majors Internet Company provides a service called *The Company Bookstore*. This is a business-to-business solution for selling books to employees of corporations. In effect, Majors puts a bookstore inside the corporation. Purchasing managers, Corporate Library Professionals, and Information Service Managers can link to a customized version of the company bookstore to offer employees access to a comprehensive database of titles.

    Majors customizes *The Company Bookstore* for the corporate intranet, processes credit card transactions, picks, packs and ships, and provides management reports. Majors is a vendor for the corporate employee as well as for information centers, training and development, and research departments. J.A. Majors Company, 4004 Tradeport Boulevard, Atlanta, GA 30354; (404) 608-2660, (800) 241-6551; Fax: (404) 608-2656, *www.majors.com/corporations/corporations.htm.*

4. **Gift to Customers.** Fiction and nonfiction titles may be the perfect gift during the holiday season, for unusual events or for special marketing periods. Mark Resnick tells us, "Some cruise ship lines, among other companies in the hospitality industry, give passengers a *thank-you* gift upon departing the ship. Sometimes they use a book about one of the destination ports as the souvenir. People are taken aback when others, particularly businesses, say *thank you*, and they will tell others about it." This creates positive word-of-mouth advertising and goodwill for your title.

    People may be willing to pay postage for a large, high-valued book—such as a coffee table book—but in most cases the company sending books pays the postage. Therefore shipping charges become a consideration when negotiating the price. Keep this in mind when you are producing your product (a CD is lighter than a book) and calculating your proposal.

5. **Public Relations.** Companies may use books to establish, repair or improve their reputations. This may be accomplished by providing books to volunteer groups or by donating them to a worthy cause.

Companies celebrating an anniversary may also use related books to help promote and celebrate the event.

Charlene Costanzo sold her title, *The Twelve Gifts of Birth*, to children's shelters to use as a fundraiser. But the image it created in the public's mind was upbeat, creating positive word-of-mouth advertising for the shelters.

Companies may use books to maintain or create an image, too. Many hospitals do this when they give a package of products to the parents of babies delivered there. If your title has information that is important to the first years of a baby's life, it might be included in this package.

6. **An Addition to the Corporate Library.** If the company has (or is interested in starting) an internal library, show them how your title could be appropriate. If it is on an applicable topic—such as selling, industry information, motivation, or marketing—you might convince the company librarians to add your title to their collections.

7. **Enhance Other Marketing Campaigns.** Laws and do-not-call lists limiting the activities of telemarketers will increase the use of direct mail to accomplish the same result. Businesses conducting direct-mail campaigns want recipients to open their envelopes, and one way to do this is to offer a "free gift inside," or an "offer for a free gift." Statistics have proven this to be an excellent way to increase response rates, and your booklet may help the rate of replies go up even more.

8. **Sales Promotional Tools.** Product managers have bottom-line responsibility for their product line and are interested in increasing their sales. Show them how they could use your titles to make this happen and you will find a willing audience. See the information later in this strategy for more tips on how to contact product managers.

According to the Advertising Specialty Institute (ASI) of Trevose, PA, North American sales of advertising specialties and promotional products were $15.6 billion in 2002. Here are ways in which companies used these promotional devices to reach their objectives:

Coupon. Manufacturers may offer a dollars-off, in-pack, on-pack or near-pack coupon entitling the bearer to a discount on your product. For example, a pet food company might include a coupon in a bag of dog food (in-pack) for a discount on your video about dog care. A coupon or product offered in-pack might be governed by strict regulations. Anything that comes in contact with food must be "food friendly," meaning that it will have to be printed with special ink. In addition, it must be odor free so it does not effect the smell or taste of the product.

Or, the manufacturer may offer the same coupon on-pack, printed on the exterior of the package and visible to the consumer. Near-pack coupons are provided at the point of sale (perhaps as a peel-off coupon or in a "take-one" container) in close proximity to where the item is being sold. For example, a coupon for a book containing holiday recipes could be placed near a display of Pfaltzgraff plates with Christmas décor.

Another benefit from coupons and rebates occurs whenever the customer is required to send any information to the manufacturer. The publisher garners information to build its database, which can offset costs of the free items.

Premium. When used as a premium (an item given away to attract, retain or reward customers or to motivate employees), a product may be offered at a relatively low cost (or free) as an incentive to purchase another product. If the dog-food manufacturer mentioned above included your dog-care video inside the package—instead of a coupon for it—your product would be considered a premium.

Companies are looking for items that would make good premiums. But they may be unaware of the high-perceived value (and lasting value) that makes books work as an excellent premium. Therefore, when you first contact a product manager about using your book as a premium, an early question should be to ask what the buyer's experience has been using books as premiums. Then you will know if you must sell the generic concept or simply the benefits of using your title as a premium.

Attend or exhibit at appropriate trade shows. The Incentive Show (held in New York annually, *www.piexpo.com* is an excellent place to display your products for use as premiums. There you can also find rep groups that may be willing to carry your line of titles. These people already have the relationships with corporate buyers and may be worth their commissions.

Prize. A high-price or high-value book might be offered as a prize in a contest or sweepstakes.

Patronage Award. Low-price items (such as booklets) might be given way with each purchase of a minimum quantity of some product, or as a reward for visiting their website.

Samples. Businesses may use your items to give to their customers or to the general public at no charge in order to build goodwill, or store traffic. They might place a sample chapter of your book on their website, offering the complete version as a self-liquidator.

Hammermill Paper Company purchased over five thousand copies of Paulette Ensign's booklet *110 Ideas for Organizing Your Business Life* as a premium for their sales representatives to leave behind with prospects after a sales call. The only change to which Paulette had to accede was to allow Hammermill to print the booklets on their paper to serve as a sample.

Self-liquidator. When a book is sold at a price low enough to entice buyers, but high enough to cover its cost, it is being used as a self-liquidator. Many supermarkets use this tactic to entice shoppers to spend more at their stores. Here, buyers may purchase a book at a discounted price with a minimum purchase. Or shoppers may be offered a continuity series at a reduced price. Other industries may find this a valid promotional tool, too.

THE SELLING PROCESS

Person-to-person salesmanship is an intuitive art, but the process of selling is somewhat more scientific. There are three steps to take that, if performed sequentially, should lead you to a successful conclusion.

The first step is to identify the industries and businesses that are likely suspects. Next, learn more about the individuals who will make or influence the decisions. As you go through this process, you will find thousands of *suspects*, which at this time are just names. So, the third step is to qualify your list, to eliminate those suspects who have no need for your content. Then prioritize those remaining, using the system described in Strategy # 29.

Idea Generator

Here are some ideas to start your innovative juices flowing. Use the creative techniques described in Chapter Two to stimulate new ways to use your product as a sales-promotional tool.

Topic	Ideas for Promotional Tool	Examples of Prospective Buyers
Pet care	In-pack or on-pack coupons for pet food containers	Pet Industry Distributors Association, IAMS; Purina
Picture book on home decorating	Self-liquidator for furniture retailers	Furniture, paint or hardware stores; Lowes or Home Depot
Barbeque cookbook	Premium for outdoor grill manufacturers	Manufacturers of outdoor grills; supermarkets; Lowes or Home Depot
Health & Fitness	Companies buy it to give to employees	Insurance companies; large businesses
	Health clubs use it as a premium for renewing membership	Gold's Gyms; Curves for Women
Motivation/Inspiration	An incentive for sales people	Sales trainers; sales coaches; companies with a large sales force; Multilevel marketing companies such as Amway; Successories and similar stores

Once you have developed your target list. Do not be intimidated by thinking you have to start calling on a corporate behemoth to create mega sales. In all likelihood, your sales will initially come from companies of less than one thousand employees. Unless you are trained in selling, there is no reason to go after large companies until you are ready.

The size of a company may or may not be an indicator of the size of the potential order, but generally speaking, small companies will be likely candidates for more orders of lesser quantities. That does not mean the selling process is shorter or less demanding. Nor should your pre-sale homework be less complete.

It may actually be a good strategy to start with a small prospect to test your persuasive techniques before going on to the larger opportunities. If you have an educational children's picture book, you might approach a local or regional chain of toy stores before calling on the national buyer for Toys "R" Us. In the process, you can practice asking questions to uncover need, making your presentation, negotiating and closing the sale. This process may also enable you to experience regular successes that will bolster your confidence.

Selling to large businesses can be lucrative in terms of the number of books they buy, but at the same time the sales process can be demanding and time consuming. Before you begin contacting prospects, learn about the industries into which you are selling. Then learn about your specific target company and then the individual decision makers and influencers.

How to Sell Books to Companies

Know your prospect's industry.

A creative exercise spurred by the examples above should provide you with a list of potential companies and industries. The next step is to whittle your list down to something more manageable. As you become more familiar with the industries, certain anomalies may become apparent. For instance, there is much talk about selling large quantities of books to pharmaceutical companies. However, this industry is under increased scrutiny for its promotional practices and companies are less likely to take on a promotional item now. In addition, these companies are especially liable to legal action. Data in all their publications must be infallible, with nothing frivolous. There is a high burden of proof placed upon the publisher seeking sales here.

Not that this industry is unapproachable. Mark Resnick observes that "you are better off starting out with an existing book and relying upon serendipity than you are to try to create one on spec. Most pharmaceutical companies have experts on staff to write their promotional literature."

> Be the type who makes mountains out of molehills, and then sell climbing equipment. IVERN BALL

Know your prospect's business.

Frank Fochetta feels that the path to successful selling in the Commercial-Sales segment is to "understand the business first, then provide content." You are not selling books but solving problems, so begin the sales process by asking questions to find out how you can help them in some way.

Before calling on a potential buyer, learn as much as you can about the company and make a list of the reasons why your content will benefit it. Review their website, or go to trade shows and talk with its salespeople. If your prospect is nearby, go there to get their literature and study it to discover more reasons why your book will help them become more profitable.

A good place to start is by showing your prospects how you can help them increase their sales—a problem common to most businesses. A creative tie-in between your title and their product may be the solution. A company that makes cribs may be open to using your children's bedtime story book as a premium. Or perhaps the character in your book could be licensed for use on another company's line of children's sleepwear. Your travel book might help a luggage company sell more suitcases. Also, look for tie-ins that do not seem logical at first. For instance a bank may be interested in your title on home décor to promote its home equity or home improvement loans.

Know the individual buyers.

Selling to corporations is a relationship business. Knowing the name of the person is only the start of the process. Prospective customers have to know and trust you before talking to you about their marketing strategies. They are planning two years into the future and they do not want competition learning of their plans. Begin by earning their trust, and that takes time.

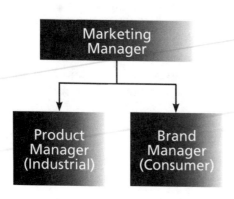

Demonstrate your trustworthiness by not being pushy. *Help them buy* the benefits of your content rather than trying to sell your books. You are also selling confidentiality, privacy. Sales in this sector take a long time to consummate because it takes an extended period to establish a degree of trust. The buyer must feel safe in talking with you, about planning marketing strategies that will be implemented two years from now.

You can build their confidence in you by knowing their industry and company background. You should also have accurate figures on the potential size of the audience for your books. Know your competition and how your title is different and better. Make suggestions on how your title may be used to stimulate their sales. Explain how they could offer a coupon, implement a continuity series, or sell it as a self-liquidator. Have an answer to the question, "Why will my customers or prospective customers be more inclined to buy my product simply because they get a free copy of your book with it?" Follow up professionally and persistently. Do what you said you would do when you said you would do it.

Learn about the person on whom you will be calling. It many cases it is a product manager (a brand manager in a consumer-products company). In either case, he or she usually has profit-and-loss responsibility for a particular line of products. Therefore, it is in his or her best interest to maximize the unit sales and profitability for their product line.

Before calling on the buyers, develop a selling strategy. Plan how you will approach, interest, persuade and close each person. If the location is nearby, visit with the prospect personally. If not, call first and arrange to send a copy of your book, cover letter, press release and fact sheet.

Get the attention of these people initially, although they may not be the ultimate decision makers. Discover the people who are decision makers and decision influencers, then convince them of your product's benefits. If the location is nearby, make an appointment to meet with the prospect personally. If not, perhaps you could arrange to meet at a trade show, or send a copy of your book, cover letter, press release, fact sheet and ideas. Then follow up with a telephone call.

Rely on others to help you. Sales' promotional agencies and premium rep groups exist to help you reach buyers who are likely to purchase your items. Many of these companies will rarely take on single-title authors/publishers, but the promotional reps might include your titles as part of their entire line. You could also hook up with other publishers with premium divisions to sell your books, publishers such as Workman, Penguin/Putnam or Simon & Schuster.

For a source of people who buy books as premiums (and for agents selling them), contact Karen Renk at the Incentive Marketing Association, *karen@incentivemarketing.org*, (630) 369-7780. The Incentive Show (*www.piexpo.com*) is another source of premium companies. Other sources of assistance include:

Corporate Events is a full service, convention and trade show management firm. They specialize in the planning and execution of conventions trades shows, special events, and incentive programs worldwide. Reach them at 7431 114th Avenue North, Suite # 102, Largo, FL 33773; (727) 548-7200; Fax: (727) 546-1956; *Corporate Events@worldnet.att.net.*

Lifestyle Vacation Incentives is the largest leisure travel agency in the country, and is one of the nation's top sales promotion and fulfillment companies specializing in consumer incentives. Reach them at 220 Congress Park Drive, Delray Beach, FL 33445; (800) 881-1900, Fax (561) 330-3369; *www.lifestylevacations.com.*

Maritz Inc. is a source of integrated performance improvement services with six operating units dedicated to improving their clients' measurable business results in critical areas, such as sales and marketing, quality, customer satisfaction and cost containment. Reach them at 1375 North Highway Drive, Fenton, MO 63099; (636) 827 4000; *www.maritz.com*. You can find vendor information at *www.maritz.com/maritz-contact-us-vendor-inquiry.asp*.

Know What You Are Selling.

It may sound odd to be reminded about knowing all aspects of *your* product line and its potential, but it is necessary. Many publishers define their product as their *books*. But your prospects are not as much interested in buying your books as they are in selling more of their products. Your book is a tool that may enable them to reach *their* goal. In the Commercial Sales sector you are less a publisher and more a consultant. As far as they are concerned, you are the expert on a particular subject of interest to the company.

During the writing phase, there are ways in which the author can demonstrate this expertise and enhance the chances of his or her books being sold. One way is to mention a brand name of a product in the text. Barbara Hemphill, in her book *Taming the Paper Tiger at Work*, mentions how a contact-management program such as ACT! can help people become more organized. This opens the doors for a potential bundling opportunity with the manufacturer. Recognize that this tactic also shuts the door to sales to competitors of brands that are mentioned.

You might actually title your book based upon a major brand. Lightbulb Press did this with their *Wall Street Journal Guide to Understanding Money and Investing* and *The Wall Street Journal Guide to Understanding Personal Finance*.

Think simples' as my old master used to say–meaning reduce the whole of its parts into the simplest terms, getting back to first principles.
Frank LLOYD WRIGHT (1869–1959) U.S. architect, writer

Know Basic Selling Techniques.

Prepare material to leave with your prospect. Prepare a one-page document listing details about your book, including publisher, title, author bio, terms, discount schedule, hard or soft cover, size, number of pages, illustrations and willingness to drop ship (See Appendix C for a template). This should be one document in a packet of material you leave with your prospect. And remember, these people meet with sales representatives from major companies and are used to seeing professional literature. Produce a multicolor catalog and put it in press-kit format that will make a favorable and lasting impression of you as a consummate professional.

Once you feel prepared, call the potential buyer and schedule a personal appointment to discuss your proposal. Most times you will be asked to leave a voice mail message, so have a twenty-second, benefit-packed message prepared, and make sure you include your telephone number and best time to call you. Once you reach the individual, begin the conversation by telling him or her that you have an idea that could make the company more profitable—or other benefit you find appropriate—and you are likely to find a willing ear.

If the company is not nearby—or if you prefer not to contact the prospective customer personally—then prepare a letter or e-mail describing your proposal. In all cases, do not assume your prospective customers realize the true value of your title. Give them ideas about how it may serve as a premium, incentive device or one of the other sales-promotional tools described above.

Communicate frequently. Build a lasting relationship with these people. Just as you do with media contacts, keep your name in front of them regularly. Meet them at trade shows, send copies of articles about your titles or their companies, and e-mail them with current news about you and the industry. Let them know that you are serious about selling books to them.

Negotiate. Begin by knowing what you want to accomplish, but be flexible deciding which path you will take to get there. Be willing to customize the cover of your book to add a notice stating, "Compliments of ABC Company." You may offer a large discount if the company participates in the cost of printing your books. Since printing costs are volume-sensitive, you might have the company pay the cost of printing their ten thousand books, but actually print twelve thousand. The incremental two thousand books that you can use for other sales will be significantly less expensive than if you printed only those two thousand.

Be patient. It takes time for these relationships to develop, perhaps six months or more. The purchasing process in large companies can be ponderous; so let the system unfold without trying to force it. And it can be frustrating when the person with whom you have been working is promoted or moved to another product line, but it may benefit you if he or she is now higher up on the decision-making ladder.

Man was born to be rich, or grow rich by use of his faculties, by the union of thought with nature. Property is an intellectual production. The game requires coolness, right reasoning, promptness, and patience in the players. RALPH WALDO EMERSON

Here are some hints to consider when talking with corporate buyers:

1. Do not sell your books, but the *benefits* your books can offer this particular buyer. Show how they will help your prospects improve their competitive position or brand profitability. Demonstrate the time period within which the buyers could experience a return on their investment.

2. The brand or product managers are usually the first level of contact. They have bottom-line authority for their brand/product line. Over the course of the negotiation process, ask what their budget is for incentives (which will help in determining your price/discount) and offer suggestions about how they can use your book to enhance their brand.

3. Another approach to the corporate market may be through Human Resources or top management. These people may use your titles as gifts to employees as a tool for motivation, education, reward or incentive.

4. Yet another entry point could be the sales manager. These people are frequently open to new ways to motivate and educate their salespeople. For instance, the manager may have a sales contest in place, the prize being a trip to the Caribbean. If your title is about the Caribbean, the manager may purchase copies of your book to give to the salespeople as a reminder of what awaits them if they reach their goals.

5. There is usually high turnover among brand/product managers. If a personnel change is made midway through the negotiation process, you may be forced to begin it all over again with the new incumbent. In any case, communicate regularly so you know if a change is about to occur. This may enable you to speak with the incoming manager and keep the momentum going.

6. Because of that turnover, premium sales can take years to close. Although the carrot of the large order may begin to lose its appeal, remain persistent and patient until you achieve the order.

7. Demonstrate to the prospective buyers that they may customize your cover, adding the company's name as the benefactor of the book.

Strategy # 54: Sell to Associations and Foundations[26]

"Sales to associations, foundations, clubs, groups and other organizations can reach 25–40 per cent of your sales," says Jan Nathan, Executive Director of the Publishers Marketing Association (PMA). "If you have the right book," she adds.

There are thousands of industry associations, charitable nonprofit associations and nonprofit trade associations around the world. Many of these use books as fundraisers, for resale and as premiums. Here are several ways in which you can work with groups to sell your books:

1. You could sell your rights to the association, which will then publish your book themselves.
2. The organization could arrange with the publisher to conduct fulfillment.
3. If the association has a bookstore on their website, it might buy directly from you to resell your titles.
4. If you are willing to donate a percentage (or fixed amount) of each sale to a charitable, nonprofit organization, you may receive high-level attention.

   Kat Shehata wrote and published the children's title, *Seabiscuit vs. War*. She augmented its distribution through IPG by contacting the National Thoroughbred Racing Association to help promote it. In exchange for advertising NTRA Charity in the back of the book, the association promoted the title in the racing community.[27]
5. You may find the association willing to copromote your book, but your title must be related to their cause for this to be most effective.

   Wiley used this approach with its title, *Bookselling for Dummies*. This was originally created to help booksellers learn more about selling books, but at the same time give them a sampling of the *Dummies* series. The initial strategy was to use it as a premium for booksellers. Wiley approached the American Booksellers Association (ABA), which "received it with open arms," says P. J. Campbell, Wiley's Director of Events. According to Dan Cullen, ABA's Director of Information, "We've sent copies to Book Sense members, and to

---

26. Special thanks to Jan Nathan, Executive Director of PMA, for information about marketing to associations included in this section.

27. *Publishers Weekly*, July 21, 2003, p. 71

ABA member stores." The ABA will also make the book a part of its initial package to all bookstores joining the association.[28]

6. Groups and associations also use books as sales promotional tools, or as rewards for joining them or renewing one's membership. Or, they might offer your books as an incentive for signing up for a conference, or purchase them to give away at a conference.

7. The primary buying criterion is price, particularly for the charitable organizations. While there is little preference for soft- over hardcover books, softcover may be preferred because if its lower price. Your book must have an ISBN and high production quality. In general, the same characteristics that would make it sell well in bookstores are essential for sales to associations.

raising item where the groups sell it to
event or project. There are fundraising
his, such as Fundraising.com, P.O. Box
388) 702-3863; *www.fundraising.com.*

ve seasonal fluctuations, but you may
fir   industry events. Find out when they
ha   ost of these have a unique theme, and
your titles may tie in with it.

According to John Kremer's *Celebrate Today* (*www.celebratetoday.com*), there are over 16,800 special days, weeks, months, anniversaries, birthdays, and other events every year providing additional marketing openings. For example, November is Child Safety and Protection Month. If your title is related to this topic, you could sell it to the International MOMS Club (*www.momsclub.org*), a nonprofit organization with 1,500 chapters and more than 75,000 members in seven countries. Likewise, July is National Corrective Posture Month. Your title on backpacking, gardening or exercise could be an excellent premium for the American Chiropractic Association (*www.amerchiro.org*) during this period.

WORKING A WEBSITE

Before contacting an association, go to its website and review it thoroughly. Become familiar with the group's mission statement and objectives, and use these in your presentation to demonstrate an understanding of their association and how your books can help them fulfill their vision.

---

28. *Publishers Weekly*, July 21, 2003, p. 75.

Associations typically have bookstores on their sites providing appropriate resource information for members. Contact the person responsible for running the store to carry your titles in it. Offer special incentives such as case discounts, autographed copies or special reports to entice them to include your titles in their store. You can do this by going to the *Publishers' Service* section and following directions. Or click on "Contact Us" which usually leads to a page listing ways to get in touch with people. Locate the person in charge of the bookstore and send an e-mail with your press release and fact sheet listing details about your book, including title, author bio, terms, discount, hard or soft cover, size, number of pages, illustrations and willingness to drop ship.

Do not go to each site with a preconceived notion that you will simply submit your title to the bookstore and then go to the next one. While this may be your only alternative at some, many websites contain an abundance of opportunities for you:

Links. Often-overlooked goldmines are the links provided on many sites to other resources or opportunities. These connections take you to related organizations and sites that offer the same chances to sell books that are described above. You can spend hours just following the links and developing the opportunities at each destination.

Networking. You will find associations' websites that list the members of its Board of Directors. Use this as a prospect list to see how you can network your way in (See Strategy #70 for more information on networking). Send each a personal e-mail describing your pleasant experience on their site and how your promotional efforts on behalf of your title will help increase traffic to their site. This traffic is likely to increase their revenue, too.

The list may also include committee chairs, one of who could be your contact for new business development (using your titles as a fundraiser) or membership (using your titles as a reward for membership renewal, or as a premium for initial registration).

There may be a committee chair for fundraising. If they have a fundraising event for which your book is particularly well suited, contact that person and offer your services to be their spokesperson. Contact him or her and volunteer to speak at their seminars and events. You can actually get paid for bringing your message to them.

Many associations provide a membership roster, making it easy to reach them individually. However, before contacting the members, ask the association for permission to do so. This will help you avoid the appearance of SPAM and to circumvent future ill will. Your e-mail to the members with the notice that the association Board approved your correspondence will enhance your image and improve your response rate.

You may also find a list of regional offices or chapters. E-mail the top person at each—particularly those nearby—and offer your services to speak at meetings or attend their events. An offer to be a last-minute substitute speaker may make you a welcome addition to their list of suppliers. Establish a good relationship with the officers of local chapters and use these to network into the national Board.

Calendar of Events. Many associations post a calendar of upcoming events on their sites with a description of the audience and exhibiting opportunities. You could exhibit at an industry trade show, speak at one of their conferences or teach a class at a seminar. You might offer to speak for free if they will allow you to sell your books (at list price) at the back of the room after your presentations. The exposure you get in their promotional literature will enhance your reputation as an industry expert, too. If you prefer not to exhibit at all the conferences, you may want to attend several to learn more about the industry and your competitors.

Awards. Some associations provide award competitions (such as PMA's Benjamin Franklin Awards). Even if you do not win the top prize, your literature can proclaim the fact that you were nominated for an award. Award competitions are particularly relevant for fiction titles, such as those bestowed by the Romance Writers (RITA Award) and Mystery Writers (Grand Master Award) Associations.

Other Resources. Periodically you will run across a site with links to other services or suppliers. Always open this to seek additional opportunities and pursue those avenues.

Newsletters. If the association has a newsletter (as most do), offer to write an article for it. As an author, you already have some credibility to be the industry specialist and an expert on the topic. They may publish your article in exchange for a mention in their newsletter or in their regular e-mail to members. If they publish reviews of appropriate titles, offer yours as a subject for a future review.

FAQs. Frequently Asked Questions tell you a lot about what interests the people in the industry. Learn what topics are important to people and address those issues in your correspondence. Let them know that you are the expert in those topics, if that is the case.

Articles. Read articles to learn what others are saying about your topic. Who else in the industry is trying to develop a theory similar to yours? How is yours different and better? If there are subjects that are not being covered with the current array of articles, offer to submit yours to be posted there. This leads to great exposure and contributes to your reputation as the industry authority.

Special reports. Many associations publish special reports and news about the industry. Read these to keep current on relevant events. This knowledge will serve you well during your media performances, too.

Message boards, chat rooms and discussion groups. Post comments to message boards and participate in discussion groups when possible. This increases your exposure and provides advertising opportunities (subtly) with people in your target market.

The PMA website serves as a good example of how one site can yield many additional opportunities for your book.

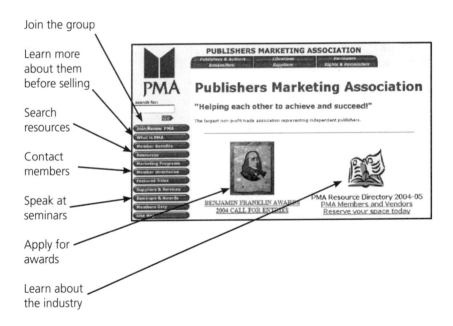

Strategy # 55: Make the Grade in the Academic Market[29]

The academic marketplace is an opportune segment for publishers, one using books as a foundation for its existence. It impacts people of all ages, from preschool through graduate school and adult education courses. Regardless of the grade, age of student, major in college or choice of home, public or private education, the need for books is ubiquitous.

The marketplace for selling books to schools is divided into three general markets: preschool, Elementary-High School (K-12) and secondary (colleges and universities). Subsegments also include adult education, distance learning, private, military and Catholic schools, among others. To give you an idea of the size of this opportunity, here are some figures from the 2003 school year:

100,255 preschools and child care centers with 59,374 directors

53,298 Elementary Schools with 1,489,380 teachers

14,723 Middle/Junior High Schools with 605,480 teachers

17,820 Senior High Schools with 858,827 teachers

1,752 four-year colleges and 1,188 two-year colleges with 95,620 department chairs

14,309 private schools and 8,312 Catholic schools with a total of 365,525 teachers

In addition there are 212 Bureau of Indian Affairs Schools, 1,268 Charter Schools, 224 Department of Defense Schools, 1,944 Magnet Schools and 14,103 Canadian Schools

Students, teachers, parents and administrators represent a target-rich audience for book marketers. In 2003 there were 47,813,003 K-12 public school students requiring a total expenditure of $296 billion to meet their needs. If each of these students required only five different titles per school year, the market need would be 240 million books.

Niche marketers know that any one title is not appropriate for all ages, especially in the diverse preschool and K–12 segments. Most of the books sold to the K-12 market are used as supplementary products rather than textbooks. The two criteria for determining the appropriate books to buy are interest level and reading level. Examples of the topics of interest for different ages and grades, are shown below.

---

29. Special thanks to Carol Waugh for information related to selling books in the academic market; Carol may be reached at 1163 Vine Street, Denver, CO 80206, *cwaugh@xcellentmarketin*

Age	Grade	Topics of Interest
Birth–2		Nursery tales, building with blocks
3–5	Pre-K	Dinosaurs, cars, trucks, humor
6–8	1–3	Fantasy, magic, planets, animals
9–12	4–7	Nature, trivia, friendship, mystery

The second criterion applied to book selection is its reading level. There are actually tests that are applied to books to determine their reading level according to the vocabulary used, the number of syllables in words and the length of the sentences.

The "No Child Left Behind Act" limits all spending to products that have proven to work based on scientific research. If not, federal money may be withheld from the school system. It becomes increasingly important for you to know these standards and make the buyers aware that your titles meet them, if that is the case.

The opportunities to target a grade level and type of school for your titles are myriad. You can multiply your chances of selling books in these segments when you consider the many ways in which they may be sold.

TEXTBOOKS

Books used in the classroom comprise a large part of the books sold in the academic market. The teachers are the decision makers in some cases, but there are usually state standards to which purchasing decisions are held. According to Pat Schroeder,[30] president of the Association of American Publishers, "Publishers are accountable to local and state education authorities for alignment of textbook content to a framework of state standards. Only instructional material that conforms to these standards will be considered."

Unfortunately there are no national standards, and each state is unique in its needs and buying procedures. However, if you can publish to the standards of CA, FL, IL, NY and TX you will reach the five top states in terms of population and budget money.

If the school board makes the final decision, then the teachers become decision influencers. In any case, the instructors are critical to the decision process, and an excellent way to reach these people is through direct mail. And the best time to reach them is when they are deciding

---

30. From a July 14, 2003 Letter to the Editor in the *Wall Street Journal*.

which books to use during the next school year. Experience shows that this occurs in late summer and early spring.

In the typical college, the instructors select the textbooks they will use. The bookstore then simply places the order (usually on a returnable basis). The habit among students of sharing textbooks often limits the sales of textbooks, and increases the likelihood of returns. Bookstores also buy textbooks back from students and resell them as used copies for an upcoming semester.

At the college level, your marketing should be directed to the instructors. What should you include in your direct-mail package to them? It would be cost-prohibitive to send a review copy to each, so your initial letter should qualify those who might be interested in using your book as a text. Then you could send a complimentary copy to those who are interested. With this strategy, your direct-mail piece should contain an informative letter, the Table of Contents, a detailed description of your title, a sales piece and a reply card requesting a "desk copy" or "examination copy." You could provide this information through your web site.

Use the reply card to obtain important marketing information as well as for qualifying the prospect. For instance, ask the respondent for full contact information, when the decision will be made and the age or grade level for which the title is being considered. Then you will know the best time to contact them and perhaps open a market you had not previously considered.

Criteria used for selection of the textbook:

1. Quality of production and content. Your book must have superior production characteristics and the information in it must be current and verified.
2. Author's credentials. Include the qualifications of the author as well as endorsements and testimonials.
3. Teacher's aids. A teacher's guide is indispensable, and additional information such as sample test questions, exercises, and assignments are helpful. You might increase your chance of selling your titles if you include overhead transparences and answer keys for grading purposes.
4. Binding. Textbooks are used repeatedly and are subject to harsh use, so most teachers prefer hardcover books. Supplementary material may be soft covered, but the primary text should have a hard cover.

HOW TO REACH THE ACADEMIC MARKET

This well-defined market segment is particularly suited to direct contact. This includes direct mail, personal visits and telephone calls. You can also reach them indirectly through school supply stores, educational dealers and suppliers, trade shows and book fairs.

Schoolbook buyers are reluctant to purchase from publishers with single titles. If you do not have a product line, consider bundling with other authors and publishers with complementary products. Then create a catalog describing your combined product line. Buyers place great significance on your catalog, so invest enough money to create one of high quality.

An excellent resource for mailing lists is Quality Education Data (QED), a research and database company focused exclusively on education. Quality Education Data Inc. is a wholly owned subsidiary of Scholastic Inc. the global children's publishing and media company. QED is located at 1625 Broadway, Suite 250, Denver, CO 80202; (800) 525-5811; Fax: (303) 860-0238; *www.qeddata.com.*

There are educational conferences held regularly throughout the year. Find those appropriate to your topic and titles and attend them. The conference planners may allow you to make a presentation, perhaps in exchange for exhibit space. This projects your image as an expert on your topic. Hand out catalogs and flyers about your titles, but avoid using your speaking time for selling. You may also write an article for the conference program, furthering the perception (and fact) of your expertise.

Go to the websites of your target schools. Many will display course outlines, perhaps including the current textbooks. The websites of some states' Departments of Education provide explanations of the requirements for each grade level. Use this information to tailor the content of your books as well as your sales approach, demonstrating the benefits of your title over their current text. You can also learn some of the industry jargon, such as the use of the terms *beginning readers, emergent readers* or *reluctant readers* in the K-12 arena.

Reviews will help you tremendously in this market, too. Send review copies to pertinent publications, especially *School Library Journal.* Personal presentations and readings at school can enhance your income (if you get paid) and sales (if you are permitted to sell your books).

Since school districts are so geographically dispersed, you will probably not find it economical to contact them personally. For that reason, most large publishers use independent sales reps to reach academic markets. These salespeople need new product every season and will not represent you if you cannot supply it.

In some cases it would be more effective to contact buyers through direct mail. Time your mailings to arrive in January and then again in the spring and summer months when the buyers are making their decisions for the upcoming school year. Once that begins there is little opportunity to sell your books until the following season.

Follett Educational Services sells a variety of products and services to educational institutions. They sell used textbooks, workbooks and teacher's editions through online or printed catalogs. They also sell paperback novels and reference books. Contact them at 1433 Internationale Parkway, Woodridge, IL 60517-4941; (800) 621-4272; Fax (800) 638-4424; *www.fes.follett.com.*

NACSCORP is a national wholesaler and services provider to college stores and campus resellers. It offers over 160,000 text and trade book titles from more than three hundred publishers. NACSCORP is an industry service offered by the National Association of College Stores (NACS), the professional trade association representing more than three thousand collegiate retailers and about one thousand associate members who supply books and other products to college stores. You can reach them at *www.nacscorp.com.*

NACS publishes *The College Store* magazine for higher education retailers. This magazine reports on topics of interest to collegiate retailers. In addition, it hosts several conferences throughout the year. NACS is located at 500 East Lorain Street, Oberlin, OH 44074; (800) 622-7498; Fax (440) 775-4769; *www.nacs.org.*

There is no typical discount structure for school buyers, and you may decide to offer a discount on volume purchased. Except for damaged books there are no returns and schools generally pay the shipping charges. Some publishers simply add 10 per cent on the invoice to cover shipping and handling costs.

You must be patient when selling to schools. You may not reach a break-even point for two to three years. But once you demonstrate your credibility, build your product line, win awards and elicit positive reviews you will begin to reap significant rewards.

OTHER POSSIBILITIES FOR YOUR TITLES

Opportunities abound in the academic marketplace for the creative marketer, particularly at the secondary level. For example, if you have a line of career-related titles you could sell them directly to the Career Development offices located at most colleges. And these people are always looking for credible speakers to help their students find employment.

You could also sell your books to alumni associations or campus chapters of the American Marketing Association as a fundraiser. Both of these groups usually have newsletters reaching their constituents, too. Who else cares about the future job of a college graduate? The parents. You can purchase a mailing list of the parents of graduating college students (American Student List Company, 330 Old Country Road. Mineola, NY 11501-4143; (888) 462-5600; Fax: (516) 248-6364; *www.studentlist.com* and send them information on your titles.

The confined nature of the campus population presents a unique opportunity for media advertising. You can promote your titles inexpensively to a highly concentrated audience through college newspapers. And you can easily test different headlines, body copy and layouts in them, but be sure to key your ads (one ad may request a reply to Dept. A and the other to Dept. B) so you can track the responses. Many schools have television or radio stations. Appear on them to market your books and practice your presentation techniques. Remember that the typical student buyer is particularly frugal. When marketing directly to them be sure to offer a compelling financial incentive.

EXPAND YOUR DEFINITION OF THE ACADEMIC MARKET.

There are even more opportunities for book sales outside the traditional academic markets, and many of these are open to fiction titles. For example, you could sell fiction or nonfiction to trade or vocational schools, day-care centers, home-schooling organizations and school libraries. Many schools have adult-education programs utilizing nontraditional textbooks. These may be books on very specific topics.

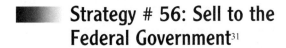

Strategy # 56: Sell to the Federal Government[31]

How would you like to sell to a customer that needs what you have to sell, has virtually unlimited funds, is required to speak to you and return your calls, must pay you in thirty days or pay you interest on the money owed, does not return your books and requires no special distribution channels, inventory or promotion? There is such as customer—and it is your own federal government.

---

31. Special thanks to Sherri Valenzuela for information on this topic. For more details, contact Sherri at *www.growusapress.com* where you can also subscribe to her complimentary monthly newsletter "Red, White & You."

Purchases by the Federal Government In FY 2001		
NAICS Code	Description	Amount
323117	Books, printing & binding, (Without publishing)	$ 4,845,000
511110	Newspaper publishing	$ 10,459,000
511120	Newsletter publishing	$ 18,671,000
511130	Book publishing	$ 11,808,000
511140	List publishing	$ 81,663,000
561410	Editing	$ 39,599,000
711510	Writers, independent freelance	$184,806,000

The U.S. federal government is the largest buyer of goods and services in the world. It signs more than 56,000 contracts per day, spending roughly $30 to $40 million each working hour. The collective value of these contracts is worth hundreds of billions of dollars, and that does not include the money spent for state and local contracts. Approximately 90 percent of government purchases are for $25,000 or less, and it must direct 23 per cent of all its purchasing dollars toward purchases reserved for small businesses.

The government is an ideal customer. Since your taxes pay for the salary of every government buyer you are in a position of authority in the buying equation. This "customer" must reveal the buying history of any service or product it is purchasing. You can even obtain the buying forecast of any agency and pre-sell yourself as the answer to their need for those items.

The U.S. Small Business Administration published the report, "Doing Business with the Federal Government" which that can be downloaded at *www.sba.gov/opc*. This, among other information, describes The Prime Contracts Program through which the SBA helps to increase small businesses' share of government contracts. It also describes The Subcontracting Assistance Program that promotes maximum use of small businesses by the nation's large prime contractors. The SBA's Procurement Marketing and Access Network, or PRO-Net, is a "virtual" one-stop procurement shop. The Internet web site *www.pronet.sba.gov* is the search engine for contracting officers, as well as a marketing tool and link to procurement opportunities and other important information. All small firms seeking federal, state and private contracts can fill out and update their own profiles at the site.

There is little seasonality in the purchasing process since it operates almost continuously, every day, all day, five days or more per week. However, there is a period coined "fiscal year frenzy" occurring at the end of each fiscal year. At this time, agencies are eager to spend their remaining budget dollars or lose them in the following budget. You might begin contacting your buyers in July, encouraging them to spend their remaining funds on your products or services.

The federal government buys through a number of vehicles. One is a blanket purchase agreement, negotiated with each vendor. However, it prefers charge cards for procuring products and services. It charges to a standard credit card for purchases up to $2,500. The General Services Administration (GSA) has already issued more than 250,000 SmartPay cards to federal employees. If your company accepts VISA or MasterCard, you can also accept GSA SmartPay cards, and the transactions can be processed through your existing merchant account.

Market to government buyers as you would any commercial prospect. Find out their needs and buying criteria. They prefer to buy locally, so make an appointment with your buyer at a nearby government office and meet with him or her. You can offer discounts and promotions, too.

CONTRACT WORK

Government agencies regularly seek people for writing documentation, books and pamphlets. The federal government can actually become your publisher when it contracts with you for a project and then buys your work. In fact, the average author stands a better chance of getting published by writing for the government than through traditional means.

Writing for the federal government is "a match made in heaven," says Sherri Valenzuela. All you need do is search for, or create, topics related to your area of expertise. Then contact the appropriate department and offer your services and ideas. This can be done even if you write fiction. For example, the core of your writing may be "the human experience." You could contact the Department of Health and Human Services and discuss ideas on how you could relate this topic to their needs. There is even a liaison in the government to help you find your niche and sell your expertise.

An excellent tool for helping you sell to the federal government is *The Fast Track Guide to Winning Government Contracts*, a system designed to help small businesspeople sell more products to the government. It includes instructions, forms, an audio set and special reports. Learn more about this at *www.growusapress.com*.

Strategy # 57: Marching to the Military

The marketplace for the armed services is made up of 1.4 million active duty personnel, more than 700,000 civilians working for the Department of Defense and almost 2,000,000 retired service people. This opportunity looms even larger when you consider the family members of these people.

The primary means of selling to the military is direct sale of existing titles. This becomes an easier task if you further segment the military market into its unique buying opportunities. For instance, you may have titles that can be sold domestically or overseas, to military libraries, Department of Defense Dependent Schools (DoDDS), on board ships, to retired military personnel, to the families of military personnel, through commissaries and direct marketing. These and others are descried below.

SELLING TO EXCHANGES

The largest buyers of books of all types for the military market are the exchange services—Army & Air Force Exchange Service, Coast Guard Exchange, Navy Exchange, and Marine Corps Exchange.

Army & Air Force Exchange Service (AAFES) provides merchandise and services to active duty military, guard and reserve members, military retirees, and family members. It donates 100 percent of earnings back to its customers. The address is 3911 South. Walton Walker Boulevard, Dallas, TX 75236-1598; (214) 312-1101; *www.aafes.com*.

You can download the entire AAFES Suppliers Handbook (pdf file-3.22MB) at *www.aafes.com/pa/selling/index.html*. If you are interested in selling books and publications within the exchange, these distributors should be contacted directly. They can answer questions regarding item selection and purchasing procedures. If you have further questions, please contact the AAFES book and magazine buyer, Yolanda Thursby, at *thursby@aafes.com* or (214) 312-6659.

U.S. Coast Guard Exchange System Headquarters, 870 Greenbrier Circle, Tower II, Suite 502, Chesapeake, VA 23320; (757) 420-2480; www.cq-exchange.com. For an updated, complete list of Coast Guard Exchanges including addresses and phone numbers go to *www.cqaux.org/cgauxweb/memtable,shtml*.

Navy Exchange Service Command includes navy exchanges, navy lodges, military uniforms and ships stores. Exchange Catalog: (800) 527-2345. Forms for dealing with the Marine Corps Exchange may be found at *www.usmc-mecs.org/dobusiness/downloads.htm*.

Navy and Marine Uniforms: (800) 368-4088, Navy Lodge (800) NAVY-INN, Navy Exchange Service Command, 3280 Virginia Beach Boulevard, Virginia Beach, VA 23452; *www.navy-nex.com.*

Furthermore, most exchanges have a book-selling section, or in some cases, an elaborate bookstore. The wide variety of products sold through exchanges creates many opportunities for cross merchandising, too. While you can contact the exchange services directly, local distributors supply the exchanges with most books and publications. Anderson News Group reaches this niche, and a more detailed list of distributors and their points of contact may be found at *www.aafes.com/pa/selling/books.html.*

According to Austin Camacho, author of *Successfully Marketing Print-on-Demand Fiction*, novels can lend themselves to special-sales markets "if you're attentive to your target audience." As an example, he cites Patrick O'Connell's 1997 clairvoyant novel *Knight Hawk*," about a rogue Air Force pilot who stole a fighter jet and used it to attack New York. After his career as an Air Force officer, O'Connell had maintained just about every type of aircraft in the U.S. arsenal and was able to fill his book with exacting and accurate details about the military, the planes and the men who flew them. Although his book was pure fiction, there was enough reality at its core that it had a particular appeal to one large target group—the men and women of the armed forces. O'Connell (*pat_o_Connell@hotmail.com*) was able to find exceptional success at book signings on military installations. At a post exchange he could meet with and talk to people who would understand the seed from which his book grew, and they in turn could buy a novel that spoke to their own experiences, filled with technical details that civilians would understand but military people could appreciate better."

In this distribution system, it is difficult to promote the sale of your titles with advertising in general print media. Magazines and newspapers have light penetration into military households. The reasons for this are that the military personnel are transient. Local news is not particularly important to them, or if it is, they subscribe to their hometown newspaper. Yet there are still ways to reach this market through military publications. Contact each of the periodicals listed below for media kits with current rate cards. These media can also supply you with up-to-date market information.

Armed Forces Journal
Defense News Media Group
6883 Commercial Drive
Springfield, VA 22159
(703) 750-9000
www.afji.com

Army Times Publishing Company
Military Markets Magazine
6883 Commercial Drive
Springfield, VA 22159

Every week, the print edition of its newspapers, *Army Times*, *Navy Times*, *Air Force Times*, and *Marine Corps Times*, deliver news and analysis about military careers, pay and benefits. In addition, each paper has community information and active lifestyle features of interest to military personnel and their families.

The Military Times papers offer over eighteen supplements throughout the year, including valuable military resource guides, a special annual historical issue, military healthcare specials and important second career and educational supplements. Visit *The Military Times* papers online at *www.militarycity.com* or at any one of their service-specific sites: *www.armytimes.com*, *www.navytimes.com*, *www.airforcetimes.com*, *www.marinecorpstimes.com*.

Family Magazine, the magazine for commissary shoppers, and Salute Magazine the magazine for active duty military *www.familymedia.com/index.lasso*.

Stars and Stripes is a newspaper for service members, government civilians and their families in Europe, the Middle East, Africa and the Pacific. *Stars and Stripes* offers national and international news, sports and opinion columns. In addition to daily pages, *Stripes* offers:

Sunday Magazine—A feature magazine that includes stories on military life and history, as well as guest columns by readers.

Timeout (Fridays in Europe, Saturdays in Pacific)—Feature articles on sports, often focusing on upcoming major events.

Stripes Travel (Thursdays)—Articles on travel worldwide.

Accent (Wednesdays)—News and information on lifestyles, including recipes and decorating tips.

Your Money (Sundays in Europe, Mondays in Pacific)—Highlighting business news.

Mini Pages—information and education exclusively for children.

The mailing address for the central office is 529 14th Street NW, Suite 350, Washington DC 20045-1301; (202) 761-0900, Fax: (202) 761-0890; *marketing@pstripes.osd.mil*, *www.estripes.com/index.asp*

Military Living
  P.O. Box 2347
  Falls Church, VA 22042-0347
  (703) 237-0203
  Fax: (703) 237-2233
  www.militaryLiving.com

ADDITIONAL SALES OPPORTUNITIES ON THE BASES

Each military base can provide myriad sales opportunities. For example, there are places in which to sell books in schools, for child- and health-care and through the base exchange. Many offer recreation such as golf, tennis, bowling, swimming, tennis and most have a base library.

Most bases offer a variety of services for the families of the people on active duty. These include family support services, employee assistance program, spouse clubs and family centers. Each provides additional opportunities in which to sell your books. Here are examples of these programs:

  The Defense Department Child Development Program is the largest employer-sponsored child-care program in the country, serving children from newborn to age twelve. It includes child development centers, family childcare and school-age care programs.

  The Employee Assistance Program is an additional avenue to help coast guard service members and their families with problems. The centers serve not only active-duty members and their families, but also reservists on active duty, defense department civilians and military retirees.

  Family advocacy programs are aimed at preventing incidents and treating victims of spouse and child abuse.

  Financial management and consumer awareness education and assistance offer help in personal finance, including budgeting, debt management and retirement planning.

  Life skills educational programs help individuals with parenting, stress management and other life skills.

  Relocation assistance helps families plan moves and manage the challenges of adapting into a new community.

  Special-needs family member assistance programs offer information and support to family members who have requirements for medical, educational or mental health services. General information on family centers can be found on the Department of Defense's Military Assistance Program at *www.dod.mil/mapsite.*

Spouse clubs are found at most military installations. Typically, bases have separate clubs for the spouses of enlisted members and officers. Clubs help spouses get acquainted with new communities, make friends and find support. Some include spouses of any personnel on base; others are specific to units. Spouses of retirees often participate in the clubs. One example is the Military Spouse Business and Professional Network, P.O. Box 80744, San Diego, CA 92138-0744.

For the contact information for specific military bases, go to *www.armytimes.com/story.php?s+0-292258-locator.php*. Here you can locate them by state, with complete contact information; this includes the number of people on active duty, their family members and civilians as well as the website for the base.

If you want to join an association that can help you sell books to the U.S. Military's commissaries (supermarkets), exchanges (general merchandise, specialty stores), and/or MWR services (sports complexes, fitness centers, clubs, etc.) look into the American Logistics Association. Its mission "is to promote, protect and ensure the existence and continued viability of the military resale systems, support other Quality of Life programs for the members of the U.S. Armed Forces and their families, provide an environment for sales that are mutually beneficial to the military and industry, provide a forum where industry and the military can explore opportunities, reach business solutions and enhance the business of ALA member companies." For more information go to *www.ala-national.org*. The ALA mailing address is 133 Fifteenth Street, NW, Suite 640, Washington, DC 20005.

MILITARY ASSOCIATIONS

Military associations represent the interests of active, reserve, veteran and retired military members, and their families. The associations perform many different functions. They provide services to their members, inform their members and the general public about issues of concern and help bring together military communities with similar interests or backgrounds. For more information on selling to associations see Strategy # 54.

Here are some of the armed services associations, what they do, and how to get in touch with them:

Gold Star Wives of America (GSW)

Chartered by congress in 1980, GSW provides members with information on benefits/programs for which they might be entitled. 5510

Columbia Pike, Suite 205, Arlington, VA 22204; (888) 479-9788; *www.goldstarwives.org, gswives2@aol.com.*

National Military Family Association (NMFA)

Serves the families of the uniformed services through education, information and advocacy and is dedicated to identifying and resolving issues affecting them. 6000 Stevenson Avenue, Suite 304, Alexandria, VA 22304-3526 (703) 823-NMFA; Fax: (703) 751-4857, *www.nmfa.org, families@nmfa.org.*

The Retired Officers Association

Aims to benefit members of the uniformed services—active duty, former and retired, National Guard and Reserve—and their families and survivors through efforts to preserve earned entitlements and to maintain a strong national defense. Membership is open to active duty, retired, National Guard, reserve, former commissioned officers and warrant officers of the Army, Navy, Air Force, Marine Corps, Coast Guard, Public Health Service and National Oceanic and Atmospheric Administration. 201 North Washington Street, Alexandria, VA 22314; (800) 245-TROA, *www.troa.org, msc@troa.org.*

United Armed Forces Association (UAFA)

Serves all ranks and branches of the armed forces—active duty, reserve, veterans, retired military and their dependents and civil service employees. P.O. Box 20672, Waco, TX 76702;(888) 457-7667; *info@uafa.org.*

Veterans of Foreign Wars (VFW)

Provides programs and services that strengthen comradeship among members, perpetuate the memory and history of fallen soldiers, foster patriotism, defend the constitution and promote service to our communities and our country. 406 West 34th Street, Kansas City, MO 64111. (816) 756-3390; *www.vfw.org, info@vfw.org.*

NONMILITARY ORGANIZATIONS

There are many groups, clubs and organizations associated with the armed services that are excellent sources for book sales. These include American Red Cross, American Retirees Association, American Overseas Schools Historical Society, Armed Services YMCA of the U.S.A., National Military Family Association and the Toys for Tots Foundation. For an exhaustive list of these organizations go to *www.military.com/NewConte nt?file=associations_newindex.*

USO clubs are affiliated with the military and provide opportunities for additional sales. For a comprehensive list of these locations, go to *www.uso.org/pubs/8_13_18.cfm?CFID=1854693&CFTOKEN=6166864* or for a list of worldwide USO addresses, write: United Services Organization World Headquarters, 601 Indiana Avenue, NW, Washington, DC 20004.

Chats—Topic rooms

Talk with others in the military community, post a message on a bulletin board or respond to a message at *www.militarycity.com/forums*.

Defense Visual Information Directorate's Discussion Forums has forums organized in conferences. These conferences provide a communication tool for the Defense Visual Information community to share ideas, many about new products, including books. *dodimagery.afis.osd.mil/dodimagery/forums/*

Military Brats Online, an online community, linking the children of the U.S. military with their heritage and each other. Military Brats can read about reunion and school announcements, link with past friends, family and online resources. *www.militarybrats.com*.

MILITARY BOOKSTORES ONLINE

Frank Cass Publishers, *www.frankcass.com/index.htm* carries titles on history, politics and international relations, military studies (including strategic studies), Middle East studies, development studies, economics and business, law. 5824 NE Hassalo Street, Portland, OR 97213; (800) 944-6190; Fax: (503) 280-8832; *marketing@frankcass.com, cass@isbs.com*,

You could also try Pentagon Books, *www.pentagon-books.com*. Online sellers of U.S. military manuals, on paper and CD-ROM. Or Military Books Online, *www.members.aol.com/vonRanke/militarybooks.html*, an Amazon.com affiliate bookshop with added information and book reviews on featured titles.

Military Times online bookstore has books on myriad topics, such as humor and battles. It has books with answers to basic computer questions such as building a website or creating worksheets; books with tips for today's competitive business world, and titles on managing change, selling successfully and motivating people. Go to *www.airforcetimes.com/subchan=sho*.

MILITARY BOOK CLUBS ONLINE

These online bookclubs focus on military titles and operate much like the general line book clubs, offering an incentive to join with discounts on books purchased over time. Examples include the Military and Aviation Book Society at *www.militarybookclub.co.uk* or the Military Book Club, a U.S.-based book club offering a range of military history and war books at discount prices at *www.militarybookclub.com.*

The Military Book Club® is a BookSpan club and the largest of all military book clubs. It features books on military history, biographies, weapons, hobbies, fiction and more. Ron Doering, Editor of the Military Book Club says, "Since its founding in the summer of 1969, The Military Book Club has grown to be the largest book club of its kind. Members now see over 170 selections annually, in more military categories than ever before." (*www.bookspan.com/doc/cor/TemplateData/clubinfo_2/cl_SP_MIL.jhtml*).

MILITARY MUSEUMS

There are military museums on many topics. For more information on selling to museums in general, see Strategy #58. Here are several examples of military museums:

USAF Museum, 1100 Spaatz Street, Wright-Patterson AFB, OH 45433; (937) 255-3286; *www.wpafb.af.mil/museum/*

Fort Huachuca Historical Museum, Endeavors to bring to the military community and general public a heightened awareness of, and an increased appreciation for, the colorful history of the Southwest and, especially, the prominent part played by the U.S. Army. Museum Director, U.S. Army Garrison, ATTN: ATZS-TDO-M, Fort Huachuca, AZ 85613-6000, (520) 533-5736. *huachuca-www.army.mil/HISTORY/museum.htm.*

General Sweeny's Museum of Civil War History, Highlights the war in the Trans-Mississippi theater. For information about selling books in the gift shop, contact Tom Sweeny, 5228 South State Highway ZZ, Republic, MO 65738. Telephone and fax (417) 732-1224. *www.civilwarmuseum.com.*

SELLING YOUR TITLES ABOARD SHIPS

There are approximately one hundred and eighty ship stores on U.S. Navy commissioned ships. Ship stores carry basic necessities such as soap and shampoo as well as a limited selection of semi-luxury items such as watches and consumer electronic items. Services aboard ship are barbershops, laundry, vending and amusement machines, and dry cleaning on the larger ships.

The mission of the Ship Store program is to provide quality goods at a discount. But, as you can imagine, space aboard a ship is very limited and only the most necessary items in each category are held in stock. However, the crewmembers may place an order for almost any item through NEXCOM (Navy Exchange, *www.navy-nex.com*).

The NEXCOM Ship Store program office, located at Naval Base Norfolk, must approve all products sold to ship stores. For information on selling to Ships Stores, write: NEXCOM, Navy Exchange Service Command, 3280 Virginia Beach Boulevard., Virginia Beach, VA 23452; (800) NAVY-EXCH (628-3924); Exchange Catalog: (800) 527-2345; review the Vendor Guide (*www.navy-nex.com/ship_stores/ss-vendor-guide.html*) for complete information on how to do business with ship stores.

MILITARY LIBRARIES

Most of libraries operated by the federal government are under the Department of Defense. Unfortunately, there is no central way for a publisher to sell to them. Librarians in each branch of the armed forces have their own process for acquiring titles, and most have separate budgets for title acquisitions. There are several opportunities for you at the following central locations:

Armed Forces Medical Library, Department of Defense Surgeon General's Office, Falls Church, VA; The National Library of Medicine's World Wide Web services provide information about library programs, services, connections to NLM online services, links to specialized NLM web servers, and multimedia features. There is a search locator at *www.locatorplus.gov.*

Joint Forces Staff College, Norfolk, VA, affiliated with the National Defense University Library (Formerly Armed Forces Staff College) at *www.jfsc.ndu.edu/library/default.asp.*

Pentagon Library, Washington, DC - Reference sources of military interest, especially "Bibliographies, Briefing Guides, and Quick Lists" on current topics including military conflicts, military statistics, and legislative histories. *www.hqda.army.mil/library.*

National Defense University Library, Washington, DC, is an eLibrary that serves the academic, research, distance learning, and professional information requirements of National Defense University staff, faculty, students and alumni through a program incorporating both print and digital information resources. *www.ndu.edu/library/ library.html*.

For a listing of U.S. Pacific Command Libraries visit *library.ad.umuc.edu/ pals/*; and for a listing of all libraries at the Service Academies, post and base libraries stateside and overseas go to *www.defenselink.mil/other_info/ libraries.html*.

The Military Librarians Division brings together those interested in the improvement of military library service. It is a forum for the exchange of ideas and information on military librarianship; it conceives and carries out projects that assist members in improving services to their constituencies; it works to promote the professional advancement of its members and to enhance understanding of the importance of libraries to a successful national defense. Military Librarians Division, Suzanne Ryder, Naval Research Lab Research Library, Code 5225, 4555 Overlook Avenue, Washington, DC 20375-0001, (202) 767-2269; DSN: 297; FAX: (202) 767-3352; *www.sla.org/division/smil*.

SELLING TO GOVERNMENT SCHOOLS

The education system operated by the Department of Defense serves the children of men and women in the services and stationed in the United States, Europe and the Pacific. This system is organized into two separate but parallel systems: the Department of Defense Dependents Schools (DoDDS) overseas, and the Department of Defense Domestic Dependent Elementary and Secondary Schools (DDESS) in the United States. In 1994 the two systems were merged under the Department of Defense Education Activity (DoDEA, 4040 North Fairfax Drive, Arlington, VA 22203-1635).

DoDEA operates 224 schools in twenty-one districts located in fourteen foreign countries, seven states, Guam, and Puerto Rico. All schools within DoDEA are fully accredited by U.S. accreditation agencies. Approximately 8,800 teachers serve DoDEA's 106,000 students. A current list of DoDEA schools may be obtained by writing the Department of Defense Dependent Schools, Hoffman I, Room 152, 2461 Eisenhower Avenue, Alexandria, VA, 22331.

The Defense Education Supplies Procurement Office (DESPO), Richmond, VA, is the DoDEA procurement office that handles educational curricula requirements for all DoDEA schools worldwide. This can include textbooks, educational software, etc. If you are interested in getting on the DESPO bidders mailing list, download the vendor data input form (*www.odedodea.edu/procure/vendorsection/Vendrwb1.doc*), fill it out and either fax it or mail it to: DESPO, Attn: Small Business Specialist, 101 Buford Road, Richmond, VA 23235; (804) 327-0505; Fax (804) 327-0671. For a copy of the DoDEA Procurement Support Guide, including procurement locations, go to *www.odedodea.edu/procure/vendorsection/procsupgd.xls*.

13

Selling to the Niche-Market Sector

NICHE MARKETS ARE MADE UP of identifiable groups of people with a common interest. This interest might be photography, cooking or playing tennis, and the practitioners may congregate in camera shops, cooking schools or tennis clubs. Marketing to these segments entails identifying groups of people interested in your topics, finding out where they seek information on that topic and making your books available in those locations.

There could be many niche opportunities to market your titles based upon its topic. You may find yourself selling it to museums, to zoos, at special events, during trade shows, through radio and television shows, via book clubs, in supermarkets, and by means of catalogs. As is appropriate, you could sell your products in home-improvement centers, pet shops, auto-supply stores, drug stores, camera shops, toy stores, garden supply stores or computer stores. The possibilities open an entire new world of opportunity as endless and as fertile as your creativity.

WHY SELL TO NICHE MARKETS?

People go to bookstores to buy books. There, your books are on a shelf, surrounded by competitive books. In niche marketing, you make your books available to prospective buyers where they seek items of interest in a noncompetitive setting. In addition:

1. You can be very specific about the people you contact and the benefits you present so your promotional dollars are more efficient.
2. Your title may be the only one available in a retail setting where there is no competition and no price comparison. You can offer your books for sale in car washes, doctors' offices, banks, restaurants, ski lodges, movie theaters, appliance stores or coffee shops.
3. It may be easier to sell to niche markets than to buyers in large corporations. Proprietors of small businesses look upon books favorably as a special service to their customers and, a source of incremental revenue.
4. Most of these venues purchase directly from the publisher, so there may be no distribution discounts.
5. The individual orders will typically be smaller than those in the Commercial Sales segment, but you will find the buying period shorter, the process less formal and access to buyers through mass communications.

You may also find the buying process different for each niche. If in doubt about the proper procedures, "visit local stores, or call major ones, to ask them how they buy products," says Dan Poynter. Must you use a distributor, and if so, which ones are the best? What are the traditional percentages on which sales are made? What are the industry operating procedures and expectations? What are the major industry trade shows, magazines and associations? Ask questions that will enable you to reach your potential buyers most expeditiously.

Strategy # 58: Sell through Museums,[32] Zoos and Parks

Every year millions of people visit thousands of museums, zoos and parks, most of which have a gift shop in which books could be sold. Museums want to inform and educate their visitors, and if you have a book that will enhance their ability to do that, you may make a good sale.

There are approximately 1,800 museums in the United States that belong to the Museum Store Association, all of which either have a store or are in the process of creating a retail operation. MSA member stores range in net sales from less than $5,000 to more than $17 million with mean net sales of $415,074. Because museum stores sell items (including books) that provide visitors with souvenirs and educational materials directly related to their museum experience, your book on any of those subjects could be ideal for sales through their shops.

The Museum Store Association (MSA) is an international organization representing museum store professionals worldwide. MSA is a nonprofit organization dedicated to the general welfare of the museum store industry, and it helps museum store managers better serve their institutions and the public. The association is located at 4100 East Mississippi Avenue, Suite 800, Denver, CO 80246-3055, and their telephone number is (303) 504-9223. You can find more information by e-mailing them at *info@museumdistrict.com* or by visiting their website (*www.museumdistrict.com/about/aboutmsa.cfm*). The Canadian Museums Association is at 280 Metcalfe Street, Suite 400, Ottawa, Ontario K2P 1R7 Canada; (613) 567-0099, Fax (613) 233-5438, *info@museums.ca* and may be found on the web at *www.museums.ca/news.htm*. Visit their bookstore while you are there.

Museums run the gamut of subjects, including ethnic groups (Polish Museum of America in Chicago), art (MOMA), science (Museum of Science and Industry, Chicago), time (Timexpo Museum, Waterbury, CT), natural history (Museum of Natural History, New York City) and many other focused topics, in large and small cities. Stores in these museums only sell books directly related to their themes, or they become subject to the Unrelated Business Income Tax (UBIT). So the more targeted your titles are to the topic of the museum the more likely they are to be purchased.

Books are considered impulse items in this market and should be priced accordingly. In addition to a low price, buyers look for quality

---

32. Tordis Ilg Isselhardt provided information on marketing to museums. *tordis@imagesfromthepast.com*

of production and content. The information in a new title is expected to be precise, and it may be subjected to a formal review process. Your submission to the buying authority should include a statement that you have checked your facts and dates for accuracy.

Their purchasing procedures are similar to those of a traditional bookstore in the sense that they buy at just-in-time inventory levels, usually in small quantities. However, you can contact one organization to sell your books to many stores at once. Eastern National is an association providing educational products and services to 150 stores in more than 130 national parks and other public trusts in thirty states, from Maine to the Caribbean. It is located at 470 Maryland Drive, Suite 1, Ft. Washington, PA 19034. You can reach them at (215) 283-6900 or by fax: (215) 283-6923, e-mail: *customer_serv@easternnational.org*. They have a bookstore on their website (*www.easternnational.org/*) as well as access to all the stores they represent. Many of their museum stores also have websites through which they market books. You may find a broader selection representing a greater opportunity for your titles there.

If you choose to sell directly to the stores, approach them as you would any other business buyer. Find out the buyers' names and make appointments to meet with them. You can usually find this information on their website, as well as other details that will help you prepare for the sale. Since you wrote a title on the museum's theme, demonstrate your knowledge of it and the museum itself.

Although there are no industry standards for purchasing books, sales are typically nonreturnable. An exception to this rule is a sale for a special event. They usually seek a 50 per cent discount, and if your titles sell well they will be reordered regularly.

If you want to learn more about how to market to museums, go to the site of the American Association of Museums (*www.aam-us.org*) where they have a bookstore with titles on how to do just that. And if you want to find out the contact information for bookstores at many national parks, go to data2.itc.nps.gov/hafe/bookshop/index.cfm and track them down.

▇▇▇ Strategy # 59: Sell Through Gift Stores[33]

Today's gift market is experiencing dynamic growth as consumers buy more gifts and home decorating products. These products are gaining more exposure to consumers through a wide range of shopping venues

---

33. Thanks to Deb Werksman of Sourcebooks for providing information on this topic. *debwerksman@sourcebooks.com*

including the national retail chains, such as Pottery Barn, Yankee Candle, Bath and Body Works, Bombay Company, Pier One, Crate and Barrel, and Kirklands, department stores, mass merchants and the Internet. In the face of these new outlets, the small privately owned specialty gift stores are losing market share and playing a less important role as a consumer source for gifts.

Still, gift shops offer an excellent opportunity to sell more of your books. This category includes major accounts such as Hallmark Stores and Spencer Gifts. It also includes regional chains, local card and gift stores as well as hotel and hospital gift shops.

One of the major benefits of selling to gift shops is that books are sold on a nonreturnable basis. Perhaps a less tangible benefit is that you are broadening your markets, reaching people where they would not normally look for books. In addition, you can sell diverse products to one company. For example, if you target Hallmark as your central prospect, there are several opportunities to be found among its subsidiary companies:

Hallmark Stories sells photo storage and memory-keeping products. If your book is related to this product line, you could sell them here. Or, if your title is related to commemorating special occasions, people, and memories, contact **Keepsake Ornaments**, another Hallmark subsidiary.

Gift Books from Hallmark. In 1999, Hallmark began expanding from cards to books that help celebrate, commemorate, and communicate. If you have a title that warms the heart and enriches the soul, your opportunity may well lie here. You can find Gift Books from Hallmark at Hallmark Gold Crown® Stores and other selected retailers as well as on *www.Hallmark.com.* Gift Books from Hallmark categories also include:

Children's Classics, beautifully packaged editions of beloved children's books.

Just For Fun books, lighthearted titles such as *Yelling It Like It Is* by Maxine.

Comfort and Encouragement, Words to Live By, and Family and Friends, all featuring inspirational and motivational titles such as *A Promise in Every Color, God Always Has a Plan B, Dear Mom: Thank You for Everything,* and *The 100 Simple Secrets of Happy People.*

Party Express from Hallmark. One of Hallmark's most important missions is to help people celebrate and honor all the special days in their lives. Therefore, Hallmark offers party ware and accessories for birthdays, holidays, and other important occasions as well as everyday and seasonal entertaining. Party Express from Hallmark could be an excellent outlet for your title on partying, since they sell their products in party, toy, discount, grocery, drug, military, and specialty card stores.

But in most cases, the gift market is highly decentralized and there are many small shops that place small orders. This increases the administrative burden, requiring you to ship and bill for many small shops.

On the other hand, this also represents an opportunity because you can reach the decision makers readily. Start locally, calling on the gift-store owners and buyers. Go to the hospital gift stores and talk with the volunteers there. Most are very willing to spend time with you, describing their buying practices.

A major decision criterion is the fit your title has with the store's image and customer base, and the types of books that sell well vary by the chain's image. For example, Hallmark generally deals in sentiment, Spencer Gifts in humor and Urban Outfitters in "hip" products for men and women. Titles that generally do not do well in gift stores are scholarly, text-driven and fiction titles.

John Hanny has been a food consultant for two presidential administrations. His title, *Secrets from the White House Kitchens* (Rutledge Books, Danbury, CT) offers recipes favored by the incumbents of the Oval Office from Franklin Roosevelt to Bill Clinton. It was a natural selection by the White House Gift Shop as well as hotel gift shops in Washington, DC.

It is not appropriate to send galleys to gift-shop buyers because they make their decisions on the finished product. They want to see your book's cover design, size, text and its general overall quality. People buying products in gift shops typically purchase on impulse. Therefore, price is important. Your book should be priced under $10.00 to penetrate the gift market. Although there is no standard size that sells best, hardcover is generally more acceptable.

Gift store sales are seasonal in nature, and if your title is appropriate to one of the major holiday periods you stand a better chance of acceptance. Buyers at key accounts will begin looking at seasonal titles six months before the holiday. Purchasing agents at local stores may buy your books up to one month before the event. In most cases, distributors will accept submissions at all times. Send them a sample of the finished book with a marketing plan and a summary of your sales to date.

Gift stores also want to carry items of current interest, and can purchase quickly under the right circumstances. Checkerbee Books capitalized on this desire after the tragic death of racecar driver Dale Earnhardt. Says Checkerbee president Len Liebenhaut, "Ten days after the accident, we had a book about him on the (gift store) shelves and sold over 400,000 copies in three months."

The gift industry is divided into subsegments. In 2002, the top-selling segment in the giftware industry was Home Decorative Accessories, with $14.9 billion in sales, a 13 percent increase over the previous year. During 2002–2003, consumers spent more money on home furnishings than they did on clothes. With this new emphasis on home decorating, consumers are not just striving to make their homes more beautiful; rather they are seeking decorative items that can positively impact the mood and emotional climate of their home. Books that have a personal, emotional link to the consumer, such as collectibles or gifts, are in demand as consumers seek to make their homes more comfortable and comforting.

Stationery, Greeting Cards, and Paper Products, the second largest segment of the giftware market, reached $13.3 billion in sales, up 10 percent over the previous year. Collectibles—figurines and dolls—is one of the slowest growing gift segments. Seasonal Decorations is the smallest category in the giftware industry. While Christmas Decor still dominates the category, Halloween Decor was the fastest-growing segment.

Catalog shopping is big in the gift industry. Contact the manufacturers directly and convince them to sell your books to the gift shops or use them as a premium to increase their sales. Use the table below to stimulate ideas on how you can sell more books to gift catalogs.

If your title is on these topics...	Submit it to these catalogs...
Music boxes	Porter Music Box
Christmas collections	Mr. Christmas, Inc.
Dolls	Annalee Mobilitee Dolls
Romantic giftware or classic artifacts	Artifacts, Inc.
Windchimes	Carson Industries
Holiday giftware and accessories	Kurt S. Adler Company
Giftware and jewelry	Reed & Barton
Toys, dolls and stuffed animals	Eden/New York City
Collectibles	Character Collectibles
Giftware, miniatures and picture frames	Continental Creations

Learn more about the gift market by reading these trade magazines:

Giftware News, 20 West Kinzie, 12th Floor, Chicago, IL 60610; (312) 849-2220, Fax: (312) 849-2174, *giftwarenews@talcott.com*, *www.giftwarenews.com*.

Gifts & Decorative Accessories, 360 Park Avenue South, New York, NY

10010; (646) 746-6400, Fax: (646) 746-7431, (646) 746-7357; *qha lford@reedbusiness.com. www.giftsanddec.com/index.asp?layout=front_ page&webzine=gda&publication=gda,*

Giftbeat, 317 Harrington Avenue Closter, NJ 07624; (800) 358-7177, Fax (201)768-3894 *http://www.giftbeat.com/about/.*

HOW TO REACH THE GIFT MARKET.

1. Direct marketing. Timing may be as important as content in gift-store mailings. Once you locate your target companies, implement your direct-mail campaign well before the major holiday period for which your title is appropriate. Create a high-quality catalog listing your titles that are appropriate for the gift trade and include it in your mailings and personal visits. Be prepared to leave behind sample books with the potential buyers. Payments are typically made in net 120 days, but you can try to negotiate more favorable terms.

2. Sales-representative groups. There are independent sales rep groups that market books to the gift trade throughout North America. While there are some national organizations, most cover a territory comprised of several states. They usually seek a 15-20 per cent commission on all books sold in their territory. Find these people at the major gift shows, the biggest of which is the New York Stationery and Gift Show, usually held in May of each year.

3. Trade shows. Your rep group may exhibit your titles at the top trade shows, but you should attend anyway for the networking opportunities. The major shows are national or regional in scope and include: National Stationery Show, Boston Gift Show, California Gift Show, New York International Gift Fair, Dallas International Gift & Home Accessories Market, The Gift Fair in Atlanta, The Gourmet Products Show, San Francisco International Gift Fair, Mid-America Seattle Gift Show, Toronto International Gift Fair and the Washington Gift Show. For a list of all major shows go to *www.com-to-us.com/redirect_10/dom/giftshow/03dom/domshow.html.*

4. Gift Marts. For a list of gift marts go to *www.com-to-us.com/redirect_ 10/mrt/CMmrt/mrt/03mrt/marts.html.*

5. Distributors. There are some publishers that also distribute to the gift trade, such as Sourcebooks and Workman. Andrews & McMeel specializes in bestsellers, humor collections, general nonfiction trade, gift books and calendars. Cogan Books is one of the top wholesalers. They are located at 15020 Desman Road, La Mirada,

CA 90638, (714) 523-0309 or (800) 733-3630, Fax: (714) 523-0796 or (800) 233-2392; *www.coganbooks.com, info@coganbooks.com,*
   Discounts to retailers will be about 50 per cent, and distributors look for 70 per cent or more. Some distributors have minimum order sizes. For example, Sourcebooks' minimum order (from the retailer) is $100, but others require up to $600 or more.

6. Co-op catalogs. Contact companies such as Gift Creations Concepts (*www.gcccatalog.com*) or Ideation (*www.ideationgifts.com/*). These firms act as a buying group and produce catalog advertising for independent gift and collectible retailers. Part of their service is negotiating with manufactures to produce items exclusively for retailers participating in their advertising programs.

EXAMPLE OF SELLING INTO HOSPITAL GIFT SHOPS

John Simone of Three Pyramids Publishing has had success selling into the hospital gift shop market with his title, *The LCIS & DCIS Breast Cancer Fact Book*. According to John, "Unfortunately, I was not able to locate an easy method for doing this. I had to contact each hospital's gift shop manager separately. This seemed to get better results."

John went on to say, "I send a short (one page) letter that introduces the book, along with my sell-sheet/brochure." If the hospital is a large one that might generate many sales, he will also send a postcard for the recipient to request a reading copy. "I mark the reading copies in several places and it is obvious that they are not to be sold," he notes.

John prioritized his list of prospective buyers in order to reach the largest number of people in his target market: women with breast cancer and those visiting them during their hospital stay or while undergoing treatments. He initially concentrated on the larger hospitals, those with breast cancer centers. He quickly discovered that almost every hospital, large and small, has a cancer treatment center, "so any hospital gift shop is a likely candidate," he adds.

John's orders are usually small, often for his minimum quantity of three books. "I offer them at 50 per cent discount if the hospital shop pays shipping, and they are nonreturnable. These are the same terms the gift shops get from most of their regular suppliers and they seem to feel it is fair and normal," he says. The book sells well in these outlets and John has had many requests for subsequent shipments. It sells at least three times more copies there than anywhere else.

John's story is also an example of how your costs can impact a promotional offer. *The LCIS & DCIS Breast Cancer Fact Book* was produced using the print-on-demand (POD) process, resulting in a relatively high production cost. This limits the number of reading copies he can send. But his strategy is to "push the hospital gift store sales and hopefully be able to generate enough sales over the coming year to publish an edition printed with traditional offset methods." That will enable him to approach another special-sales opportunity: oncology offices. His objective in this segment is to send reading copies to each doctor for display in his or her office, with ordering information included, so that a patient can easily order the book.

Strategy # 60: Selling to Specialty Stores

Gift shops represent only the tip of the iceberg when it comes to selling books to specialty stores. Every store that sells a product on your topic can be a source of sales for your books. You can sell your cookbooks at food stands or gourmet shops, your book about dogs or cats to pet shops, your book about foot care in shoe stores. Your opportunities are limited only by your creativity.

Look at your product not as a book, but as an accessory to a particular industry. Bruce Lansky increased his sales of his parenting books when he sold them in maternity shops. It was then he realized he wasn't in the book business. He was in the baby-accessory business. If you have a title on motivation or one that serves as a solution for business people, sell it through stores that have similar products such as Franklin Covey (2200 W Parkway Boulevard, Salt Lake City, UT, 84119-2331; (801) 817-1776, (*www.franklincovey.com*), or Successories (2520 Diehl Road, Aurora, IL, 60504; (*www.successories.com*).

Think inside the box if everyone else is thinking outside the box. If you have a title on how to dress for success, office-supply stores might be a good outlet (Staples Inc., 500 Staples Drive, Framingham, MA 01702; (508) 253-5000; *www.staples.com*. You also might consider stores that sell clothes to business executives, such as Burberry (350 Avenue of the Americas, New York, NY, 10019; (212) 246-2570), or Brooks Brothers (346 Madison Avenue, New York, NY, 10017; (212) 682-8800).

Do not limit yourself to brick-and-mortar stores, either. Think online stores, too. If you have educational children's books, why not sell them through Learning Express at *www.learningexpress.com*. If yours is a patriotic topic, sell your products at *www.hngifts.com/huttohammo.com*. If you have a topic related to relationships, money or health for baby boomers, sell it in the Marketplace at BoomerCafe©, *www.boomercafe.com*.

Here are examples that should stimulate your creative juices to come up with more places in which to sell your books. Apply these ideas to a creative session as described in Chapter Two.

If Your Title is About:	Consider Selling it Here:
Pets	Pet stores, veterinarians, aquariums, kennels, companies that sell pet supplies, gift shops, discount stores, book clubs, catalogs
Cooking, Diet	Gourmet shops, dieticians, nutritionists, department stores, supermarkets, cookware stores, Williams-Sonoma, food stores, health food stores, companies whose products could be ingredients in your recipes, food stands, campgrounds, book clubs, catalogs, fish markets, houseware shops
Health, Fashion and Beauty	Drug stores, doctors' offices, airport stores, barber shops, beauty salons, clothing stores, college stores, book clubs, catalogs, fitness centers, gyms, plus-size stores, health food stores
Child Care, Children's Topics	Toy stores, home schooling, day-care centers, nannies, au pairs, children's hospitals, children's museums, zoos, parks, Christmas shops, book clubs, catalogs, companies that produce children's items (apparel, vitamins, toys), maternity shops, school-supply stores, educational stores, novelty stores, libraries, video stores
Travel, Regional Titles, Recreation	RV dealerships, travel agents, airport stores, cruise ships, luggage stores, camera shops, gas stations, book clubs, marinas, catalogs, libraries, hotel gift shops, tourist shops, chambers of commerce, automobile dealerships
Religious, Family Life, Inspirational or Spiritual Topics	Meditation centers, retreats, churches, book clubs, catalogs, church libraries, hospital gift shops, prison libraries, religious stores
Sports, Recreation, Games	Sporting-goods stores, country clubs, pro shops, Little League, stadiums, tennis club, gun shops, book clubs, catalogs, fitness centers, gyms, department stores, hobby shops, toy stores

Dan Poynter offers sage advice for those wanting to increase their sales to specialty shops. He instructs us to "make dealers out of the stores." Give them displays and get them to buy in case quantities. Dan believes publishers should go to the retail stores and ask, "Who is your distributor? Then contact that firm to get it to carry your products, too."

When you contact small retailers, sell to them in terms that are important to them. Describe how your products will increase their profit per square foot. Tell them how your media promotion will stimulate traffic through their store. Prove that you know what their customers want, and that your titles will help increase their overall sales.

"But I do not want to call on all those stores," you say? VendorPro is a company that serves as a wholesale marketing company to help you sell more products without making the contacts. Once you post your products on the VendorPro site, you have the opportunity to sell their products instantly through thousands of retail stores, mail-order catalogs, and web shopping sites.

Every one of your products will have its own page that they create for you. You can post as many products as you like, and you can even upload images. Your products are instantly emailed to purchasing agents who are looking for products just like yours. Find out more about this service at *www.vendorpro.com*.

Strategy # 61: Sell Through Book Clubs

One of the benefits of niche marketing is that it offers you an alternative using the major players in each category. That is certainly true with book clubs, which are seen as the province of major publishers, and subsequently overlooked by independent publishers. Book clubs actually represent a practical means of reaching your target markets. There are book clubs for business titles (*www.sohojobs.org/bookclub.html*) as well as titles in New Age (*www.newageuniversity.org/new_age_book_club.htm*), romance (*romancereport.com/bookclub/*), mystery (*www.mysterythriller.co.uk/*), religious (*www.omnicbc.com/*) and science fiction (*http://www.sfbc.com/*) genres.

Look at book clubs as you would a distributor, helping you reach specific markets more economically than you could yourself. In reality, they sell your books and charge you a percentage of the sale. However, sales to book clubs are made on a nonreturnable basis. And there are number of other advantages to working with book clubs:

1. Acceptance by a book club adds credibility to your title as well as an opportunity to send a new press release. Note the fact on all your

literature that your title is a selection of the book club. Tell producers and editors and you may enhance your chances of getting on a show or having a story written about you. The book club will sing your praises, giving you additional, free exposure.

2. In some cases a book club may help cover part of your printing costs. If the book club purchases while you are preparing for your initial print run, you can order a larger quantity (including the books for your inventory) and your unit production costs will be significantly lower. If they buy copies from your stock, they will generally pay production costs plus a royalty of 10 per cent to 15 per cent.

3. When the clubs send their literature to their members, they are advertising for you. It also builds credibility for your title once a club accepts it.

4. Book club sales typically enhance bookstore sales rather than detract from them.

The royalties you can expect for book-club sales are approximately 10 per cent of the club's list price (which may be 70 per cent off your book's list price). The royalty may be less if your book is used as a premium. A typical advance against royalties offered by the niche book clubs is minimal.

Tim McCormick[34], helped successfully market hundreds of thousands of copies of the title *How to Behave So Your Children Will, Too*. According to Tim, "Book clubs may demand discounts up to 80 – 90%. If they give you an offer, take it. Then figure out how to do it." He goes on to explain, "You're likely to lose money on a book club sale. But fifty thousand people may see your book. That is pretty inexpensive advertising."

When negotiating with book clubs, do not offer a price first. Instead, ask for their standard terms. "I learned that lesson the hard way," Mr. McCormick laments. "I offered one company 80 per cent off and later found out that they only needed 65 per cent."

The term for most book club contracts is two to three years, during which time the book club has the right to distribute the book to its members as they see fit. Generally, the major book club licenses require exclusive book club rights. Most of the niche clubs do not require exclusivity.

Bookspan has many book clubs with catalogs of thousands of titles that have been hand selected by editors in tune with what people like to read. Bookspan focuses its book clubs in four categories: general interest, lifestyles, specialty and professional.

---

34. Greentree Publishing, *www.howtobehave.com*, *greentreepub@earthlink.net*.

The general interest clubs offer fiction and nonfiction books at discount prices. Books and other merchandise offered through general clubs encompass a variety of areas such as diet, exercise, self-help, spirituality, reference, biography, autobiography, cooking, history, and children's books. Clubs include The Book-of-the-Month Club, Doubleday Book Club, Doubleday Large Print, The Literary Guild, Quality Paperback Book Club and Reader's Subscription ("serious books for the serious reader").

The lifestyle clubs include Black Expressions (dedicated to celebrating the voices and visions of African Americans), Children's Book-of-the-Month Club, Country Homes & Gardens, One Spirit (committed to personal growth, wellness and spiritual development), Outdoorsman's Edge.

The specialty clubs offer books and related merchandise specific to certain genres such as mystery, science fiction, individual religious beliefs and practices, hunting and fishing, gardening, romance etc. Examples include Crafter's Choice, Discovery Channel Book Club, Equestrian's Edge, The Good Cook, History Book Club, The Military Book Club, Mystery Guild, Rhapsody and the Science Fiction Book Club.

The professional clubs focus on computer sciences, Mac programs/computers, teaching segments by student age, speech pathology, nursing, antiques, architecture, gardening or specific sciences (astronomy, behavioral, natural, etc.). Clubs in this category are Architects & Designers Book Service, Behavioral Science Book Service, Computer Books Direct, Early Childhood Teachers Club, Library of Science, Library of Speech-Language Pathology, Nurse's Book Society and the Primary Teacher's Book Club.

Author Eric Gelb has some advice for publishers seeking book-club sales. Eric says, "Join the book clubs and catalogs in your genre. These outlets continually seek new product. When you can, make a purchase, even a small one; this tactic will upgrade you on the mailing lists and when the list manager sells your name, other catalogs will arrive in your mailbox (you may want to get a post office box). Several years ago, the now defunct Money Book Club (AOL Time Warner) featured my *Personal Budget Planner* and *Checkbook Management* as a joint alternate selection for over two years. That was a huge win. Most catalogs feature a telephone number, Internet address, and sometimes the editor's name. Locate the acquisition editor and pitch your offering."

When submitting books to various book clubs for consideration, it is best to contact them six months before your title's publication date. Call first to find out their submission guidelines. Review their website and look for competitive books and examples of the copy they use to describe the books. Provide the book-club buyers with a sample of the selling copy you think would be most effective in presenting your book favorably.

■■■ Strategy # 62: Get Reviews

People read magazines and newspapers to learn more about subjects of interest to them. It is expensive to advertise in all these, but you can still reach the readers through book reviews. Reviews in these publications are free, and they give the message more credibility because it is an objective source saying how great (or not-so-great) the title is. Reviews also stimulate word-of-mouth advertising, another source of credible—and free—promotion.

Most publishers seek reviews of their titles among the major reviewers, which is not a bad idea if you are selling through bookstores. Those media receive many entreaties for reviews, and the competition is stiff. An exhaustive list of reviewers, organized by category, can be found at *www.bookmarketing.com/reviewers/*. Jim Cox at Midwest Book Review has consistently been a good source of reviews for independent publishers. Contact Jim at *www.midwestbookreview.com/*.

Instead of, or in addition to, sending your review copies to the major book-review media, send them to other sources of reviews. These can be more likely to reach your target audiences.

It is not always best to submit your review copies to the book-review editor of a newspaper or magazine. Instead, send it to the section editor (for sports, travel, leisure, etc). These people receive far fewer books and may be more likely to write a review. They may even publish a more complete article about the author and his or her title.

There are book reviewers online seeking titles to review for fiction and nonfiction work. For

Sending Review Copies
Send to every niche newspaper, newsletter, e-zine, specialty shop and magazine of relevance.
Send a fact sheet with each submission (Author, publisher, ISBN, price, sales outlets, contact information).
Send news releases to broadcast media.
Be persistent and always follow up.
Personalize each submission.
Time your submission with special sections/theme issues of media.
Print the flag *Unedited Advance Copy* on the cover of review copies (or, print stickers with the same message).
Send advance galley copies to niche reviewers (three to four months before publication date).

example, *The Mystery Reader* reviews thrillers, suspense and historical mystery novels. And there are sites that post reviews of books on science fiction, romance, business, religion, sports and many other topics. Submit your titles to those reaching your niche markets.

Niche magazines are often overlooked as sources of reviews. There are magazines that review books for people interested in subjects as diverse as stay-at-home dads, minority executives, home schooling, skydiving, health, celebrities, fiction and an almost endless array of topics. *The Journal of Communication* publishes articles and book reviews on a broad range of issues in communication theory, research, practice and policy. *Astronomy & Astrophysics Annual* publishes annual reviews of scholarly research in the fields of astronomy & astrophysics.

The library market places ...... ence on reviews. In addition to book revi ...... rary news, online librarianship, collect ...... s. *Choice* magazine reviews books for hig ...... aries. Submit your books to Choice, Edit ...... er, Middletown, CT 06457; (860) 347-69 ...... *a.org/acrl/choice/home.html.* *submissions@*

Do not ig ...... source of reviews, either. There are mai .... television stations with shows devoted to alerting their audiences to the latest books of possible interest. The Christian Television Network even has online shopping. Find it at 15565 Northland Drive, Suite 900W, Southfield, MI 48075; (248) 559-4200; *www.ctnusa.org/.*

Poets of the Tabloid Murder conducts weekly interviews with mystery writers, every Tuesday at 5 pm Eastern Time. Broadcast from the University of Connecticut at Storrs, on WHUS 91.7 FM and webcast via Real Audio; contact WHUS at 2110 Hillside Rd, Unit 3008, Storrs CT 06269-3008 Phone: (860) 486-2958, Fax: (860) 486-2955. *www.whus.org.*

BookCrazy Radio has programs featuring author interviews with live broadcasts, Saturdays at 12:00 noon on KCTK 960 AM, Phoenix, Arizona. Broadcasts are also available on the website via streaming audio; contact the producers at 2601 E Bell Road #14, Phoenix AZ 85032, (602) 508-0960, (888) 960-9696. *www.bookcrazy.net, iambookcrazy@aol.com.*

Even though review copies can be expensive, do not be miserly about sending them. Be selective, but send your material to as many prospective niche reviewers as possible. The results could generate broad exposure, awareness and sales in your niche markets.

Strategy # 63: Enjoy Back-of-the-Room Sales after Speaking Engagements

If you are proficient at speaking before groups, you can sell your products at list price following your presentations. This is called back-of-the-room selling and can be very profitable. Companies hiring you as a speaker will often purchase your books, tapes or booklets in advance for each attendee. And superior speaking skills make your library tours more effective, as Jerry Labriola described in Chapter Eleven.

You may feel that your product line is not complete enough to stimulate sales in quantities sufficient to make this process worthwhile. In that case, look into INTI Publishing's Mentor Study Program. INTI Publishing is a personal development company that can provide you with a customized subscription program that you can offer your audience. For more information go to *www.intipub.com/mentor_study_programs.html* or call INTI at (813) 881-1638.

You can still make money from back-of-the-room sales even if you abhor public speaking by having other speakers sell your products for you. Professional speakers earn their living making presentations to groups of people, but their speaking fees are only part of the income they receive from each engagement. The other part comes from selling books and tapes after their presentations. Although many have their own products to sell at the back of the room, many do not. Contact speakers who are knowledgeable on your topic to see if they would be willing to sell your titles for a percentage of the sale. Locate speakers in a chapter of the National Speakers Association nearest you by visiting *www.nsaspeaker.org/search/chapter_directory.xpl*.

Strategy # 64: Conduct Author Events

An author does not have to be a media performer or professional speaker to conduct promotional events. Nor does he or she have to suffer through a lonely booksigning at a bookstore. Authors can hold events that dwell on their topic of interest, such as demonstrations, workshops, readings or in-home parties, with product sales occurring as a result of imparting important information.

Have fun while conducting business at these events. Jehan Clements (*www.storytellercompany.com*) is a storyteller, musician, author/illustrator, and inventor. He does not simply *read* his two children's books, *Alfred the Ant* and *The Banana That Ate New York* in schools, he *performs* them. He dresses as Alfred and the infamous banana, turning the tales into humorous environmental stories. While performing for the children, "I demonstrate my invention to the teachers. It is my very own, do it yourself *Storytelling Flip-Over Picture Book*." This device allows the teacher to keep the illustrations in full view of the children while maintaining unobstructed access to the words.

John Harnish[35] recounts another example of an author event. "Jane M. Martin's, *Breathe Better, Live in Wellness: Winning Your Battle over Shortness of Breath*, (Infinity Publishing, 2003) is a print-on-demand (POD) published title that was written to help improve the quality of life for people suffering with some form of chronic lung disease. Instead of doing a traditional reading at a bookstore, Mrs. Martin, a certified Respiratory Therapist, conducted in-services for the patients and staff of the Martha Jefferson Wellness Center, Charlottesville, Virginia. It would have been physically challenging for some of the pulmonary patients to go into a bookstore, so Jane took her book directly to its target audience at the patient-friendly wellness center."

▰ Strategy # 65: Participate in Award Competitions

The winner of an award competition can benefit in many ways, including increased sales, greater recognition, help in selling subsidiary rights and perhaps even a cash reward. There are myriad such contests ranging from the Pulitzer Prize to those of lesser notoriety. PMA's Benjamin Franklin Award has become prestigious among independent publishers. There are awards for children's titles, romance books, cookbooks, westerns and mysteries.

Participants in award competitions gain added prestige in their genre, often leading to greater sales. Enter as many as are appropriate, especially in all your niche markets. Include on all your literature and correspondence the notice that the title is an award-winning work, or one nominated as a title recognized for its quality of writing or design.

Author Ron Clark, a sixth-grade teacher in East Harlem, New York, was chosen to become Disney's Teacher of the Year. Armed with that recognition, and knowledge that people are more concerned about education than ever before, he wrote *The Essential 55* (Hyperion, April 2003). His plain spoken emphasis on teaching children basic social skills, plus a mention on *Oprah* and NPR, led him to a # 2 spot on Amazon.com and a #3 position on the *Publishers Weekly* nonfiction bestseller list after its first week on sale.

---

35. Author of *Everything You Always Wanted To Know About Print-On-Demand Publishing But Didn't Know Who To Ask*.

Strategy # 66: Sell Through Mail Order Catalogs

Many of the benefits of selling to book clubs accrue to selling through catalogs. They can sell a lot of books for you, but they exact a fee for doing so, sometimes as much as an 80 per cent discount. However, the exposure catalogs give your books to all their customers will often result in spillover sales through book stores. The catalogs deliver your book cover to thousands—or tens of thousands—of potential buyers. This gives you additional hits on people in your target markets.

There are over 10,000 printed catalogs in existence and there are thousands more on the Internet. Many of these are niche catalogs sought by groups of people potentially interested in your topic.

Just as you think of book clubs as distributors, think of catalogs as an extension of your direct marketing capability. They create a sales brochure in the form of a catalog and mail it to a targeted list of addressees. Once these recipients become loyal customers, they buy repeatedly from the catalog company. This enhances your credibility as well as your sales. Catalogs rarely require an exclusive and most pay in 30 days. Sales are generally non-returnable and the catalog company usually pays for shipping. When you think of the services they perform for you, their discount structure seems easier to endure.

Catalogs that specialize in selling books are little different from bookstores. The competition is too intense for your title to stand out. Instead, seek specialty catalogs that sell complementary products. Here, your book becomes an accessory item. As Dan Poynter says, "I do not sell a book about parachuting, but a parachute accessory." This strategy removes your title from the *book* category and places it in a *specialty* category, commanding a higher price.

You will have little difficulty finding a catalog that suits your product line. For example, if you go to *www.catalogsite.catalogcity.com/* and select a subcategory for beauty, you will be given these choices: 256 catalogs for bath and body gift sets, 815 for bath and shower supplies, 282 for body art, 2,410 for cosmetics, 2,917 for fragrances and perfumes, 611 for grooming aids, 1498 for hair care, 390 for hair removal and bleaching, 266 for nail care and hundreds of other catalogs from which to choose. You can find an even larger selection of catalogs at *www.catalogs.google.com.*

The *Directory of Mail Order Catalogs 2003 Edition* contains over eleven thousand mail order companies selling consumer products throughout the United States. The directory indexes catalogs by geography, catalog, product line and company name. Find this at *www.namoa.org/catalog/*. Other online sources of catalogs include *www.buyersindex.com/* and *www.cataloglink.com*. LTD Commodities is a business-to-business mail order catalog company and does not solicit residential customers. LTD is located at 2800 Lakeside Drive, Bannockburn, IL 60015; (847) 295-6058, Fax: (847) 604-7600; *www.ltdcommodities.com*.

If you have a product that might sell in Canada, search the Catalogue of Canadian Catalogues published by Alpel Publishing, P.O. Box 203, Chambly, Quebec, Canada J3L 4B3 (450) 658- 6205; *www.mailordercanada.com* *alpel@videotron.ca*.

Tom Woll[36] describes the steps in selling to catalogs as, "Start early, target, send material, follow up and negotiate." Before selling to catalogs, become familiar with those reaching your target markets by calling to request a copy. At the same time, request a sample of their submission guidelines and forms. Then when you contact them you can relate your product to the other items offered in the catalog, according to their procedures. Follow up persistently and professionally.

Send each prospect a proposal when they are in the decision-making period for the products that will be included in the catalog. If it is a catalog of gift ideas for the fourth-quarter holiday season, the choices are made in the first quarter of the year.

Your submission should include a cover letter and a data sheet with all the details about your book, from its shipping weight and size to its major features and benefits. If their guidelines require a sample book at this stage, include it with your package. Otherwise, follow up a few weeks later on the telephone and send a sample if requested.

Cover design is particularly important in catalog sales. "When reduced to a size of about one square inch, it must be clear and legible," Mr. Woll affirms. Small or script type is not always readable under these conditions, and a good title may be rejected for that reason.

There is no standard discount among catalogs, so you have some negotiating flexibility. Make a counter proposal if you feel the discount offered is unfair. However, they will probably require a discount greater than 60 per cent because they can sell a large quantity of product.

Do not expect a large order immediately since most catalog companies will do a smaller-scale test first. The term *smaller-scale* is relative because a test may move five hundred or more copies of your product. The time period in which this occurs varies with the frequency of the catalog's publication (some publish monthly, others quarterly) and the applicability

---

36. Cross River Publishing Consultants, *twoll@aol.com*.

of your product to the buying period and complementary products.

Catalogs may fear that a small publisher cannot stock to their demand. According to Tom Woll, "You may be required to hold inventory sufficient to meet their expected sales. You may also have to guarantee your price for the period of your contract." Offer them proof that you will do so, or that you can reprint and deliver within a suitable time. If you cannot meet their requirements you may have to reconsider using catalogs as a selling tool.

BE CREATIVE

Buyers at the Lillian Vernon catalog company sought a licensing deal for Paulette Ensign's booklet *110 Ideas for Organizing Your Business Life*. They purchased over 250,000 copies of the booklet to use as a premium to reward purchases. They tracked a 13 per cent increase in sales related directly to the premium offer.

"Selling fiction to catalogs is more difficult than selling nonfiction," says Mr. Woll. But it can be done. Souvenir Press sold over five thousand copies of cartoonist Ronald Searle's book, *Wine Speak* through U.S. catalogs. Tom continues with, "You can sell fiction to catalogs if you tie the theme of your novel in to the theme of the catalog." If your story focuses on gardening, for example, you might sell it to White Flower Farm (*www.whiteflowerfarm.com*) to sell in their catalog or to use as a premium for ordering.

Most catalogs present their items in enticing displays. If they will not sell your book in their catalog, why not include it as background in one of the presentations? If your title is about gourmet foods, the exposure would be enormous in a catalog such as Harry and David (*www.harryanddavid.com*). If they receive many inquiries about purchasing your book, they may later add it to their product offering.

■ Strategy # 67: Use Free Webrings to Target Your Markets

According to Hajni Blasko[37], "A Webring is a community of Websites united by a common interest and organized into a circular *ring* of mutual links. Webrings permit you to go from site to site, traveling the entire Webring. Links also permit you to access the list of member sites and to join the Webring. This type of promotional exposure is *tar-*

---

37. Hajni Blasko is a web promoter at Substance Books, *www.substancebooks.com*.

geted marketing since you will introduce yourself to a group of people already focused and interested in the subject matter of your book or services. Webrings will bring you traffic from your listing on the HUB page (homepage of the ring) and bring you traffic from the *ring flow.* "All Webring providers feature a directory on their sites. These directories are well constructed and easy-to-navigate pools of sites around the same subject matter. You can search around the directories to locate Webrings of interest by 1) date created, 2) size (number of member sites), 3) alphabetical order, or by 4) popularity (number of visits). Your book's short description and a well functioning link to your site placed on a popular Webring's HUB page is a winning promotional tool.

"All Webrings have a specific banner-sized navigation bar created by the ringmaster. This navigation bar connects the sites of the ring by creating a virtual doorway between them. If your site doesn't include this navigation code (SSNB), the flow of traffic will be shut down and your ring will be as functional as a dead-end highway."

Strategy # 68: Hints for Selling to Niche Markets

Richard Harris, President, New Mexico Book Association (*www.nmbook.org*), relates this story about the wisdom of niche marketing:

Nearly twenty years ago, a psychotherapist wrote a book about pregnancy and birth—from the father's point of view. A major East Coast publisher published it, and it sold steadily for a number of years, until the publisher went out of business. The author bought the four hundred copies in stock at remainder prices and sold them at workshops, raising enough money to self-publish a new edition of the book.

Working with me and a team of professionals including an editor, a designer, a graphic artist and a photographer, he put together an expanded and more attractive edition, lined up publicity and distribution services, and sold out two print runs in his first year.

Feeling the urge to get back to writing, he decided to place the book with a real publisher. A well-known East Coast media conglomerate offered him an impressive advance, apparently figuring that if he could sell more than ten thousand copies of the book on his own, they should certainly be able to sell many more.

The publisher put out a beautifully designed and illustrated hardcover edition. But it totally bombed, selling only a few hundred copies. In the end, the author took the rights to the book back (again), self-published it (again) and got it back on the market. It has been selling just fine ever since.

His secret? He does his major distribution through sales reps that wholesale product lines to maternity shops—where no big publisher's sales rep has ever set foot.

The reality is that of all the customers who visit a Borders or Barnes & Noble store on any given day, it's unlikely that even one is looking for a book on expectant fathers. But just about every customer who walks into a maternity shop knows that her husband should read this book. And unlike bookstores, maternity shops will carry the book for years to come.

Author Eric Gelb offers another niche-marketing suggestion: "Search out magazines for marketing opportunities." He continues, "Some magazines sell books, which can be another terrific outlet for you. Many magazines use unsold ad space for book clubs, book catalogs and to sell books that relate to articles they feature in that issue. We have sold copies of our books to numerous publications including *Ladies' Home Journal*, *Success magazine*, and *The Crafts Report*. Study the masthead and contact the publication by telephone to verify the person's contact points. When you can, speak to the editor or marketing director directly to pitch your idea. Then follow up with a letter and sales kit."

Additional Hints for Selling to Niche Markets

1. Make it easy for people to buy from you and to then sell your books. Provide the business proprietors with free countertop displays with the purchase of a minimum quantity. Include instructions for reordering your books to refill the displays.
2. Give the retailers ideas for cross selling, such as suggesting that they place your barbecue cookbook near the display of outdoor grills.
3. Contact the department buyers in large stores rather than the people purchasing general store items. The buyer for cookware may be amenable to purchasing your cookbook when others may not see its value.
4. Research each niche to learn the idiosyncrasies, discounts, terms and distribution methods of marketing to each. How do you find this information? Go to a nearby store that is appropriate to your title and speak to the manager. Ask him or her for insight on how to sell to the industry. Then follow up on the leads you are given.

Read magazines and attend trade shows to learn about the industry, and to network with and contact the exhibitors and attendees. For example, if your title is on a topic associated with music, you might attend the American Music Therapy Association Conference (AMTA) (*www.musictherapy.org*), the Music Industries Association of Canada (MIAC) Annual Conference and Trade Show (*www.miac.com*), and subscribe to *DJ Times* magazine (*www.djtimes.com*). You can find trade shows and magazines devoted to almost any topic on which books are published.

5. Be willing to customize your products (cover and content) for an industry or customer if the quantity ordered makes it worthwhile. Some stores may want a special size to fit their shelves or existing display racks. Other may prefer a hard- or softcover book. Sell people books they want to buy.

6. Sell benefits. Prove to them that your titles can help them improve their store traffic, profits or provide some advantage that is important to *them.* Demonstrate that you have successfully sold your books through similar outlets, if that is the case.

7. Generally you will sell to niche markets on a nonreturnable basis.

Strategy # 69: Consider Dual Distribution

At this point you may assume that you must choose between implementing a Special Distribution network or a strategy of selling directly in Commercial Sales or niche markets. Or, you may be thinking about ignoring the traditional segment. A better strategy is to find the optimum combination of bookstore and non-bookstore marketing that will maximize your sales and profits for each title.

You do not have to—nor should you—choose between traditional and special-sales marketing. In most cases, some combination of the two will optimize your profitability. The key is to choose the best marketing strategy for each title and market.

	Traditional Distribution	Special Distribution	Direct Distribution
Title A	•	•	•
Title B		•	•
Title C	•		

Title D	•	•	

The impact of your marketing decisions on your net revenue is demonstrated below. This example illustrates how changes in your distribution system impact net revenue. In this case, the title is priced at $14.95 with 1,000 books printed. The Cost of Good Sold (COGS) is $4,500, for editing, cover design, layout and printing.

In the first exhibit all one thousand books are sold to bookstores through a distributor charging a fee of 65 per cent of sales. The net revenue of $732 is determined by deducting the COGS and the distribution discount from the total revenue.

Marketing to Bookstores Only							
	List price	Quantity Sold	Revenue	COGS	Distributor's Percentage	Distribution Deduction	Net Revenue
Traditional	$14.95	1,000	$14,950	$4,500	65%	$9,718	$732

How would your net revenue be affected by a change in distribution? The chart below shows the increase in net revenue if you sold these same books (with a promotional discount of 20 per cent) directly to niche markets. If this were the case, you could make ten times the net revenue, or $7,460.

Marketing to Bookstores Only							
	List price	Quantity Sold	Revenue	COGS	Distributor's Percentage	Distribution Deduction	Net Revenue
Traditional	$14.95	1,000	$14,950	$4,500	20%	$2,990	$7,460

Many things that seem too good to be true are too good to be true, and this is one of them. If you decide to forego bookstore marketing and concentrate in special sales, the onus is upon you to perform all the services otherwise performed by your distributor. The costs for carrying inventory, shipping and handling and selling are now deducted from your revenue. Your investment in money, time and labor increases, and these costs reduce your profitability. You must decide if you have the time and skill to make that investment.

> Much of our American progress has been the product of the individual who had an idea, pursued it, fashioned it, tenaciously clung to it against all odds; and then produced it, sold it, and profited from it.
> HUBERT H. HUMPHREY

One answer to this dilemma is to combine traditional and nontraditional distribution to optimize your profitability. With an assorted distribution strategy you could sell some books through bookstores while focusing more of your efforts in the non-bookstore segment. The table below demonstrates that your total net revenue would be less than that shown above, but this may better suit your budget, skills and time constraints.

Marketing to Bookstores and Special-Sales Markets							
	List price	Quantity Sold	Revenue	COGS	Distributor's Percentage	Distribution Deduction	Net Revenue
Traditional	$14.95	500	$7,475	$2,250	65%	$4,859	$366
Special Sales	$14.95	500	$7,475	$2,250	20%	$1,495	$3,730
Total		1,000	$14,950	$4,500		$6,354	$4,096

A template to help you plan the best combination of dual distribution for your circumstances is included in the Distribution Profitability Calculator found in *The Marketing Planning* CD-ROM. Use it to experiment with different combinations and percentages to help you decide the best one for your circumstances.

> When you sell a man a book you do not sell him just twelve ounces of paper and ink and glue you sell him a whole new life.
> CHRISTOPHER MORLEY, *U.S. novelist, journalist*

14

How to Contact
Prospective Buyers

A N INTERESTING DILEMMA in the book-selling world is that the author must get involved in the sales process, but most authors do not like to sell. They want only to write and leave the marketing up to the publisher. Of course, some authors want to get involved, and they are welcome to do that to their heart's content. And there are ways to involve reluctant authors by using them where their presence is needed in a minimally threatening way.

Therein lies the twofold beauty of special-sales marketing. First, authors can sell by using the communication technique with which they feel most comfortable and experienced. This may entail networking at business or social events, calling potential buyers, writing or e-mailing them, or talking with them personally in their offices or at trade shows. As the publisher, you may have an in-house person or staff to do the selling, in which case the following sales techniques still apply.

The second point is that you do not need to know all the selling skills of handling objections and closing the sale. All it takes is a thorough knowledge of your products and the needs of your prospective customers. Since you already know and believe in your titles, and after applying the information from the last few chapters you know your prospects. Now you need only to transfer your passion to the solution of your prospects needs, so both parties reach their objectives. This occurs in four steps, and they apply in personal selling or when using mass communications.

STEP ONE: Prioritize. Did you ever try to get a job? If so, you did not call on every company in the country (although it may have seemed like you did at the time) because not every one could satisfy your criteria. So you probably narrowed down your list of potential employers according to their ability to meet your needs of geography, price and job content. Then you sent a cover letter and resume to each of them in hopes of arranging a personal interview.

The same process applies to selling books. There are over 7,000,000 million business entities in the United States, and it would take more time and money than you have to contact them all. Besides, it wouldn't make sense to even try because most have no need for your products. But it does make sense to find out which ones could use your content and call upon them. Use the strategies described in Chapter Eight as well as the *Fastart*™ Checklist in Appendix B to prioritize your suspects into a qualified list of prospects.

STEP TWO: Network. Large sales are based on trust. People like to buy from people they know. It gives them a sense of security and a feeling that they will not be ill treated. If you can get referred to a potential buyer by someone he or she already knows, you begin with an element of reliability. A proven way to make that connection is through networking, or establishing relationships in a nonthreatening atmosphere.

Much of this ground-laying work can be accomplished in the Author Questionnaire, where authors are usually asked for names of people they know. There may be potential customers among previous schoolmates, former or current employers, club or association memberships or from other personal sources. Some of these people may be prospects, or could lead you to a product manager or buyer in a target company, a museum curator or gift-shop owner.

Strategy # 70: Improve Your Networking Skills

Right now you are, at most, five contacts away from anyone you might want to reach, whether it is a buyer at Wal-Mart or the curator of a national museum. A key to building a successful special-sales business is to learn the name of the first of those five people. Do that by networking with people, finding out whom they know and how they can help you. Each contact brings you one step closer to your ultimate objective.

Networking helps you build a file of names. Then when the need arises, you have a ready list of people who can serve as sources of information and sales. The more contacts you have, and the broader their spheres of influence, the more likely you are to acquire the right information when you need it.

WHERE TO MAKE CONTACT

> ### The Networker's Oath
>
> Regardless of where you network, there are several rules to which you must adhere if you expect to create a list of beneficial contacts:
>
> **Be creative.** People offer information from their own perspective. Learn to analyze and manipulate their feedback to address your particular circumstances. Frequently ask "What if..." questions.
>
> **Be positive.** Use networking meetings to discuss opportunities, not problems. Accept help graciously, criticism constructively and rejection in stride.
>
> **Be prepared.** Before attending a trade show, make a list of the people you want to reach and their booth numbers. Arrange appointments beforehand and carry a large supply of business cards.
>
> **Be reciprocal.** Networking is more effective if it is not one-sided. Willingly share any (nonconfidential) information you have that might be helpful to others.
>
> **Be resourceful.** Look for networking opportunities everywhere, such as on airplanes, at your gym or even online.
>
> **Be respectful.** If you call people, make sure it is a convenient time for them to talk.
>
> **Be thorough.** Keep records of all your contacts in a form that is easy for you to use. This could be on index cards, in a loose-leaf binder or on your computer.

Begin by narrowing down the total number of possible contacts to those most likely to help you. For example, if you are looking for marketing assistance, associate with people who have that knowledge by joining PMA or a nearby group of publishers.

In addition, trade shows provide fertile ground for making helpful contacts and renewing old relationships. Attend the ALA, BEA and other major events, but do not ignore regional and local bookseller shows (see Strategy #10 for a list). Register for seminars and workshops. Join listserves to increase your visibility among your colleagues. Go where your fellow publishers congregate, and you will see your network of contacts grow quickly.

HOW TO MAKE CONTACTS

Most networking is informal and may be conducted at business or social gatherings. Other events are planned, structured meetings that go through a typical series of stages.

1. Introduction. The extent of this phase depends on the level of familiarity you have with the person. Mention who referred you in order to create rapport.
2. Present a one-minute summary. Provide an adequate frame of reference so the individual knows the context in which to give his or her recommendations.
3. Keep the conversation moving. Ask pertinent questions, listen responsively and take notes.
4. Summarize and close. Once you have all the data you need, summarize the main points and list the names of the people you wish contact. Be sure to ask whether or not you may use your networker as a reference.
5. Send a thank-you note. Send your contacts thank-you notes and let them know if their referrals were productive.

Your networking will be productive if you use common sense and courtesy. Do not interrogate people, but conduct a friendly conversation for a mutually beneficial exchange of information. Your objective is to obtain information and referrals. Network consistently and soon you will find the person who will lead you to your goal.

STEP THREE: Establish buying criteria. A recurring theme throughout *Beyond the Bookstore* is that people buy for their reasons, not yours. Your sale will come more easily if you find out what those reasons are before you start describing what you have to sell. Try to determine these criteria during your networking meetings or research.

If you cannot determine the buyer's hot buttons beforehand, begin each meeting by asking questions that bring them to the surface. Selling is basically a question-and-answer process to find out what and why the prospect wants to buy. For example, you may try to sell your 6" x 9" book on dieting. Even though the prospect likes its content, he or she may think a book is too large for the store. You will lose the sale if you persist in pushing your book. A successful dialogue might go like this:

PROSPECT: That is great information, but I was looking for something smaller that I might use as a premium.

YOU: If this information were available as a booklet, would you be interested in buying it?

PROSPECT: Yes. Sales are down this month and that would be more likely to fit my budget. A booklet would help my customers learn…

Now you know that the buyer likes your content, cost is important, the buyer wants to use a premium to inform the customers about something so that sales will increase, he or she does not want a book, and you have a verbal commitment to buy your booklets. It is no longer a question of *if* the sale is made, but what size the booklets should be and how many should you print. An added benefit to you is that you now have another product to sell to similar prospects.

Learn, then earn. Find out why each prospect wants to buy and then describe how your products will help them. You will earn more by getting people to buy then you will by trying to sell.

STEP FOUR: CUSTOMIZE AND MAKE YOUR PRESENTATION.
Did you ever watch golfers look through the assortment of clubs in their bags seeking just the right one for each particular situation? Think of your title's benefits as individual clubs, each to be brandished as circumstances warrant. When your prospects tell you what they want to buy, pull out that club and describe what is important to them. Do not use a driver when a putter is the better choice.

Customize your presentation in personal or mass communication. It is easier to do when face to face because you can choose the right "club" for each person. In mass communication, such as a direct-mail campaign, you should choose the benefit that is most likely to appeal to the largest number of recipients.

Strategy # 71: Create Direct-Mail Campaigns

Direct mail has been given a bad reputation because of overuse, misleading offers and poorly designed mailing pieces. Unfortunately, people perceive all direct mail as *junk* mail, and its Internet equivalent as *spam*.

In reality, direct mail is a targeted marketing weapon that that can help you sell more products, test new titles, generate sales leads, or communicate the benefits of your products. When you have a finite, identifiable group of people who are potential customers for your books, direct mail may be the most effective and efficient marketing tool you can use to reach them. It gives you control of the timing, delivery and content of your promotion, a predetermined fixed cost and the means to forecast and measure the return on your marketing investment. *The Marketing Planning* CD-ROM has a tool to help you calculate and control your direct mail costs and break-even point.

Unfortunately, direct marketing is too often implemented by simply purchasing a mailing list and then sending an existing brochure to the people on it. Unless you first prepare a tactical plan, including a way to evaluate your relative success, you will probably end up wasting money and becoming disillusioned in the potential effectiveness of a strategic direct-mail campaign.

Your plan can be a simple document that describes the benefits of your title to a particular market niche and the proposition you will offer to entice people to purchase your books. It should outline the actions you intend to take in six key areas. These areas are 1) the books/products you offer, 2) the target market, 3) the special offer you are proposing, 4) the format you present 5) the ways in which you test and 6) how you evaluate your implementation.

1. **The product.** Is your product one that can be sold successfully with direct marketing? Before you decide, ask yourself several questions. First, is it a real value for the price you are asking? If you are trying to deplete your inventory of overpriced books simply by offering a reduced price via direct mail, you may be disappointed. Instead, think about your titles from the recipients' perspectives. Is the point of difference important to them? Does the cover design create a good first impression?

   Continue your checklist by evaluating the titles you will include in the package. Can your potential customers buy something more current and less expensive from your competitors? If you are bundling several titles, how will you package them? What is the shipping cost? Will that cost be passed on to the buyer or be included in your price? Will the title's cost structure support the discount you intend to offer? The more value your product has for your prospects, the less significant its price becomes.

2. **The target market.** There are two general groups of people to whom you could mail your package: customers and prospects. In either case, if you mail to an outdated list, your results will be unsatisfactory. When mailing to existing customers, make sure your list is cleaned (obsolete names removed) regularly.

   Organize your list of customers according to their purchasing history. Those who normally purchase one portion of your titles may be interested in the remainder of your line if they had a pleasant experience dealing with you in the past. In that case, they may be open to working with you to create new product forms, too.

Segment your customer list by those who have purchased recently, those who purchase frequently and by the dollar value of their orders. Each group could be receptive to different repurchase incentives. You might inquire of those who have not purchased for a long time to find out why.

If you intend to mail to prospective customers, you may have to buy a list. Before doing so, make sure the list has been cleaned recently. Not all mailing lists are created equally. Some contain recipients by name, others by title.

When you purchase a list, it is usually for onetime use. Do not attempt to use it twice, since most are seeded with the name and address of people who monitor how many letters they receive from you. If they receive multiple mailings from you, you can be charged for another use of the list and perhaps excluded from buying it again.

3. **The offer.** By now, you should not be surprised to learn that the most important part of your direct-mail package is not your book, but the value that surrounds it. There are several basic propositions you can use by themselves or in various combinations, depending on your objectives to communicate that value.

  1. **Free information.** This is often the most effective offer, particularly when your objective is to generate leads for future business. Tell people that when they send for a copy of your book they will also receive a special report or booklet with free, useful information. You can also direct people to your web site for answers to frequently asked questions.

  2. **Samples.** If you are selling booklets or other low-cost items, a sample will show people the level of information and quality they may expect when purchasing from you. Perhaps making an excerpt available on your web site will accomplish the same result for your books. Or if you are selling inexpensive accessories or supplies, free samples represent a continuous reminder of your product offering.

  3. **Conditional sale.** If you are selling a subscription to your newsletter, or perhaps a continuity book program, you could increase the possibility of long-term acceptance based on a sample. For instance, you would offer the premier issue of your newsletter

for free if the prospect agrees to a one-year subscription.

4. **Yes-No.** This is an involvement proposition where the prospect is asked to respond by indicating whether he or she accepts or rejects your offer. Historically, more favorable responses are received from making a choice then when no rejection option is provided.

5. **Time limit.** Setting a time limit on a given offer forces action, either positive or negative. Usually it is more effective to name a specific date rather than a time period. Allow enough time for deliberation, but not so much as to cause inertia.

6. **Discounts.** A discount is a popular lure and is particularly effective where the value of your book is well established. Three types of discounts are typically offered: for cash, for an introductory order or for volume purchases. Providing free shipping could be considered a discount if the customer is used to paying for freight.

   Not only is the discount itself a key to success or failure, but also the manner in which it is presented can have an equally dramatic effect. For example, below are three ways to state the same proposition. Which of these do you think would be most effective?

   1. Half price!
   2. Buy one—get one free!
   3. 50% Off!

   The one most likely to draw a higher response is Number 2 because of the power of the word *free*.

7. **Negative option.** This offer prearranges for shipment if the customer does not cancel it by mailing a rejection form prior to the deadline.

8. **Positive option.** In this case, every shipment is based on a direct positive action by the customer. Front-end response is likely to be lower, but long-term sales are likely to be greater.

9. **Load-up.** This is a favorite of publishers of continuity series. For example, you would offer a set of twelve books, one to be released each month. After the customer has received and paid for the first three books you would invite him or her to receive the remaining nine all in one shipment with the understanding that payments may continue to be made monthly. This invariably results in more complete sets of books being sold.

10. **Free gift.** For best results, test several gifts to determine the one most appealing to the target audience. The most important criterion for gift selection is 1) appropriateness of the gift, 2) its effect on repeat business and 3) net profit per thousand including the cost of the gift. Create a booklet that could serve as the gift.

11. **Secret gift.** If the prospective customer completes all the information on the reply card or order form he or she will receive an extra free, unnamed gift.

12. **Advance payment.** If you want the customer to order with a credit card or to send a check with the order you could offer an incentive for doing so. This might be a special report or free gift.

13. **Add-on offers.** If you want your prospects to call you, tell them to ask for your *special offer* when they speak to your sales person. A variation of this might direct more traffic to your web site.

14. **Deluxe alternatives.** Give the customer a choice between your perfect-bound book and your special leather-bound edition. An autographed copy could be considered a deluxe alternative, too.

15. **Offer a guarantee.** The words *satisfaction guaranteed* are at the heart of all mail order selling. If you include a buy-back option it becomes even more effective.

16. **Bounce-backs.** This offer succeeds on the premise that the best time to sell people is right after you have sold them. Forms offering more of the same item, related books or items totally different from that originally purchased are included in shipments or with the invoices.

17. **Optional terms.** Here, the objective is to give the prospect the option of choosing terms at varying rates. The bigger the commitment the better the bargain.

4. **The format.** The standard format for direct mail is a three-piece package consisting of a cover letter describing the offer, a brochure and a reply mechanism. However, you can create many variations of this traditional package. Before you get too creative, make sure your piece is in character with the image of your publishing firm and the titles offered.

Many mail envelopes have a teaser written on them to get the recipient to open it. While this can be an effective strategy, do not demean the envelope with unnecessary clip art that could distort the impression you want to make. When in doubt, remember the KISS principle: Keep It Straightforward and Simple. Make your letter informative and persuasive, your flyer attractive and descriptive and your reply mechanism complete and easy to use.

Your direct-mail pieces in general will be more productive if you customize the letter and flyer to the needs of the target audience. Niche markets are defined and organized around a common interest in your subject. Write the copy to connect the benefits of your product with the needs of the recipients (see Strategy #74 for more information on creating effective literature, and Appendix D for a suggested layout template).

5. **The test.** Before you embark on a one-hundred-thousand-piece nationwide mailing, test on a smaller scale your choice of titles, the list you will use, the offer you will make and different formats you plan to use. Also test the timing of your mailing and alternative geographic areas. Invariably you will learn ways to fine-tune the four key areas listed above and more accurately forecast the results you can expect on the larger mailing.

6. **Evaluation.** Before you conduct your direct-mail campaign, decide if it will be profitable for you. *The Marketing Planning* CD-ROM will calculate the break-even point. Typically, mail campaigns for low-priced titles are les likely to be profitable than those for bundled titles or products. After the campaign, analyze your profitability. You could expect a mailing to draw a response rate of 1–2 per cent of the total number of recipients. Did you reach or exceed that level? Why or why not?

Strategy # 72: Attend Trade Shows

A trade show is an event where a group of specialized sellers displays their products to a group of corresponding buyers over a period of several days. Hundreds or thousands of industry people, including media people, potential customers, suppliers and networking contacts congregate at these expositions looking for new products, information, contacts and ideas.

PLAN

Participation in a trade show will be more successful if you begin by deciding exactly what it is you want to accomplish. Inexperienced exhibitors believe it is necessary to sell enough books at each show to cover their costs of attending. Although sales are important, you will rarely sell enough books at a show to defray all your expenses. Orders received should not be your sole criterion for success because the true benefits of exhibiting accrue after the show is over.

Objectives for any book-industry exposition should be to initiate contacts and perform other activities that will give you the best long-term return on your investment. These include performing market research, discovering new ideas and trends for future books, continuing your education, networking, socializing, stimulating publicity, creating national or international distribution and uncovering opportunities for special sales or foreign rights. An objective to sell should not be overlooked, so keep a keen eye out for converting suspects to prospects, and then to customers.

Next, decide which specific shows will help you reach these objectives. Depending on the products you are selling and your target markets, there are many conventions from which you could choose. Of course, there is the annual BookExpo America (BEA), which is the largest of all the book-related exhibitions in the United States. Or, you might want to exhibit at a show with a more specific audience such as the Natural Products Expo West, the Gourmet Products Show, or the Incentive Show. Visit your local library for a directory of expositions called *Trade Shows Worldwide* (Gale Publications) to find a list of most major shows as well as their costs, dates and locations.

Before you decide to exhibit, attend the show to see if it will be worthwhile for you. If there is not time to do so, contact the show management and ask if it attracts the right audience for your product line. How many people will attend? What is the cost to exhibit? If you attract 1 per cent of the potential audience, will it be cost effective for you (keeping in mind the long-term ROI)? Where will the show be held? Will the show be adequately promoted among your potential customers?

PREPARE A BUDGET

Next, calculate a budget to determine how many shows you can attend. While the cost of the exhibit space is a large part of a show's budget, it is not the only expenditure to consider. Estimate transportation and living expenses, the cost of the display, literature, shipping and promotional costs. Below are examples of expenses you are likely to incur at a major trade show, such as BEA. *The Marketing Planning* CD-ROM has a format for forecasting and recording your trade show expenses.

    Exhibit Space (Main Floor) $3,600   (10′ x 10′)

Space in Small Press Section	$ 995	(6' x 8'; includes carpeting, 2 chairs and 6' table)
Carpeting	$ 100	
2 chairs, waste baskets	$ 60	
8' Table	$ 110	
Display	$ 500+	
Hotel, meals	$ 200	per person, per day
Round-trip transportation	Varies	
Car Rental/Parking	$ 70+	per day
Electricity	$ 100	
Booth cleaning	$ 65	
Shipping to/from the show	$ 250+	
Giveaways	$ 100+	
Literature	$ 200+	
Promotion and publicity	$ 500+	

There are ways to reduce the cost of the booth space. You could share a booth with a noncompeting company. Or, you could purchase exhibit space from groups such as PMA or from your distributor. There are also ways to conserve out-of-pocket expenses. Use frequent-flyer coupons for airfare, or contact the sponsoring association for special rates on airfare, car rentals and lodging. Stay with friends, relatives or in a hotel room with a kitchen for preparing your meals.

IMPLEMENT YOUR PLAN

Now that your strategy and budget are complete, it is time to begin executing your trade-show plan. This occurs at two major times, the first of which occurs prior to the exposition, and the second is during it.

Before the Show

Contact the sponsoring company and request an exhibitor's kit. This has all the information you need regarding the floor layout, prices and services available (i.e., electrical, cleaning, etc.). If you are interested in exhibiting at BEA you can contact Reed Exhibition Company at (*www. bookexpo.reedexpo.com*). Here you will find a list of current exhibitors, information for potential exhibitors and advertising, website and sponsorship information.

As early as possible, decide upon the location of your booth space on the show floor. Generally, you are given a first, second and third choice for your preferred location. Most inline spaces provide ten feet of aisle access and are usually eight or ten feet deep; but there are also corner, island

and peninsula locations available for those with larger budgets. Choose a space that is visible from a high-traffic zone such as an entrance, restaurant or autographing area. BEA clusters exhibitors by topic. For example, there is a separate section for children's/educational items, audio/video, remainders and publishers' supplies and services. BEA also offers a Small Press Section with smaller, more economical booth space.

Once you know your location you can create your physical display. Fortunately, you have several options from which to choose. You can build a display to your specifications, buy a used one or rent a portable exhibit.

Building one may be a wise option if you have many shows in your exhibit schedule. It is also the most expensive choice, particularly when you consider the need for shipping containers for the display and transportation costs. Large, bulky exhibits must be shipped well in advance and may require expensive laborers to install for you.

There are also portable exhibits available. These come as a complete backdrop or in smaller, tabletop sizes. They are generally lightweight and may be checked as luggage on your flight or shipped in advance to your hotel. These may also be rented if you anticipate attending only one or two shows annually.

How to Attract Attention

It is not necessary to have the biggest, loudest or flashiest booth at the show to attract attendees. It is better to have a theme that is consistent with your topic and company image. What is it you want to accomplish? What do you want to say? To whom? What one impression do you want visitors to have about your books? Then everything you do should support your objective so there is no confusion among people passing by as to what you are selling.

Think of your display as a billboard, vying for the attention of people walking down the aisle who are not necessarily looking for what you are promoting. Your exhibit should have one focal point, one element that will attract attention. Use graphics and copy to encourage eye movement to your book or product. For example, at a recent BEA a publisher demonstrated a pop-up children's book with a mechanical device that kept opening and closing the book. Show rules may place restrictions on height, noise or distance from the aisle. Investigate them before you decide upon an attention-getting device.

Attracting the attention of potential customers wandering past your exhibit is a key to success. Plan demonstrations or events that will make people stop and look. For example, magicians and celebrities (or celebrity impersonators) usually attract attention. Hold a raffle or conduct a game that awards prizes on the basis of participation. Sound and motion are typically good at stimulating awareness. The closer your demonstration is to your theme, the more likely it will be to contribute to your sales objective.

Your exhibit should be distinctive, creative and attention getting. It should also be appropriate, tasteful, clean, inviting, neat and attractive, always projecting a first-class image. Photographs, signs or other elements used in the display should look professionally prepared. Hand-printed banners or homemade posters pinned against a backdrop will make you look unprofessional and will not attract people passing by.

Conduct Preshow Promotion

As soon as you are assigned a booth number, begin promoting the fact that you are exhibiting and place your booth number on all your communications. Prepare literature specifically for each group of attendees. For instance, if you are exhibiting at the American Library Association's annual convention, your literature should not describe how your book would increase traffic in a bookstore. It is not necessary to print as many brochures as there are attendees. Less than 10 per cent of the attendees will probably visit your exhibit and most of them do not want to carry excess literature with them. Get their names and addresses so you can send your literature to them after the show.

Also create press kits to leave in the pressroom and to hand out at your booth. These should include backgrounds on each author, a fact sheet on every title and any information making your exhibit newsworthy.

Prior to the show, send out mailings and announcements inviting your customers and prospects to visit your booth. Let people know you are exhibiting, where you will be located and why is it of value to them to seek you out. Also place announcements on your web page. And several weeks before the event, arrange appointments to meet with prospects and customers at the show.

You may be traveling a great distance to the convention, so do not waste your money. Schedule booksignings and appointments with prospective customers or distributor sales people for the time you are in the area. Arrange media appearances on local stations and interviews with editors of newspapers and magazines in the city hosting the trade show.

During the Show

If your preshow promotion was successful, you should draw at least 1 percent of the attendees to your exhibit. But the quickest way to turn these visitors away is to make them feel unwelcome. Your prospective customers expect knowledgeable salespeople to staff an exhibit. People working your booth must know about your titles as well as their authors, prices and discounts. It will help if they memorize a thirty-second descriptive sound bite for each title.

Similarly, do not smoke, sit down, talk on the telephone or read in your booth. Keep breath mints on hand and use them regularly. And do not appear overanxious by standing like a vulture at the edge of your booth space saying "How are you today?" to every person who walks by. If you are located midway in the aisle, the people walking past have heard that question twenty times by the time they get to you. In fact, do not ask any question that could be answered with a *yes* or *no*. These are usually sentences beginning in verbs: "Are you a buyer at a bookstore?" or "Do you sell (your topic) books in your store?" People will answer in one word and then walk away. Instead, ask questions that will get them to stop and talk with you. Do this by asking open-ended questions beginning with *who, what, where, when, why* or *how*. For instance, you could say, "What type of books are you looking for?" This will make someone stop and answer you. Look at their badge for the city or state in which they reside and use that as a conversation starter ("Oh, I used to live in Cincinnati. Is XYZ restaurant still there?").

Badges are usually color coded so you can tell if the person is an exhibitor, bookstore owner, press member, visitor or author. But judging the relative importance of a person (in the context of your objectives) by the color of his or her badge may be misleading. Many people switch or borrow badges, and you may neglect a major sales opportunity by ignoring someone with an exhibitor's badge. Be professional and courteous to everyone.

If used properly, a giveaway item may get people to stop and talk with you. It does not have to be big or elaborate. Novelty items such as key chains, pencils, pads of paper with your company name and/or book title usually work well. Many companies offer free services, or they make water, coffee or candy available. Create a special booklet for each show's audience, based on your topics. Your promotion will be most effective if it is inexpensive, of interest and value to those in your target market and related to your theme.

There are other tips to help you reach your objectives for exhibiting. Work with at least two people at your booth. This will give each time to rest, walk the show, network, look for new ideas and perform research. You will talk with many potential customers during the show, and the likelihood of you remembering every conversation is not high. Ask people for their business cards, and on each, note the nature of the conversation and any follow up that is required. Keep snacks, water and fruit at your booth your refreshment. Attend and network at social events, but do not "party hearty." Show up alert and energetic each morning, and always greet people with a *smile*.

Nanette Miner (BVC Publishing) was exhibiting at a salon trade show in Orlando, Florida and traffic at her booth was slow. According to Nanette, "I got bored sitting behind my booth so I took an armful of my books with me and started dropping them off at other vendors' booths. Within a week of returning to my office, the publisher of *Salon Strategies* newsletter called me and asked if he could purchase 750 copies of my booklet *101 Media and Marketing Tips for Salon Owners, Stylists and Managers* to use as an incentive for subscriptions or renewals to the newsletter."

Follow up

Follow up starts before you leave for home. Each night, review your daily performance and plan how you can improve tomorrow. Write thank-you notes and mail them from the show. Take pictures of people with you at your display and send them a copy. Also, photograph your exhibit when it is teeming with visitors and send one to your local newspapers, customers and distributors.

Evaluation

Once the show is over, evaluate your experience while the information is still fresh in your mind. Should you exhibit again next year, and if so, what would you change? What booth locations seemed to get the most traffic? Which displays seemed to attract the most people? Did you see a large number of people walking around with a giveaway item from one particular company? What was your cost-per-inquiry and is that acceptable? What new ideas or trends should you act upon? What new relationships did you make and what old friendships were rekindled? If you were seeking opportunities for special sales or foreign rights, were you successful?

Participate in every trade show with a strategic plan of action. Plan your exhibit carefully, implement your plan, follow up and then evaluate the relative success of your actions. Decide what you can do to improve next time and then begin the process all over again.

Strategy # 73: Contact Prospects by Telephone

The telephone can help you economically locate new prospects, follow up, conduct market research and sell books ... if you know the fundamentals of using a telephone properly. One word can remind you to use all the facets of oral communication to maximize your effectiveness particularly when using the telephone. This word is **VOICES**. It is an acronym (**V**olume, **O**thers' viewpoints, **I**nflection, **C**onfidence, **E**nthusiasm and **S**peed) that will help you improve the content and delivery of your message.

VOLUME. Your volume projects your voice and makes it easy or difficult to hear. Nervousness can make you feel less sure of yourself, reflected through lower volume. Similarly, if you hold your hand over the telephone mouthpiece, you won't sound loud enough. Or if you place the phone on your shoulder with the mouthpiece under your chin (while you are writing something), the other person may not hear you as well. The listener will have to press the phone to his or her ear, which may then become sore. He or she will cut the conversation short before that occurs.

If you have a speakerphone, do not use it for making your prospecting calls. At times these are difficult to hear and may make you sound as if you are talking through a tunnel. The listeners are trying to assess you by your voice, and any distortion can bias their image of you. Also, the person on the other end of the phone has no idea who *else* is listening, and therefore may be less willing to be candid.

OTHERS' VIEWPOINTS. Your goal is to convince each potential customer that he or she will be better off by purchasing your product or content than not. Use your voice to convey your sincerity and belief in how your content can help the listener in some way.

Additional hints

Personalize the conversation. Use your prospect's name when possible. People like to hear their name, and it gets their attention. One theory has it that you should say the person's name three times in the beginning of the conversation (Ms. Jones? Ms. Mary Jones? Good morning, Ms. Jones.). It sounds awkward, but you may be able to use it effectively.

Use the prospect's name. During the conversation, refer to your prospect's name occasionally. Write it at the top of your script or note pad, and (without overdoing it) refer to it as you speak. Use the title Mr. or Ms. until told to use the first name. You will find your listeners will be more amenable to your proposition if you treat them with the respect they think they are due.

Stick to one strong idea. When you finally get through to someone who is willing to listen to you, your first reaction is to tell him or her everything you know about your book. You may think if you say enough things, one of them is bound to be that which will cause him or her to buy.

But this is not the case. You have only a few seconds to provide enough information that will pique their interest. You must keep your focus on your objective, and drive home the connection between their need and your book's ability to satisfy it. If you are trying to convince people to add your title to their gift shop, tell them how your book and your promotion will increase traffic to their store and make them more profitable. If you try to throw as many details as you can at the wall—hoping something will stick—all you will end up with is a messy wall.

Deja vu. If you have met with the person previously, remind him or her of it. A simple statement such as "we met at last year's trade show" may prompt him or her to remember who you are. The fact you remembered will flatter the listener, and it will make you seem less like a salesperson and more like an associate calling to discuss a business issue.

INFLECTION. Avoid a monotonous tone of voice by varying your vocal qualities. This will keep the listener more attentive and interested in what you are saying. Speak in an enthusiastic tone, regularly moderating your volume, speed and emphasis on important words and phrases. Changing the accent to different words adds impact. For example, you could emphasize the benefits of your titles by saying "they have proven to be excellent fund-raising tools *and* they can make your event more profitable."

CONFIDENCE. Have you ever been on an airplane during a turbulent storm? If so, you will understand the reassured feeling of the passengers when the captain confidently announces everything is under control. Your voice must project this same confidence in your abilities.

Many of your prospective customers equate *confidence* with *competence.* If your temporary nervousness makes you sound like someone with no self-confidence, the prospect may look upon your request with less favor.

Do not use words such as "I'll try," " maybe" or "I'll do what I can." They create the impression you aren't sure whether or not you can do what you say.

"I wanted to, ah, ask you, um, for an appointment, um ..." if you allow non-words (such as *"um, uh"*) to creep into your speech pattern, you are less likely to project confidence. Frequent use of *OK* and the words "you know" may alienate the recipient of your call as much as unnecessary sounds.

NOTE: Eliminate these glitches by talking into a cassette recorder and listening to your voice. Do you express the reason for your call confidently and enunciate your title's benefits? Record several of your telephone calls (with the other party's consent), and critique your performance. Or call a friend and give him or her your presentation. Then evaluate it together. If you have three-way calling, have another friend listen to, and assess, your performance. Also, consider writing beforehand what you want to say, but allow for departures from your script.

ENTHUSIASM. Too much confidence might make you come across as being egotistical and not speaking with the customer's best interest in mind. To reduce the likelihood of this happening, temper your self-confidence with enthusiasm. This is an intangible quality, communicated through your voice. Smile as you speak. Your smile can be *seen* over the telephone and adds a pleasant, friendly quality to your voice.

Transferring enthusiasm doesn't mean you must jump up and down, emphasizing every word. You can achieve it by speaking slowly and articulately, but with conviction. It can be communicated by pausing before answering a question, speaking with a smile in your voice and being prepared with responses to questions.

You can have some fun as you speak in the telephone by watching yourself in a mirror. This will enable you to practice gesturing (to add inflection to your voice) and smiling, since you are having a conversation with yourself, not a potential customer. You may also find it helpful to stand as you speak. Doing so opens up your diaphragm and allows you to speak with a more resonant voice.

SPEED. Your rate of speech can interfere with effective communication. If you are nervous making telephone calls you may speak a little more quickly than you would normally, distorting your articulation and in-terfering with effective communication. And the faster your vocal cords move, the higher your voice will pitch. Slow down your speech and your tone will drop, giving you a confident, resonant voice. If you talk too quickly, your pronunciation will suffer. The prospective customer will ask you to repeat yourself regularly, which becomes irritating to both parties. In addition, you may sound either nervous or untrustworthy.

On the other hand, if you speak too slowly, the listeners may become impatient. They may get the feeling you are wasting their time and try to finish your sentences for you. Or, if they think you have ended a sentence, they may begin talking and interrupt you. Since you can not see the expression on the listeners' faces, you can not tell if they are paying attention to you, if they have a question or if you are speaking too slowly or swiftly. If you pause now and then you can recapture their attention and address any areas of misunderstanding or concern.

The normal rate of speed is about 130–140 words per minute. You can learn where you fit on this scale by counting 130 words and reading them into a cassette recorder. Then play it back, timing your reading. If you speak too quickly or too slowly, practice until you get a good feel for your most comfortable and effective rate. Enunciate better by reading aloud to yourself and to your family or friends.

Strategy # 74: Create Professional, Benefit-Oriented Sales Literature and Catalogs

Your literature and catalogs are sales tools that are used to present your titles in the most compelling way. You cannot have a simple listing of your titles with the expectation that a prospect will choose from among them. Your literature must be planned and customized as selling tools to be used during your presentations, as trade-show handouts and as persuasive leave-behinds to continue selling in your absence.

In this sense, your promotional material projects an image of you, your titles and your company. Business people are used to seeing professionally prepared literature and anything of lesser quality will detract from your sales efforts. There is a template for sales literature in Appendix D, but here are some tips that will help you create effective selling sheets, flyers, mail inserts and catalogs.

1. **First impression.** Your literature not only describes your product line, it describes your definition of quality. A black and white Xerox copy on twenty-pound paper will do little to convince a buyer that you have produced a quality book.

   Four-color printing is no longer the expensive proposition it was in the past, available only to the largest companies. Improved technology and lower prices have made this process accessible to the masses, relatively economically.

2. **Use a professional designer.** You can probably take one look at a book and know if the layout was prepared by a professional designer or by a self-published author on a tight budget. Special-sales buyers will know the difference, too. They are using your product to project the proper image to their customers, and they want to be confident that you will add to, and not detract from, that image.

    Designers have been trained to communicate a message and image using the nuances of layout, type, photography, illustrations, color and white space. Use their knowledge and skills to create sales literature of which you can be proud, and that will help you sell more books.

3. **Provide a path.** Some promotional material draws the reader into it, caressing the words and layout with emotionally charged subtleties. A definite starting point with an easy-to-follow path will lead the reader through a field of benefits to a logical and positive conclusion.

    If using a four-page layout, include the following information on your front cover: date, special offer inside, anything that is new or free and the type of product (CD-ROMs, books, software, etc.). The rear cover is also an important selling area. Highlight your new titles, best sellers or award winners.

    Present information sequentially. Grab the readers' interest with an attention-getting opening statement. Use captions to draw attention or to help the reader to understand your visuals. Then describe how your titles will benefit them. Bring them up to a boiling point with a blazing description of reasons why and how they will be better off with your books than without them. Then ask for the order.

    Use color, bold headings or tabs to separate sections and draw the reader to the information. Tell your designer what you want to accomplish with your literature and let him or her make it happen.

4. **Talk benefits, not features.** As you begin selling outside the provincial boundaries of traditional booksellers, the prospects do not care about features such as an ISBN. They want to know how your title will benefit them. Remember the words of Charles Revson stated earlier, and stop selling your books. Your literature must sell what your books will do *for the buyer* (refer to Strategy #24).

    You may have to create different literature for different audiences. Buyers in the Special-Distribution segment may have different hot buttons than buyers in the Commercial-Sales or Niche Markets.

Similarly, you may have to create new literature for special occasions. A flyer designed to offer a special promotion at an association conference may have little application to a corporate product manager.

5. **Form follows function.** A two-sided sales piece may not be necessary unless you need that much space to make a persuasive presentation. Nor should you feel obligated to produce a multipage flyer if one page will suffice. In the words of Thoreau, "Simplify, simplify, simplify."

   Use the proper paper. There are so many options available that it becomes difficult to choose. If you are creating a mailing piece, you may opt for a lightweight paper to reduce your mailing costs. If you integrate a business reply card (BRC) into your literature, you will need heavier paper to meet postal-service requirements.

6. **Make it easy to order.** Show the reader how to take some positive action in the form of writing, e-mailing or calling for more information or to place an order. In addition to all necessary information (address, telephone and fax numbers, URL, e-mail address), provide some assurance of quick delivery. If you provide a guarantee of any kind, make sure it is displayed prominently.

   Provide a form to complete and return. Make sure you get all the information you need to complete the order, including the expiration date on a credit card and a valid signature. Always ask for a telephone number, because there will be times when illegible handwriting may make it necessary to call the buyer for clarification.

7. **Offer a discount or an incentive to order.** Organize your products in associated groups to encourage larger orders. Then offer a discount for volume purchases. Or, use a premium to encourage an early decision.

Strategy # 75: Conduct a Special-Sales Marketing Tour As You Would a Media Tour

You are probably familiar with the process of creating a media tour, but why not do the same thing for a special-sales tour? You can organize and concentrate your selling efforts geographically and use your time effectively.

This is particularly simple to do if you have a "day job" in which you travel and your employer pays your expenses. This is not to suggest that you have your employer pay for your time selling your books. But when you take a business trip, leave a day or two early and stay a day or two later (even over a weekend or use vacation time if necessary) then you had planned. Use that time to call on prospective buyers. *The Marketing Planning* CD has a special template to help you plan your expenses and determine the break-even point for a special-sales or media tour.

If you plan a media tour, combine it with a special-sales tour and call on potential buyers between media events. Your media events may even enhance your selling activities if potential buyers hear you on the air before your appointment with them.

A sample day on a combined tour might be constructed of a morning drive-time radio show with the remainder of the morning spent calling on corporate buyers. A noontime booksigning could be followed by an afternoon contacting local retail stores, capped by a late afternoon television show. If you could fit in an evening personal presentation with back-of-the-room sales, you would have a productive day. Put enough of those days back-to-back and you will sell a lot of books.

15

Scrutinize Your Relative Success and Make Necessary Corrections

DID YOU EVER TRY TO LOSE WEIGHT? If so, you may have set a goal to lose 24 pounds in one year, broken down into twelve monthly two-pound increments. Then you probably weighed yourself regularly to see if you were on track to reach your goal.

Let's say your objective was to lose six pounds in the first three months. If at the end of that period you weighed yourself and found that you lost only *three pounds*, you would have to revise your second quarter's weight-loss goal to three pounds per month in order to stay on target. You may have also found it necessary to make adjustments to your diet or exercise program.

This same process can be applied to your special-sales marketing efforts. Just ask yourself a few questions. Are your book sales on target? Are you reaching your objectives? Are you as profitable as you had forecast? How do you know? Regular evaluation of your progress can show you if you are on track to reach your objective and points out areas in need of strategic or tactical adjustment.

Strategy #76: Measure Your Progress

Your marketing objective was written to be, among other things, measurable. That implies that you have some procedure in place to measure your relative success at reaching your objective. There must be a system for accountability, or your marketing effort becomes an exercise in futility.

WHEN TO MEASURE

Just as it is not necessary to weigh yourself every day, you shouldn't measure your progress too often. How often is too often? Measurement of any period less than one quarter is probably too frequent. Your marketing activities need the chance to develop, to make an impact. Conversely, you can't wait too long or you may not have sufficient time to respond.

Some activities are difficult to measure. Publicity, media appearances and advertising are three of those. These are meant to generate exposure and awareness, which in turn should translate into sales. This promotion process takes time to evolve, and your efforts will succeed if you tell people frequently enough that your book is available and how it will help them. However, if you measure your sales after the seventh or eighth time you run your ad, send your press release or appear on the air there may not have been time for your promotion to take effect. If you stop promoting short of the point at which your efforts make an impact. Then all you have done is wasted money.

Just because your ad has appeared ten times does not mean everyone in your target audience saw it ten times. You may have to run it twenty times to get everyone to see it ten times and take action. Give your marketing actions time to work.

After one quarter you should have some feel for the effectiveness of your communication. If your sales do not increase after three months of perpetual promotion, what should you do? Maybe the culprit is not the medium itself, but the execution of your plan. Just because you are on a television or radio show does not guarantee sales. You may perform poorly, or the show's audience may not be in your target market. Similarly, you may be sending hundreds of press releases weekly, but what if they are poorly written or sent to the wrong person? Not only must you measure at the right time, you must know what to measure.

WHAT TO MEASURE

A thermometer measures temperature. It doesn't control the temperature. It gives you an indication that the heating or cooling elements are working properly. If the room is too warm or too cold, you simply make adjustments to remedy the situation.

Evaluation acts as your marketing thermostat, measuring your sales and/or profits and telling you if your marketing efforts are working properly. If your indicators are off target, then you must go into more depth and look at the various elements of your marketing mix to find the culprit. Luckily, there are only four areas in which you need to look.

Product. Look at your product mix. Is your information presented in the form best suited to the needs of your target market? Are you spending too much time trying to breathe new life into a title that should be abandoned? Which titles are your stars, those with an exponential return on the marketing dollars invested in them? Did you cut too many corners trying to save money in the production stage?

Place. Did you implement a dual-distribution strategy? Did you properly investigate all the possible niches in which your books could be sold? Are you spending enough time nurturing long-term opportunities in the Commercial Sales sector while stimulating revenue-producing, short-term sales in the Niche Markets? If you are concentrating in the Special-Distribution segment, do you have the right distribution partners?

Price. If you applied a strategy of income averaging, check to make sure your sales are not inordinately skewed toward bookstores and Special-Distribution customers. If so, these discounts will eat into your profitably quickly. Are your negotiated prices too low? Are you offering too many (or not enough) financial incentives?

Promotion. The promotion category is subdivided into publicity, advertising, sales promotion and personal selling, and these all have both short- and long-term implications. Some of your efforts i.e., direct marketing, provide immediate feedback and results. Others are less prone to being measured accurately. In these cases, the best defense is a good offense. Test all your promotional tools before you use them. Utilize those showing the best promise and make them work.

When you are contemplating what to measure, the quick answer is *everything*. But if you spend too much time evaluating your actions you won't have time to implement your plan. Work with the adage that says, "What gets measured gets done." Evaluate your efforts in the four elements of the marketing mix to see if your efforts are properly directed and implemented. Now, how do you do that?

HOW TO MEASURE

When a helicopter is at rest, the dials on its dashboard are all askew with arrows pointing in all directions. But when that helicopter is flying straight and level, with no problems, all the arrows are pointing straight up. The pilot can glance at the instrument panel and quickly see if any dials are out of order, indicating that a problem exists. The pilot immediately knows when something is wrong without wasting time evaluating that which is working correctly.

Special-sales marketers can save a lot of time by setting up a system that points out where problems exist and that leaves well enough alone. There are two ways to do this. The first is with a quantitative audit and the second is with a qualitative audit.

Strategy # 77: Conduct a Quantitative Audit

A quantitative audit is objective in nature, comparing sales that were forecast with sales that were actually achieved. Here are examples demonstrating how to track your sales (in both units and dollars) on a quarterly basis (1Q = First Quarter; YTD = Year to Date).

Unit Sales vs. Forecast								
	1Q	1Q			YTD	YTD		
	Forecast	Actual	Diff.	%Diff.	Forecast	Actual	Diff.	%Diff.
Current Bookstore Customers Distributor A Wholesaler A Online Bookstore A								

New Markets
Libraries
  Wholesaler A
  Customer A
Gift Shops
  Customer A
  Customer B								

Dollar Sales vs. Forecast								
	1Q	1Q			YTD	YTD		
	$ Forecast	$ Actual	$Diff.	%Diff.	$ Forecast	$ Actual	$Diff.	%Diff.
Current Book-store Customers Distributor A Wholesaler A Online Bookstore A								
New Markets Libraries Wholesaler A Customer A Gift Shops Customer A Customer B								

Strategy # 78: Conduct a Qualitative Audit

Special-sales marketing is similar to traditional marketing in the way your judgment impacts the results of your quantitative analysis. For example, the quarterly analysis statements above may point out that while unit sales are on track, revenue is below forecast. But the chart below identifies many of the topics discussed throughout *Beyond the Bookstore* that can cause this situation. This list should stimulate a qualitative thought process that will help you identify and respond to possible causes.

Possible Causes of Results		
Poor Results	**Good Results**	**Excellent Results**
Product Driven	Market driven	Market driving
Mass-market orientation	Segment oriented	Niche/customer oriented
Product focus	Augmented product	Focus on customer solutions
Average product quality	Better than average product	Excellent product quality
Average service quality	Better than average service	Excellent service quality
Function oriented	Process oriented	Outcome oriented
Reacting to competition	Matching competition	Leading competition
Supplier exploitation	Supplier preference	Supplier partnership
Distribution exploitation	Distributor support	Distributor partnership
Price driven	Quality driven	Value driven
No plan	Written plan	Implemented plan

COMPONENTS OF A QUALITATIVE MARKETING AUDIT

Some people respond more favorably to a list of questions to kick-start their strategic thinking. Use the questions below, combined with the creative process described in Chapter Two to identify and respond to the forces denying attainment of your goals.

Business/Personnel Factors.
- Do you have enough of the right people employed to implement your special-sales plan?
- Are your physical facilities sufficient to perform all your activities?
- Do your people have the proper equipment and training to perform as you have asked?
- Have you invested sufficient capital?
- Is your mission clearly stated in market-oriented terms?
- Are your objectives stated clearly enough to guide marketing planning and performance measurement?

Marketplace Factors.
- What is happening to the size, growth, geographical distribution of the markets in which you have chosen to compete? Consider a combination of Special Distribution, Commercial Sales and Niche Markets.
- Have the needs of your customers changed? Did you properly recognize and respond to them?
- Have any new competitors entered the arena? If so, how are their products, distribution, pricing and promotion different from yours?

Planning Process.
- Are the strategies appropriate to the stages of the titles' life cycle stages?
- Is your plan written and in a form that supports easy use?
- Have you identified and defined your market segments carefully and completely?
- Have you developed an effective marketing mix for each target segment?
- Are enough resources budgeted to accomplish marketing objectives?
- Are your objectives reasonable and attainable?

- Are the sales to each special-sales sector (Special Distribution, Commercial Sales and Niche Markets) distributed as forecast or does one overpower the others?

Implementation / Product Development.
- Is the current product line sufficient to meet objectives?
- Which products should be phased out? Added? Changed?
- How might you improve your product array?

Distribution.
- Are your distribution partners working out as expected?
- Are you acting as a partner to your distributors, communicating with them regularly?
- Do you have adequate market coverage in the Special-Distribution sector?
- Is your fulfillment operation sufficient to the task?
- How might you improve your distribution?

Pricing.
- Are your pricing objectives and strategies suitable to market and competitive conditions?
- Do prospects make a connection between your pricing and the value your titles offer?
- Are discounts and incentives sufficient to motivate your distribution partners?
- How might you improve your pricing strategies?

Promotion.
- Do enough people know your titles exist? If so, what are their opinions of your titles?
- Are you conveying the benefits of your titles?
- Are you communicating the proper message to the right people by means of the correct medium (publicity, advertising, sales promotion and personal selling)?
- Have you budgeted sufficient funds to promotion?
- Are you making enough use of direct, online and database marketing?
- How might you improve your promotional activities?

Strategy # 79: Interpret Results and Make Changes

Simply knowing what is wrong does not correct the situation. Given the degree of success in reaching your goal, you may need to make some changes in your marketing efforts for the remainder of the planning period. Do not be too quick to make adjustments until you have adequate information, sufficiently analyzed.

For example, your sales in the first quarter may be well below the figure that represents one-fourth of your annual sales. But if the title under consideration is a gift item, the bulk of the sales may not occur until the fourth quarter. In this case, no strategic adjustments may be necessary now, but may be required in the planning period following the peak season.

Look to your bread-and-butter titles. Where are deviations the most severe? Which customers or titles are straying from predicted sales? Why is that happening? What trends do you see developing? How must your forecast be changed for the remaining periods in order to reach your annual goal? This analysis will give you advance warning of potentially dangerous trends and give you the chance to respond accordingly.

Revised Strategy and Unit Sales Forecast				
	Amended Strategy	2Q Forecast	3Q Forecast	4Q Forecast
Current Bookstore Customers Distributor A Wholesaler A Online Bookstore A				
New Markets Libraries Wholesaler A Customer A Gift Shops Customer A Customer B				
Current Titles Title A Title B Title C Title D				

An airplane has what are called *trim tabs* on its horizontal and vertical control surfaces. These are used to make minor adjustments that allow the plane to fly with little overt action by the pilot. When you feel that your strategy is taking you a little off course, do not think you have to make major changes in strategy. Unless you see a large problem, begin by fine-tuning your existing actions.

For example, if your first-quarter unit sales are approximately at forecast levels, but your profits are below what was expected, you may have a pricing problem. Perhaps your price incentives were a little too aggressive and need to be trimmed. On the other hand if you allocated all your production costs to the first printing, the second printing will be more profitable, bringing your forecast back on track.

Plan a quarterly strategic brainstorming session right after your quarterly evaluation occurs. Analyze and discuss your results and think of possible remedies. Maybe you are not reaching your objectives because they were unrealistic. Was the plan ill conceived or was poor implementation at fault? What are possible causes of your shortfall? Poor design? Bad timing? Not enough time? No differentiation? Not enough promotion/budget? Try to pinpoint the cause, make changes in your strategy and/or implementation, and then try something different.

It does not make good business sense to continue doing the same thing, but expecting different results. If what you are doing works, do more of it. But if what you are doing does not work, try something else. The question is, how do you know if it is working or not? You know this by scrutinizing your progress, making changes as necessary and then implementing your new programs. Then next quarter you start the entire process again.

If you're climbing the ladder of life, you go rung by rung, one step at a time. Do not look too far up, set your goals high but take one step at a time. Sometimes you do not think you're progressing until you step back and see how high you've really gone. DONNY OSMOND, *U.S. actor, singer*

16

Realize Your Goals

A SHOE MANUFACTURING COMPANY once sent two of its sales-people to different regions of a third-world country. After a few weeks one of the representatives reported, "Everybody here goes around barefoot. There is no chance of selling shoes, so I am returning home." The other sales person looked at the situation in his region differently saying, "Nobody here wears shoes. There is nothing but opportunity."

This story relates as much to selling books as it does to shoes: the opportunity you find depends on what you see and how you interpret it. If you search for sales where others see only car washes, beauty salons, restaurants and jewelry stores, then you will sell more products. You can sell more books by finding out where people buy them, or could buy them, and then making them available there. This is simple, but not necessarily easy.

Something hidden. Go and find it. Go, and look behind the Ranges. . .
Go! RUDYARD KIPLING, *English poet, novelist*

There are two important concepts that might make the process of realizing your objectives a little less formidable. The first presupposes that you have sales or profitability goals, as discussed in Chapter Three. The second probes a little deeper, seeking an answer to the question,

"What is your ultimate goal?" That may be to make a difference in peoples' lives, a contribution to some cause, or to gratify your professional pride. What matters is that it matters to you. Whatever it is, the journey to realizing your professional goal can be enhanced by selling to special-sales markets.

In addition to applying all the tips and techniques described in *Beyond the Bookstore*, there is more you can do to fulfill your publishing mission. The first of these additional actions recognizes that to do what is necessary to be successful selling your books to non-bookstore markets could be intimidating. It requires a move outside most publishers' comfort zones into a realm of unknown possibilities. Begin by simply admitting that it is possible to for you to do it.

Some publishers may jump into the sea of special sales with arms and legs flailing. Others want to test the waters before diving in. It matters less in which group you reside than it does that the route you choose fits your needs and personality.

If you are one of the reluctant publishers, start by taking small steps into territory that is somewhat familiar. Continue selling to bookstores, and then add libraries to your list of target markets. Contact one of the wholesalers to this market and work with it to increase your sales. Next, call on government agencies whose buyers are required to return your calls and who are obliged to be courteous and professional with you.

Once these become routine operations, submit your titles to participants in the Special Distribution sector. Here the channels are similar to those in the traditional distribution system. Work from the familiar to the less familiar, and then to the more challenging arenas of Commercial Sales and Niche Markets.

Another hint is to ask yourself empowering questions. Instead of "What else could go wrong?" seek answers that stimulate your creativity to find solutions to your problems. Begin your questions with "What if…?" followed by words with positive intent. "What if we sold our books to military exchanges? What if we communicated this information as a DVD instead of a book?" Follow these questions with others that seek multiple responses, such as "In how many ways could we make that happen?"

Do not prejudge your options because in most cases you will probably downplay your chances of success and magnify the possible obstacles. If you find yourself thinking, "Why bother calling them. They will probably never buy this title anyway." change your direction of thought. Ask, "What if they did buy?" or "What is the best thing that could happen?"

Gain from your pain. You may make mistakes; anyone going into uncharted waters does. But learn from them. If your inquiry to Anderson

Merchandisers is rejected, find out why. Is the topic not suited for mass merchandisers, or was your submission incomplete? Perhaps you could resubmit it as an applicant for supermarkets or drugstores to Anderson News Group.

If you have a problem, find a solution. Work with the ideas presented here to increase your sales and profitability. Use *The Marketing Planning CD-ROM* to help you plan, implement and evaluate your actions. It's all up to you. Make it happen.

Don't bunt. Aim out of the ballpark. Aim for the company of immortals.
DAVID OGILVY, *U.S. advertising executive*

APPENDIX A
Outline for a Marketing Plan

Part One—Analysis and Direction

1. INTRODUCTION
1.1 Mission Statement
1.2 Executive Summary
1.3 Objectives

2. THE BUSINESS
2.1 Business Background
2.2 Product Line Description
2.3 Distribution

3. MARKET ANALYSIS
3.1 Market Definition
3.2 Market Segmentation
3.3 Customer Needs
3.4 Competition

4. MARKETING ISSUES AND OPPORTUNITIES
4.1 Marketing Strengths
4.2 Marketing Weaknesses
4.3 Marketing Opportunities

4.4 Marketing Threats
4.5 Resulting Issues

5. GOALS

5.1 Financial Objectives
5.2 Marketing Objectives
5.3 Innovation Objectives

Part Two—Implementation

6. GENERAL MARKETING STRATEGIES

6.1 Positioning Strategy
6.2 Product and Packaging Strategies
6.3 Pricing Strategies
6.4 Distribution Strategies
6.5 General Promotion Strategies
6.6 Personal Selling Strategies
6.7 Advertising and Direct Marketing Strategies
6.8 Sales Promotion Strategies
6.9 Publicity Strategies

7. SPECIFIC MARKETING TACTICS

7.1 Positioning Tactics
7.2 Product and Packaging Tactics
7.3 Pricing Tactics
7.4 Distribution Tactics
7.5 General Promotion Tactics
7.6 Personal Selling Tactics
7.7 Advertising and Direct Marketing Tactics
7.8 Sales Promotion Tactics
7.9 Publicity Tactics

B

Fastart™ Checklist

How to Get a Quick Start Selling Your Books To Special-Sales Markets

☐ Prioritize the companies listed in your plan according to their likelihood of buying your books. Place them in an A, B or C category.

☐ In order to help you rank your potential customers, organize them by making lists of those...
  - ☐ likely to purchase in large quantities.
  - ☐ decision makers and influencers.
  - ☐ with whom you are familiar.
  - ☐ with similar reasons for buying.
  - ☐ you will contact by phone or mail.
  - ☐ knowledgeable of your title.

☐ List the benefits to each group of prospective customers (reasons why the information in your book is important to *them*).
  - ☐ Ten benefits for buyers in the Special Distribution category.
  - ☐ Ten benefits for buyers in the Commercial Sales section.
  - ☐ Ten benefits for buyers in the Niche Marketing segment.

☐ Create a one-page letter describing your book in terms of the benefits for each target segment listed above.

- ☐ Cut and paste it to a blank email and make format changes.
- ☐ Create a telephone script to use when calling prospects in each target segment.
- ☐ Contact those prospects with a long decision-making process.
- ☐ Create a package to send to distributors.
- ☐ Submit your package to distributors in the Special-Distribution segment.
- ☐ Contact decision makers and influencers in the Commercial Sales segment.
- ☐ Submit your package to the Home-Shopping Networks.
- ☐ Contact prospects with a long lead time. Magazines sometimes have a 90–120 day lead-time before their pub date.
- ☐ Submit your package to reviewers.
- ☐ Submit your package to book clubs, catalogs and newsletters.
- ☐ Continue to work your prospect list by contacting those most likely to purchase quickly.
- ☐ Contact all remaining prospective customers according to your priorities.
- ☐ Regularly visit and participate in relevant chat rooms and discussion groups.

APPENDIX C
Marketing Information to Send to a Distributor or Wholesaler

PUBLISHER'S NAME, ADDRESS AND CONTACT NAME:

NUMBER OF TITLES PUBLISHED IN A YEAR:

INFORMATION ABOUT YOUR TITLE:
- Title:
- Author:
- Size:
- ISBN:
- LCCN:
- Series?
- Binding:
- Author's credentials:
- Photographs:
- Number of pages:
- Number of copies printed:
- Pub Date:
- Description of competitive titles:
- Fifty-word description of why your title is different and better than competition:
- Testimonials:
- Awards:
- Covers available for samples?

PRICING
- List price:
- Discount schedule:
- Examples of competitive prices:

PROMOTION

- Overall strategy: What will you do to stimulate sales and make their reps' jobs easier?

PROMOTIONAL BUDGET:

PUBLICITY

- Attach reviews or send a list of those to which you have submitted.
- Print coverage sought or expected: names of magazines, newspapers:
- Broadcast media events: appearances made or scheduled on television and radio: Where?
- Tour planned?
- Publicity firm with which you are working:

ADVERTISING

- Willing to co-op with distributor?
- Advertise in their catalog?

SALES PROMOTION

- How do you plan to support their sales representatives?

PERSONAL SELLING

- Availability for booksignings:
- Plans for personal presentations that will drive people into retail stores.

D

APPENDIX D
Template for Sales Literature

Headline that quickly and clearly tells the recipient why purchasing this title will improve his or her situation in some way

First paragraph should expand on the primary benefit described in the headline. Remember that the reasons some people have for buying your book are different from others'. In two or three sentences respond to the Five Ws: *Who, What, Where, When* and *Why*.

Image of the cover of your book

The second paragraph should introduce additional benefits and reasons to purchase your book. Justify the column and do not use a type size that is less than 12 points. Use a sans serif typeface with sufficient leading (space between the lines).

The third paragraph should introduce the author(s) and state his, her or their credentials for being an authority on the topic (if it is nonfiction) or writing experience and previous titles if the book is fiction.

Include all the information the recipient needs to purchase your books. Resellers will need the ISBN, your discount information and shipping costs. Consumers will expect an order form to fill out and return. If you accept credit cards, state which you will take and make provisions for people to include the card number, expiration date and signature (most people will send this information rather than fax or e-mail it). You may choose to include space for a form that the ordering person can complete. This will typically provide space for the buyer's name, address, number of books ordered and total price.

Provide a testimonial or celebrity endorsement, especially if the author is unknown to this buying segment. It is not necessary to use quotation marks if you italicize the quote. Use quotations by people with whom the recipients will relate and believe as credible. If the person is not well known, include a prestigious title. You may have to change the quotation for different markets. Name the person making the statement and his or her credentials

---

Close with a statement telling the readers what you want them to do:
Call Today for More Information

Make it as easy as possible for the recipient to contact you, so include your company name, address, phone/fax numbers, email address and website.

E

APPENDIX E
Special-Sales Action Plan

First Quarter Action Plan				
	Start Date	Finish Date	Person Responsible	Next Steps
Create Promotional Programs				
1. Publicity				
Contact magazines for periodical rights for excerpts				
Contact magazines about serial rights				
Celebrity endorsements				
List of Pre-Publication Book Reviewers				
Press Release				
Press Kits				
List of Post-Publication Book Reviewers				
Send announcement to key buyers				
Send press kits to media				
2. Advertising				
Prepare prepublication announcement ads				
Develop your brochure and literature				
3. Personal selling				
Plan author tours				
Plan book signings				
Contact broadcast media				

Contact print media				
Contact syndicated columnists				
Contact wire services				
Telephone follow-up				
4. Sales Promotion				
Business cards (Title/ISBN on rear)				
Letterhead with book cover				
Post cards				
Bookmarks				
5. Direct Mail				
Implement targeted mailing campaigns				
Participate in co-op niche mailings				
Determine break-even point				
Follow-up larger wholesalers with mailing				
Mail brochures/flyers to smaller wholesalers				
Mail brochures/flyers to major bookstore chains				

F

APPENDIX F
A Special-Sales Planning Simulator

	Special Distribution	Commercial Sales	Niche Marketing
Product Design	Produce library binding; produce soft or hard cover as required	Demonstrate your willingness to customize your content to meet their needs: cover design, size or even text to add their product's name	May need booklet-size version for specialty shops that look for lower-priced items
Distribution	Generally through distributors, but some companies may buy direct at a substantial discount	You negotiate directly with decision makers; do not print books for inventory but for orders; Network-marketing companies resell to their distributors	Many small stores buy directly; may ask for consignment but avoid doing so; look for groups of buyers to purchase large quantities

	Special Distribution	Commercial Sales	Niche Marketing
Pricing	Companies such as Books Are Fun may pay for a print run; If company contributes to print run offer a price of cost plus X%	Price discounts are negotiated on a customer-by-customer basis, usually based upon quantity purchased.	Usually small discounts; some buy at list price; offer quantity discounts that increase with purchase size
Promotion	Demonstrate to retailers that you plan to promote heavily to the target readers to drive people into their stores	Requires significant face-to-face contact; long decision-making period but sales are usually in large quantities; focus on benefits of content	Demonstrate to retailers that you plan to promote heavily to the target readers and drive people into their stores
Publicity	Seek reviews in *Library Journal*; media performances; high-visibility publicity	Use magazine articles and media coverage as examples of the quality of your content	Demonstrate local publicity or plans to contact local media to communicate to people in the store's buying area.
Advertising	Co-op advertising with the distributors	Usually no advertising is needed here because of the reliance on one-on-one selling	Advertise in the newsletters of associations and others; trade ad space for articles that you write and submit
Sales Promotion	Generally trade promotions; distributor sales' support	Coupon or insert in customers' packages	More likely to use your display material; shelf-talkers, etc
Sales Literature	Flyer should stress how you can increase store traffic and therefore profits	Individual presentations supported by professional literature	Flyer should stress how you can increase store traffic and therefore profits

	Special Distribution	Commercial Sales	Niche Marketing
Personal Selling	Getting books into these markets takes consistent follow-up; media performances	Getting books into these markets takes personal sales calls; consistent follow-up; media performances; may reach them at trade shows or by exhibiting at the Premium and Incentive shows; attend these shows to find P&I reps and groups; heavy networking to form relationships with buyers	Available for personal appearances

Index